FINANCIAL MANAGEMENT
PRACTICES IN INDIA

Efficient financial management is the essence of business. This book analyses and evaluates core financial management practices of corporate enterprises in India across diverse sectors including realty, fast moving consumer goods, pharmaceutical, automobile, IT, chemical and business process outsourcing (BPO) sectors. It emphasises the importance of the integrated process of capital investments, financing policy, working capital management and dividend distribution for shareholders for a developing economy such as India. It further highlights the need for financial viability both in totality and segmental performance. The volume also offers a comparative study of the practices of the companies in different sectors to allow a better appreciation of the issues and challenges regarding management of finances.

Rich in case studies, this book will be an indispensable resource for scholars, teachers and students of financial management, business economics as well as corporate practitioners.

Sandeep Goel is Associate Professor of Finance at the Management Development Institute (MDI), Gurgaon, India. He has double doctorate, one in finance and another in accounting, from the Faculty of Management Studies, University of Delhi. He has twenty years of industry and academic experience in different organisations and institutions of repute, including the Shri Ram Group, University of Delhi and MDI. His areas of teaching and research interests are financial reporting and analysis, corporate finance, corporate governance and earnings management. He has authored six books and published over fifty articles in national and international journals.

FINANCIAL MANAGEMENT PRACTICES IN INDIA

Sandeep Goel

Routledge
Taylor & Francis Group

LONDON AND NEW YORK

First published 2016
by Routledge
2 Park Square, Milton Park, Abingdon, Oxon OX14 4RN

and by Routledge
711 Third Avenue, New York, NY 10017

First issued in paperback 2017

*Routledge is an imprint of the Taylor & Francis Group,
an informa business*

British Library Cataloguing-in-Publication Data
A catalogue record for this book is available from the British Library

Library of Congress Cataloging-in-Publication Data
A catalog record has been requested for this book

ISBN 13: 978-1-138-48840-3 (pbk)
ISBN 13: 978-1-138-96322-1 (hbk)

Typeset in Sabon
by Apex CoVantage, LLC

CONTENTS

CONTENTS

CONTENTS

FIGURES

TABLES

PREFACE

'Everything boils down to finance' – business or non-business activity. Therefore, 'financial management' is undoubtedly one of the most important areas of any organisation. Indian corporate is no exception to it. It needs to be financially viable not only in totality but also in segmental performance as far as possible. This altogether becomes more important in the context of economic development of a country like India. Besides meeting their financial requirements from their own internal resources, they are also supposed to generate surpluses for financing the needs of other priority sectors.

It is against this backdrop that the present book has been penned down. Its focus is to highlight the importance of an efficient financial management in a corporate enterprise. It evaluates the financial management practices of corporate enterprises in India in diverse sectors. The attempt is to study and analyse the practices of the companies in these sectors on comparative basis in order to better appreciate the various issues and challenges regarding management of finances. The period covered in the present study is a span of five years, ranging from 2006–7 to 2010–11. It has been taken as it is reasonably a good period to analyse the financial performance of the companies under study and its impact on the shareholders' return, particularly in the context of pre- and post-global turmoil. The main data used are secondary in nature and they have been collected from the annual reports and other relevant documents of the undertaking. The data collected have been analysed by applying various accounting and statistical tools such as, ratio analysis, correlation analysis, beta analysis, sensitivity analysis, graphs (time-series) and pie charts.

The objective of the book is to develop not only an understanding of the concepts of finance but most importantly also to help managers to use it as an effective tool for communication, monitoring, analysis and resource allocation.

The present book is a real 'case-based' book on financial management practices in India with relevant text interwoven in the discussion.

The present book is divided into five parts. Part I gives an overview of the conceptual framework of financial management. Part II presents the long-term investment decision of the companies under study. It examines their fixed assets structure to see the level of investment made in fixed assets and their efficiency in utilisation. Here five sector case studies from realty, FMCG, pharmaceutical, automobile and power sector are discussed. Part III discusses the financing decisions made by the units. It analyses their financial structure and its various components to see how the different units finance their respective assets. There are six sector case studies from steel, diversified, construction, auto, IT and BPO sector. There is also a discussion on shareholders' wealth maximisation using DuPont model in FMCG sector.

Part IV comprises a detailed discussion on the aspect of working capital management. The chapter mainly includes (a) analysis of working capital with particular emphasis on its level of investment as a whole and in various components individually, (b) financing of working capital of each of the units, (c) liquidity analysis and short-term solvency position of the concerned units and (d) utilisation of current assets. It has five sector case studies from auto, mix, textile, cement and IT. In addition, there is a discussion on implications of positive and negative working capital in corporate India. Part V investigates the dividend decision in detail. It analyses the dividend disbursement in the enterprises; that is, it examines whether the earnings of different units are adequate or not. If they are sufficient, then how the dividend policy and retention policy are determined? If they are not, why so? What are the reasons behind it? It contains three sector case studies from FMCG, chemical and power. In last, there is an analysis of relationship between dividend policy on market return.

It is hoped that it would create a fresh knowledge base thereof and provide direction to the academia, business makers and policymakers to effectively cope with emerging financial challenges enveloped in a haze of mystery.

I wish to thank God almighty for everything in life! The work would be incomplete if I do not acknowledge my parents' contribution. They have been a constant source of inspiration for me and have always stood by me through thick and thin. My wife provided her unstinted support and encouragement in completing the book. My little daughter Maanya is my soul whose smile always keeps me going in life.

Last, but not the least, I am thankful to the entire team of Routledge, New Delhi, for their tremendous support and wholehearted cooperation at all stages of publication of this book.

I am confident that the readers will find this book truly valuable in terms of its quality and presentation. Any constructive comments and suggestions for improving the contents of the book will be highly appreciated.

Part I

INTRODUCTION

1

NATURE OF FINANCIAL MANAGEMENT

Introduction

Almost everything in life eventually boils down to the rupee sign. Money, and therefore, finance, is an integral part of life.[1] It is equally applicable to a business organisation. The success of business depends on the efficient financial management. All functions of business revolve around finance. Therefore, every business enterprise needs to be efficient in managing its finance. They need to ensure that enough funding is available at the right time and invested into the right projects.

What is financial management?

Financial management is the process of acquiring and disbursement of funds. It includes all the activities relating to planning, organising, directing and controlling the funds of the enterprise.

Elements

1 *Investment decision*: It implies the allocation of funds in various assets. The investment in fixed assets is called *capital budgeting decision*. The investment in current assets is called *working capital decision*.

2 *Financing decision*: It refers to the process of raising funds from various sources depending on factors, such as the cost of funds, control, liquidity and so forth.

3 *Dividend decision*: It is the decision about distributing net profit. The finance manager decides what percentage of profits would be distributed as dividend to shareholders and how much profits would be kept aside as reserves for future contingencies.

INTRODUCTION

Objectives of financial management

The main objectives of financial management are as follows:

1 *Profit maximisation*: It is the primary objective of financial management. Every business enterprise tries to earn maximum profit, both short term and long term.
2 *Wealth maximisation*: Shareholders' value maximisation is the key objective of financial management and *is preferred over profit maximisation on account of market interest*. Wealth maximisation is a combination of regular return to shareholders in the form of dividend and appreciating market returns.
3 *Liquidity*: Liquidity maintenance is one of the most important objectives of financial management. The firm must have a sound cash position for meeting day-to-day expenses; otherwise, there might be a threat to the survival of the firm.
4 *Solvency*: Long-term soundness is a key objective of financial management. The company must be solvent to pay interest and repay loans at regular intervals. Lack of solvency can be a big blow to the firm in this competitive scenario.

Functions of financial management

Following are the main functions of financial management:

1 *Estimating financial requirements*: Proper estimation of financial requirements is an important function of financial management. The finance manager must determine accurately how much finance is required for business operations, keeping in view the long-term and short-term requirements.
2 *Mobilisation of funds*: Funds acquisition is another important function of financial management. After estimating the financial requirements, the finance manager must decide on raising the funds from various sources of finance, such as shares, debentures, bank loans and the like. There must be a proper balance between owned funds and debt funds.
3 *Proper utilisation of finance*: The next task of finance manager is to utilise these funds efficiently. Long-term funds should be invested in fixed assets and short-term funds should be used for current assets. The finance manager should not invest the company's funds in unprofitable projects.

4

4   *Distribution of profits*: The distribution of net profit has to be decided by the finance manager regarding dividend and reinvestment of earnings. The finance manager must consider the requirements of shareholders and expansion plans of the company.

5   *Cash management*: Finance manager must ensure enough liquidity and should plan out the cash required for various requirements of the firm, such as payment of salaries, bills, meeting current liabilities and the like.

6   *Financial control*: Sound financial control is the prerequisite for the growth of business. The finance manager must exercise proper control with the help of techniques, such as budgetary control, cost analysis, financial forecasting and the like.

Financial management scene in India

Traditionally, a single manager would manage the entire operations of a business. With business going global, the finance function has become a specialised function. There are finance specialists now to manage your operations.

Since liberalisation in 1991, the face of Indian corporate has changed tremendously, making finance as the essence of every business. Today every company has specialist set of people shouldering the responsibility of finance managers in their organisation, called Director-Finance, Chief Finance Officer and Financial Controller and the like.

The finance manager is not merely concerned with maintaining accounts of the business. He or she has to perform multi-tasks, including fund raising to procurement of assets to distribution of profits to ensuring safety of the financial assets of the company. He or she has to plan the operations of a business in such a manner so that there is a positive cash flow and the firm keeps on growing. He or she is expected to generate maximum profits for the company and keep shareholders satisfied.

Financial management is continuously progressing. A good finance manager must see all updates, changes in the fields of financial management. He or she should be interested to know what new sources of funds are developed at international level. What new projects are in current period? What amendments are done by government in tax laws? A good finance manager must be aware of what is happening around.

Following are the main changes which have tuned the field of financial management in India during past few decades:

Interest rates. Interest rates are controlled by the Reserve Bank of India (RBI) and other commercial banks' rates are affected from RBI's action. To ascertain cost of debt, one should know this.

Value of shares. Value of shares now can be determined at premium or discount freely. One should determine its shares value at optimum level because it directly affects the earnings per share (EPS).

Mergers and acquisitions. As good finance manager, one should keep one's eye on who is taking over which company. To merge with other company may be sometime profitable than going alone.

In conclusion, financial management has changed with the changing times and has become very scientific with the latest principles and practices of management around.

Financial management problems

Some of the problems relating to the financial management faced by corporate enterprises are discussed below:

1 Due to poor planning, the enterprises *do not maintain a desirable combination of sources of funds.* This leads to shortage of equity and then they depend too much on borrowed capital. Hence, sound financial planning is required for an optimal financial structure.

2 *Inadequate combination of assets* results in the problem of either underinvestment or overinvestment in total assets. This is more pertinent to current assets, such as inventories and receivables. For a manufacturing undertaking, these problems need an immediate check by adopting appropriate inventory controlling techniques and sound credit and collection policies.

3 *Inaccurate projection of revenues and costs* results in improper investment in inventories, receivables and plant capacity. These factors ultimately result in poor earnings of the enterprises. So, there should be an efficient and effective profit planning for better utilisation of resources and enhanced earnings.

4   The enterprises *lack a definite and stable dividend policy*. There should be an adequate balance between payment of dividends and retention of earnings. Dividend payments should be more regular and consistent in proportion to the paid-up capital.

5   The enterprises *should be managed by only professionally competent, qualified and experienced personnel* for better result orientation.

Discussion questions

1   Define financial management. Explain its elements.
2   What are the objectives of financial management?
3   'Shareholders' wealth maximisation is the key objective of financial management'. Justify.
4   Discuss the function of financial management.
5   'The financial management scenario in India has undergone a sea change of late'. Elaborate.
6   What are the various financial management problems faced by the corporate enterprise? Discuss with solutions.

Note

1 Douglas R. Emery, John D. Finnerty, and John D. Stowe, *Principles of Financial Management*, Upper Saddle River, NJ: Prentice Hall, 1998, p. 2.

Part II

INVESTMENT DECISION
Capital budgeting

2

CAPITAL BUDGETING

Nature and scope

Introduction

Capital budgeting decision is the decision of investment in long-term assets. The major criterion for selection of a capital investment project is its financial viability in terms of expected cash inflows over initial cash outflows. They should meet a target benchmark. Capital budgeting techniques are applied in order to determine which projects will yield the maximum return over a given period of time.

The various types of capital investment decisions are:

* replacement of an asset;
* expansion of the production capacity;
* diversification of business;
* modernisation of existing facilities; and
* research and development (R&D) activities.

Capital budgeting process

The capital budgeting process includes the following steps:

1 *Identifying investment needs*: The first step is to identify the need or opportunity for a capital investment. This involves the evaluation of various available opportunities by the management. There are various factors which are considered while arriving at a decision, like financial, non-financial parameters, market factors and most importantly risk–return trade-off.

2 *Capital project evaluation*: After deciding on the proposed project, its evaluation is done regarding its viability. The estimated cash

flows, target cost of capital and potential risks are identified for the evaluation. Calculating appropriate discount rate is a critical part of this process. Following measures are used for the appraisal:

1   *Initial cash outflows*: It is the amount of cash flows to be invested initially in the project.
2   *Net cash inflows from operations*: the amount of cash inflows to be generated from the capital investment decision.
3   *Terminal cash flows*: the salvage value of an existing asset at the end of the life.
4   *Depreciation*: the usage charge of an asset.
5   *Income tax effects*: tax shield on account of sale of an asset.
6   *Discounting rate*: the funding rate in computation of cash flows.
7   *Risk considerations*: political risk, monetary risk and other risks should be considered in the evaluation process.

Finally, various capital budgeting techniques are applied to test its feasibility (discussed in the next section).

Capital project evaluation methods

Following are the most widely used methods for evaluating the capital investment projects.

- *The payback period*: It is the period of recovery of initial investment. The project with the shortest payback period is selected. But, this method does not consider cash flows after the payback period and also does not consider the time value of money.
- *The discounted payback period*: It is an improved version of the payback method as it considers time value of money. It discounts cash flows and then computes the investment recovery period. In simple words, it is the time period required to reach net present value (NPV) = 0.
- *The accounting rate of return (ARR)*: It uses accounting income information for calculating the average return from a project. The return from the project is compared with target ARR based on the firm's cost of capital for arriving at a decision.
- *The NPV*: It is based on the time value of money and is a popular discounted cash flow (DCF) method. It discounts future cash flows (both inflows and outflows) using a target cost of capital

12

and determines the difference between the present value of net cash inflows and cash outflows. A positive value implies that the project is profitable and vice versa.

- *Profitability Index*: It is a ratio of the present value of inflows to the present value of outflows. The index is used instead of NPV in case of evaluating mutually exclusive proposals with different costs.
- *The internal rate of return (IRR)*: It is also DCF method. It finds out the discounting rate that equates the present value of cash outflows and cash inflows. This rate of return is then compared with the budgeted rate of return to determine the viability of the capital project.
- *The modified IRR (MIRR)*: It overcomes the deficiencies in the IRR method. MIRR method calculates the present value of the cash outflows, the future value of the cash inflows (to the end of the project's life) and then solves for the discount rate that will equate the present value of cash outflows and the future value of the benefits.

Evaluating risk of capital projects

Risk is an inherent element of any project and therefore needs to be analysed carefully. Risk exists because of the inability of the decision maker to make perfect forecasts. In formal terms, the risk associated with an investment may be defined as the variability that is likely to occur in the future returns from the investment.

The most commonly used risk assessment techniques include margin of safety, risk-adjusted discount rate, certainty-equivalent coefficient, sensitivity analysis, scenario analysis, decision-tree analysis and Monte Carlo simulation.

- *Margin of safety*: It signifies the strength of a business during uncertain periods. A project with higher margin of safety is preferred. It is calculated as the difference between total sales and break-even sales.
- *Risk-adjusted discount rate*: It is the sum of the risk-free rate and the risk-premium rate reflecting the investor's attitude towards risk. Higher K is used for riskier projects.
- *Certainty-equivalent coefficient*: It involves reducing the forecasts of cash flows to some conservative levels. Following steps are required:
  - Cash flows are multiplied by certainty-equivalent coefficient.
  - Certain cash flows are discounted at risk-free rate.
  - Decision maker calculates the NPV and arrives at the decision.

- *Sensitivity analysis*: It is also called 'what if' analysis. It analyses the change in the project's NPV (or IRR) for a given change in one of the variables. Accordingly, it helps the management in decision-making.
- *Scenario analysis*: It analyses the impact of alternative combinations of variables, called *scenarios*, on the project's NPV (or IRR). The three scenarios used are optimistic, pessimistic and most likely.
- *Decision-tree analysis*: It is a graphical portrayal of potential scenarios and their expected profitability based on the project's cash flow. It involves following steps:

  - define the investment plan
  - identify decision alternatives
  - draw a decision tree

    (i) decision points, and
    (ii) chance events

  - analyse data.

- *Monte Carlo simulation*: It uses econometric/statistical probability analyses to calculate risk.

Discussion questions

1 Discuss the process of capital budgeting.
2 What are the various methods of evaluating capital investment and objectives of financial management?
3 'NPV method is considered to be superior to IRR method for shareholders' interest'. Explain.
4 Discuss various risk mitigation techniques of capital investment.

3

CAPITAL BUDGETING PRACTICES OF REALTY SECTOR IN INDIA

Indian realty sector

The real estate industry has significant linkages with several other sectors of the economy and over 250 associated industries. One rupee invested in this sector results in 78 paise being added to the gross domestic product (GDP) of the state. A unit increase in expenditure in this sector has a multiplier effect and the capacity to generate income as high as five times. If the economy grows at the rate of 10% the housing sector has the capacity to grow at 14% and generate 3.2 million new jobs over a decade.

Historically, the real estate sector in India was unorganised and characterised by various factors that impeded organised dealing, such as centralised title registry, non-availability of bank financing, high interest rates and lack of transparency.

In recent years, the sector has exhibited a trend towards greater organisation and transparency accompanied by reforms such as

- Government of India support to repeal of the Urban Land Ceiling Act;
- modification in Rent Control Act to provide greater protection to homeowners;
- rationalisation of property tax; and
- proposed computerisation of land records.

India is currently the second fastest-growing economy in the world. The Indian construction industry has been playing a vital role in overall economic development of the country, growing at over 20% compound annual growth rate (CAGR) over the past five years and contributing 8% to GDP.

Scope

In this unit, we have analysed the following three major players in the Indian realty industry.

1. DLF Ltd

DLF has over sixty years of track record of sustained growth, customer satisfaction and innovation. DLF's primary business is development of residential, commercial and retail properties. The company has a unique business model with earnings arising from development and rentals. Its exposure across businesses, segments and geographies, mitigates any down-cycles in the market. DLF is credited with introducing and pioneering the revolutionary concept of developing commercial complexes in the vicinity of residential areas

2. Unitech Ltd

Established in 1972, Unitech is today a leading real estate developer in India. Known for the quality of its products, it is the first developer to have been certified ISO 9001:2000 in North India and offers the most diversified product mix comprising residential, commercial/information technology (IT) parks, retail, hotels, amusement parks and special economic zones (SEZs).

3. Parsvnath Developers

Parsvnath has emerged as one of the most progressive and multifaceted real estate and construction entities in the country. With a pan-India presence in over forty-four cities in fifteen states, they are steadfastly focused on continuing to create and build dreamscapes that transform lives and the world around us – be it through contemporary residential spaces, state-of-the-art office complexes, affordable housing, luxurious, shopping malls and hypermarkets, posh hotels, futuristic multiplexes and ultra-modern IT parks and SEZs.

Analysis and discussion

1. Investment pattern

The trend of investment in long-term assets of the units is analysed to find out whether they are growing or stagnant? It is further evaluated to determine the risk strategy of the management in the environment within which it operates.

(a) DLF Ltd

The investments of DLF Ltd for the past five years are given in Table 3.1 and Figure 3.1.

From Figure 3.1 we can state that, the investments by DLF are increasing every year. DLF unlocked about Rs 1,270 crore during 2010–11 by divesting certain non-core assets and businesses. The overall divestment target for non-core assets has now been increased to Rs 10,000 crore, implying that between Rs 6,000 and Rs 7,000 crore would be realised through divestments over the next two to three years. The cash flow from divestment would be utilised primarily for debt reduction.

Table 3.1 Investment pattern of DLF

Year	2011	2010	2009	2008	2007
Investments (Rs crore)	7,037.24	6,558.88	2,956.32	1,839.83	769.17

Source: DLF Annual Reports.

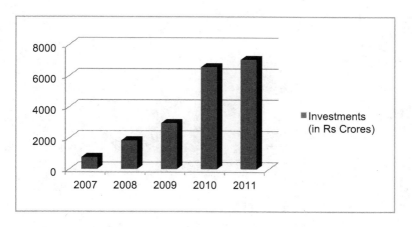

Figure 3.1 Investment trend of DLF

17

(b) Unitech Ltd

The investments of Unitech Ltd for the past five years are given in Table 3.2 and Figure 3.2.

As we can see from the data in Figure 3.2, the company's investments increased in 2009 and have been almost constant since then. The company is exposed to specific risks in connection with the management of investments and the environment within which it operates. The company aims to understand and wants to measure and monitor the various risks to which it is exposed and to ensure that it adheres, as far as reasonably and practically possible, to the policies and procedures established by it to mitigate these risks.

(c) Parsvnath Developers Ltd

The investments of Parsvnath Developers for the past five years are given in Table 3.3 and Figure 3.3.

Table 3.2 Investment pattern of Unitech

Year	2011	2010	2009	2008	2007
Investments (Rs crore)	2,054.02	1,654.15	1,954.94	1,397.99	518.92

Source: Unitech Annual Reports.

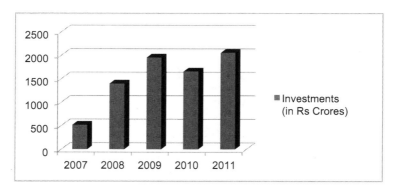

Figure 3.2 Investment trend of Unitech

Table 3.3 Investment pattern of Parsvnath Developers

Year	2011	2010	2009	2008	2007
Investments (Rs crore)	428.22	220.83	99.34	80.57	82.86

Source: Parsvnath Annual Reports.

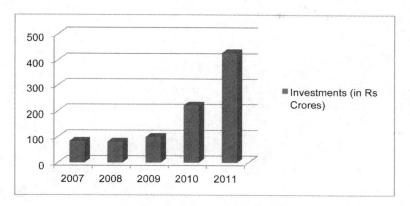

Figure 3.3 Investment trend of Parsvnath Developers

It is evident here that over the past five years, investment in the above company has been building up and gaining a real momentum, particularly in tier I cities.

2. Operating risk

Operating risk indicates the operational efficiency of business units. To measure the degree of operating risk, current to fixed assets ratio has been used as it determines the resources' utilisation by a business and thus evaluates the operational efficiency.

(a) DLF Ltd

Current to fixed asset ratio: Current assets are important to businesses because they are the assets that are used to fund day-to-day operations and pay ongoing expenses. Depending on the nature of the business, current assets can range from barrels of crude oil, to baked goods, to foreign currency (Table 3.4).

The current to fixed asset ratio is quite low; meaning the company's operating risk is on a higher side.

(b) Unitech Ltd

The current to fixed asset ratio is high, meaning the company has money to fund its day-to-day operations, and is functioning at low operating risk. But, it also implies low efficiency in utilisation of current assets (Table 3.5).

(c) Parsvnath Developers Ltd

The current to fixed asset ratio is adequate, meaning the company's level of operating risk is almost negligible (Table 3.6).

Table 3.4 Assets composition of DLF

Ratio	March 2011	March 2010	March 2009	March 2008	March 2007
Net current assets (Rs crore)	17,955.29	15,521.99	15,618.55	14,588.51	5,679.57
Net fixed assets (Rs crore)	1,743.1	1,729.02	1,815.53	1,474.37	328.57
Current to fixed asset ratio	10.30	8.98	8.60	9.89	17.29

Source: DLF Annual Reports.

Table 3.5 Assets composition of Unitech

Ratio	March 2011	March 2010	March 2009	March 2008	March 2007
Net current assets (Rs crore)	12,626.15	11,006.33	8,430.43	7,862.74	4,176.75
Net fixed assets (Rs crore)	104.49	107.07	107.84	100.73	69.63
Current to fixed asset ratio	120.84	102.80	78.18	78.06	59.98

Source: Unitech Annual Reports.

Table 3.6 Assets composition of Parsvnath Developers

Ratio	March 2011	March 2010	March 2009	March 2008	March 2007
Net current assets (Rs crore)	3,144.57	3,218.23	3,351.44	3,207.32	2,281.64
Net fixed assets (Rs crore)	149.02	106.94	127.24	119.47	71.29
Current to fixed asset ratio	21.10	30.09	26.34	26.85	32.01

Source: Parsvnath Annual Reports.

Conclusion

All three companies have an increasing trend of fixed assets, an indication of expansion. They have a current to fixed asset ratio of more than one. This means that all the companies can finance their day-to-day activities and short-term liabilities with their current assets (i.e., less/no risk firms). But Unitech Ltd has a huge current to fixed asset ratio of 120 which means they can not only finance their activities but also pay their long-term liabilities. They are the company with least operating risk (according to current to fixed asset ratio) followed by Parsvnath Developers Ltd and then DLF Ltd. But, they need to check their mix of assets.

Discussion questions

1   Which type of capital budgeting decision is discussed in the present case of realty sector in India?
2   Discuss the investment trend of DLF, Unitech and Parsvnath Developers with regard to capital budgeting decision.
3   What are the various capital budgeting appraisal methods used by businesses?
4   Discuss the techniques used for incorporating the risk factor in capital projects?
5   Analyse the operating risk of the above units with the help of CA/TA ratio.
6   Comment upon the capital investment management of the above units.

4

CAPITAL BUDGETING PRACTICES OF FMCG SECTOR IN INDIA

Fast moving consumer goods sector overview

The fast moving consumer goods (FMCG) industry in India is currently valued at US$27 billion and constitutes roughly 2.2% of the Indian GDP. It is expected to reach US$47 billion by 2013 and US$74 billion by 2018, growing annually at 10–12%. The FMCG sector is one such sector that touches the life of almost every individual on a daily basis.

A well-distributed supply chain network spread across 6 million retail outlets, low penetration levels, low operating costs and competition between the organised and unorganised segments are the key features of the Indian FMCG sector.

The FMCG sector is the world's fourth-largest sector in India and provides employment for over three million people in the country. This sector primarily includes the production, distribution and marketing of consumer packaged goods, that is those categories of products which are consumed at regular intervals. The sector is growing at rapid pace with well-established distribution networks and intense competition between the organised and unorganised segments. It has a strong and competitive multinational companies (MNCs) presence across the entire value chain. The FMCG's promising market includes middle class and the rural segments of the Indian population, and gives brand makers the opportunity to convert them to branded products. It includes food and beverage, personal care, pharmaceuticals, plastic goods, paper and stationery and household products and the like.

The FMCG sector has seen high growth in the past few years owing to the increased rural incomes, rising consumption culture in India, changing consumer patterns and proliferation of consumer awareness campaigns. By 2025, the total consumption in the sector is expected to quadruple making India the fifth-largest consumer market in the world.

On the basis of products the FMCG industry can be broadly classified as shown below.

Category products

Food and beverages: health beverages, soft drinks, staples, cereals, bakery products (biscuits, bread and cakes), snack food, chocolates, ice cream, tea, coffee, soft drinks, processed fruits, vegetables, dairy products, bottled water, branded flour, branded rice, branded sugar, juices and so on.

Household care

Fabric wash (laundry soaps and synthetic detergents), household cleaners (dish/utensil cleaners, floor cleaners, toilet cleaners, air fresheners, insecticides and mosquito repellents, metal polish and furniture polish).

Personal care

Oral care, hair care, skin care, personal wash (soaps), cosmetics and toiletries, deodorants, perfumes, feminine hygiene and paper products.

Five trends that drive growth in FMCG sector currently[1]

- *Rural and new consumer segments*: Benefitted by various government schemes (like National Rural Employment Guarantee Act and minimum support price (MSP)) the spending power of a rural non-agricultural consumer has increased and has hence become the new target consumer of the FMCG companies.
- *Sales, promotions and discounts*: Retailers from food and groceries, electronics, home furnishings and apparel and lifestyle are likely to increase the number of promotions and sales that they run in a bid to lure consumers shying away from buying.
- *Expansions and new launches*: The year will see consumer companies increase their reach into the interiors of India. Firms will also

launch more products and widen their portfolio as they get into new segments and categories.

- *Emerging segments and trade channels*: Growth will come from the fringes – categories that are not among the mainstays – such as oats, conditioners, liquid fabric conditioners and liquid soaps and face wash compared with staple soaps and deodorants.
- *Premiumisation*: Researches indicate that consumers are willing to adopt a new premium category, even at a higher price, in the space of convenience, health and wellness. Sale of commodities like cornflakes and muesli, baked potatoes and 100% juices are rising.

Five factors that affect the growth in FMCG sector

- *Increasing rate of inflation*: This has led to raw materials becoming expensive, putting a pressure on the margins of these companies.
- *Steadily rising fuel costs*: Rising fuel costs have increased distribution and transportation costs. Along with raw materials, these expenses make up close to 25% of the expenditure for the companies.
- *Present slowdown in the economy*: Although the slowdown has not directly affected the FMCG sector, there has been a slowdown in the pace of growth.
- *Declining value of rupee*: The declining value of rupee against other currencies may affect the margins of Marico, Godrej Consumer Products Ltd (GCPL), Dabur and Marico who import raw materials from other countries.
- *Affected by budget changes*: The recent budget has not increased the spending power of an average middle-class consumer; as a result the foot fall from this section is likely to decrease.

Scope

In the present discussion, we have analysed the following three major players in the Indian FMCG industry:

- GCPL
- Hindustan Unilever Ltd (HUL)
- ITC Ltd

1. Godrej Consumer Products Ltd

GCPL is involved in the manufacturing and marketing of FMCG. It operates in the segment of household and personal products. Apart from India, the company has its subsidiaries in the Netherlands, the United Kingdom, South Africa and Mauritius. The company operates in three major segments – home care, personal wash and hair care. Company is into oleo chemicals which are used in a variety of applications including personal care (hair care, skin care, oral care and cosmetics), home care (laundry detergents) and pharmaceuticals. The growth in India's GDP/per capita has led to a strong growth in the personal and home care market. Additionally, the significant size of the global personal and home care ingredients markets also represents a potential opportunity. The current environment has, however, seen fluctuating raw material costs (i.e., crude oil, palm and vegetable oil), which impact the Oleochemicals business.

2. Hindustan Unilever Ltd

More than 100 years old, Hindustan Unilever Ltd (HUL) is a major FMCG company in India with brands such as Dove, Lux, Lipton and Lifebuoy among others. In 2010, the company was troubled by volatile and rapidly changing commodity markets but managed to pull through with a concerted focus on the rural market in India. It rolled out cross category rural marketing efforts in financial year (FY) 2010–11 through three major programmes, namely, Perfect Stores, Project Shaktimaan and Project Khushiyon ki Doli. By FY 2012, HUL's rural outlets accounted for almost 90% of HUL's turnover in retail outlets.

3. ITC Ltd

ITC is an Indian diversified conglomerate with operations in four segments, namely, FMCG, agribusiness, paperboards, paper and packaging and hotels. It is the largest FMCG company in Indian market in terms of market capitalisation. Although primarily known for its vast cigarette and tobacco business, some of its major brands include Mangaldeep, Goldflake, Sunfeast and Vivel, among others. ITC's net revenue grew by 17.2% in FY 2012 primarily driven by a 23.6% growth in the non-cigarette FMCG business. Its profit after tax (PAT) increased by 22.4% and the net profits registered a growth of 23.6% in FY

2012. The earning per share also went up to Rs 7.93 in FY 2012 compared to Rs 6.49 in FY 2011.

Analysis and discussion

1. Investment pattern of long-term assets

The long-term investment trend of the units is analysed to determine their growth pattern. It is further evaluated components' wise to determine the management approach for future expansion.

(a) GCPL

The investments of GCPL for the past three years are given in Table 4.1 and Figure 4.1.

Table 4.1 Investment pattern of GCPL (Rs crore)

Year	March 2009	March 2010	March 2011
Leasehold land	1.71	3.6	22.43
Freehold land	9.89	13.84	23.86
Buildings	96.38	129	178.6
Plant and machinery	523.98	548.06	575.41
Other fixed assets	151.34	142.22	160.59

Source: Godrej Annual Reports.

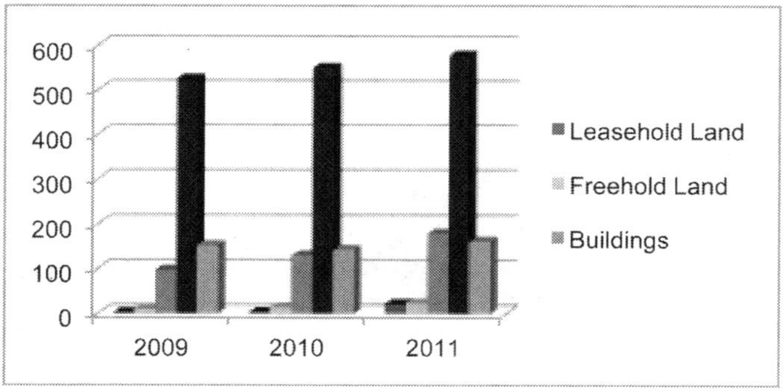

Figure 4.1 Investment trend of GCPL

26

We can see that Godrej is incrementally increasing its investment in long-term assets. Increase in plant and machinery is not very significant but substantial investment is made in building in past year which is done keeping in mind the long-term increase in demand in a growing economy like India. The investments in other assets remain constant.

(b) HUL

The investments of HUL for the past three years are given in Table 4.2 and Figure 4.2.

We can see that HUL is progressively increasing its investment in long-term assets especially plant and machinery. The investment in buildings is also increasing progressively. This is good sign as the company is looking to expand. The investments in land and other fixed assets remain almost constant.

Table 4.2 Investment pattern of HUL (Rs crore)

Year	March 2009	March 2010	March 2011
Leasehold land	33.7	33.13	57.35
Freehold land	57.63	79.23	75.92
Buildings	692.22	938.8	969.64
Plant and machinery	1,737.78	2,139.02	2,260.94
Other fixed assets	125.23	137.84	139.91

Source: HUL Annual Reports.

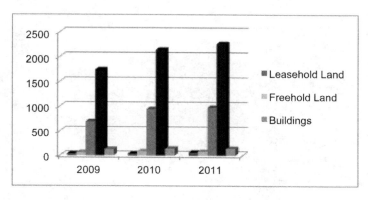

Figure 4.2 Investment trend of HUL

27

(c) ITC Ltd

The investments of ITC Ltd for the past three years are given in Table 4.3 and Figure 4.3.

As we can see, considerable amount of long-term investment is done by ITC in plant machinery and buildings. ITC is looking to expand capacity to cater to increased demand. Investment in other areas remains constant and this is a further indication of ITC's increasing production plans.

2. Strategy for long-term growth

This section specifically discusses the strategy adopted by the management of the units to achieve the desired long-term growth. It could be cost-related or efficiency-related or funds-related, as evident in the following discussion.

Table 4.3 Investment pattern of ITC Ltd (Rs crore)

Year	March 2009	March 2010	March 2011
Leasehold land	0	0	0
Freehold land	907.42	960.97	1,059.93
Buildings	2,156.27	2,639.07	2,803.70
Plant and machinery	7,109.49	7,871.08	8,428.05
Other fixed assets	200.27	237.1	342.25

Source: ITC Annual Reports.

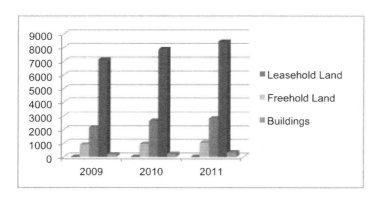

Figure 4.3 Investment trend of ITC Ltd

(a) GCPL

Company's approach is called CREATE, which represents the focused set of businesses that they participate in, along with some of the key imperatives that they are pursuing across the group – competitively growing its core businesses, building an environment for transformation and nurturing emergent businesses of the future. CREATE stands for:

- Consumer and Chemicals
- Real Estate
- Agrisector
- Transformation
- Emergent

Company's continued strong focus on cost reduction and operational efficiency improvement initiatives, which included reduction in the net working capital employed and reduction in the variable costs of production have been yielding good results. The specialty and value-added products have contributed to the improvement in margins and expected to improve further going forward. Such products accounted for 33% of the turnover of the division.

Company has developed a customer relationship management website (eCRM) that enables customers to track their orders and transactions and also receive updates through personalised web pages 24 × 7. This has now been extended to international customers also.

(b) HUL

At a time when input costs remain high and price volatility brings added challenges, HUL will continue to focus on the best value for their consumers and customers through innovations and strong cost efficiency programmes.

HUL will manage business dynamically to deliver consistent and profitable growth; they also recognise that responsible growth is as important. In 2010, HUL launched the Unilever Sustainable Living Plan globally. The Unilever Sustainable Living Plan seeks to double the size of the company while reducing its environmental impact. In an increasingly resource-constrained world, this decoupling of growth from the impact on the planet is the model that consumers will ultimately demand.

Key strategies of HUL are as follows:

1   *Winning with brands and innovations*: Great products, superior innovation and effective marketing are essential for building world-class brands.
2   *Winning in the marketplace*: Outstanding customer service and great in-store execution helped sustain winning relationships with customers.
3   *Winning through continuous improvement*: Delivering competitive, profitable and sustainable growth requires a mindset of continuous improvement. This means being fast and flexible in the supply chain while keeping end-to-end costs competitive. This involves the following:

    a   Leveraging global scale and knowledge to make our supply chain most competitive. Regular benchmarking with global and local competitors.
    b   Reduction in inventories and reduced time-to-shelf improves its product freshness and deliver superior consumer value.
    c   Prioritising speed and flexibility in the supply chain to deliver growth.
    d   Driving total productive maintenance (TPM) to continuously reduce business waste and eliminate losses in the supply chain.

4   *Winning with people*: The company's people agenda comprises building a robust talent and leadership pipeline which helps the organisation win in the present and the future, build capabilities and engage employees across all levels and foster a high performance culture in the organisation.

(c) ITC Ltd

The company's continuing leadership position and market standing was nurtured by successfully fortifying the business and growing its portfolio of brands catering to diverse consumer preferences across segments. 'Innovation' across all areas of operation was the central theme around which enhanced market standing and competitive superiority was achieved. Inherent expertise in the areas of contemporary product development, cutting-edge technology and robust go-to-market processes, combined with the company's deep consumer insights saw the launch of several new and exciting offers, in line with the strategy of continually meeting emerging consumer needs.

The business continued to focus on supply chain improvements to enhance market servicing and margins. Product development and brand-building will be critical to drive sales. Innovative interventions will continue to be essential for building strong consumer franchise. Well researched and robust product development processes will continue to be leveraged to launch innovative and differentiated products across all segments. With effective and cost-efficient servicing of target markets continuing to be a key success factor, the business will continue to leverage the company's sales and distribution network to achieve deep penetration, visibility and availability for its products.

There is an increasing demand for suppliers with 'end-to-end' capabilities having complete custody of the supply chain, supported by appropriate technology to deliver quality and product assurance. The company seeks to harness this opportunity by building a business model based on customised products and services with requisite crop development, state-of-the-art infrastructure and tailor-made products and processes to garner an increasing share of the fast-growing domestic and export market.

In the past year, the company launched an initiative to strengthen and expand the distribution reach of its e-Choupal network for FMCG products in the rural markets. The company now proposes to synchronise its rural marketing and rural distribution businesses. The company has many other social initiatives in the rural sector which helps them reach the grass-roots level for their products and also to improve their image.

Conclusion

It is evident from the above discussion that among three companies, HUL is going for good amount of capital investment for future expansion. They are eyeing major growth avenues in the coming times. GCPL and ITC are incrementally increasing their investment in long-term assets.

Discussion questions

1 Critique the investment pattern of GCPL, HUL and ITC for their capital budgeting decision.
2 Discuss the strategy adopted by the above units for long-term growth.

3   How do you evaluate the capital investment management of the above units?

Note

1 Available at http://www.livemint.com/Industry/LyNBizkuOMdmThw6iao GbN/Five-trends-that-will-drive-FMCG-growth-in-2013.html (accessed on 25 June 2012).

5

CAPITAL BUDGETING PRACTICES OF PHARMACEUTICAL SECTOR IN INDIA

Pharmaceutical industry background

Indian pharmaceutical industry is one of the fastest-growing segments of Indian manufacturing sector. The pharmaceutical industry has experienced a growth rate of 12%, with the annual turnover of the sector crossing US$14.6 billion, in 2008–9. Globally, Indian pharmaceutical industry stands at fourth position in terms of volume with a share of 8% in the world pharmaceuticals market. Indian pharmaceuticals industry ranks fourteenth in the world in terms of value; in the Asia-Pacific pharmaceuticals market, India holds a share of 6.6%. Japan is the biggest player in the Asia-Pacific region accounting for 67% of the total market value. The sector produces almost 70% bulk drug requirements of the country. The key therapeutic segments include anti-infective, gastrointestinal and cardiovascular segments. In India, acute therapies make up about 60% of the pharmaceutical market. However, it is expected that with the changing lifestyle and aging population, sales of medicines for chronic therapies (e.g., diabetes and cardiovascular) is growing rapidly. A study has estimated that by the year 2010, the central nervous system and cardiovascular segment would have a market share of 33%. The industry is fragmented with more than 25,000 registered units, of which 300 units are large- and medium-scale units. In terms of value, however, top twenty players control more than 50% of total market.

Scope

In this discussion, we will analyse the following three major players in the Indian Pharmaceutical industry

1. Sun Pharmaceuticals Industries Ltd

It is a speciality pharmaceutical company, with a large presence in the United States and India, and a spread across forty other markets. Sun Pharma began in 1983 with just five products for psychiatry ailments. Since then, they have emerged as a leading pharma company in India and presently they are the sixth-largest company by sales.

2. Novartis India Ltd

Novartis is a world leader in the R&D segment. The company has core businesses in pharmaceuticals, vaccines, consumer health, generics, eye care and animal health. The group is headquartered in Basel, Switzerland, and is present in India through Novartis India Ltd.

3. Cipla Ltd

Cipla was set up on 17 August 1935 as a public limited company with an authorised capital of Rs 6 lakh. Its exports for 2010 were more than Rs 29,000 million, comprising raw materials, intermediates, prescription drugs, over-the-counter products and veterinary products. It is also into technology services for products and processes.

Analysis and discussion

1. Financing and investment pattern of long-term assets

This section evaluates the investment trend of long-terms assets of the units and their financing policy. The investment composition has been further analysed component-wise to find out relative contribution of each asset in the total assets. The financing policy of long-term assets indicates the financial risk of the company and its dependence on type of funds, that is, do they go for owned funds or borrowed funds or mix and in what proportion?

(a) Sun Pharmaceuticals Industries Ltd

Long-term assets can be analysed by looking at the gross block and the capital work in progress (Table 5.1).

Figure 5.1 shows the trend of the long-term assets for the past three years of the said company. It has been on a continuous increasing trend. When we break down the gross block (Table 5.2), it is found

Table 5.1 Long-term investment of Sun Pharma (Rs crore)

	2009	2010	2011
Gross block	1,061.90	1,159.76	1,268.76
Capital work in progress	75.95	92.15	228.06
Share capital	103.56	103.56	103.56
Reserves total	5,047.86	5,614.42	6,576.97
Secured loans	23.6	29.49	50.53
Unsecured loans	0	0	0

Source: Sun Pharma Annual Reports.

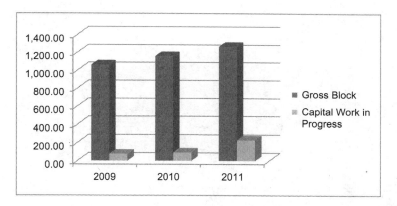

Figure 5.1 Long-term investment trend of Sun Pharma

Table 5.2 Composition of gross block of Sun Pharma

Break up of gross block (Rs crore) Year	March 2011	March 2010	March 2009	March 2008	March 2007
Buildings	252.85	236.71	214.05	199.3	188.84
Plant and machinery	919.31	829.27	756.33	653.17	571.27

Source: Sun Pharma Annual Reports.

that the major investments in the gross block have been in the *buildings* and the *plant and machinery*.

Sources of fund: Now if we see at the sources of fund (Table 5.3), we see there is no increase in the share capital over the past three years

Table 5.3 Sources of funds of Sun Pharma (Rs crore)

	2009	2010	2011
Share capital	103.56	103.56	103.56
Reserves total	5,047.86	5,614.42	6,576.97
Secured loans	23.6	29.49	50.53
Unsecured loans	0	0	0

Source: Sun Pharma Annual Reports.

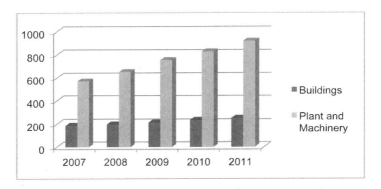

Figure 5.2 Gross block trend of Sun Pharma

and the secured loans have increased on account of bill discounting (which might be used for short-term financing of work in capital), so the logical conclusion we can make is that the *long-term assets are being financed by the reserves and surpluses.*

(b) Novartis India Ltd

Long-term assets can be analysed by looking at the gross block and the capital work in progress (Table 5.4).

Here also the trend is an increasing trend, indicating reaction to the market requirements. When we break down the gross block, the major investments in the gross block are found to be made in the *buildings* and the *plant and machinery*. These are the major item in fixed assets which are required for production requirements (Table 5.5 and Figure 5.4).

Table 5.4 Long-term investment of Novartis India (Rs crore)

	2009	2010	2011
Gross block	22.80	23.3	24.15
Capital work in progress	0.07	0.76	0.73

Source: Novartis Annual Reports.

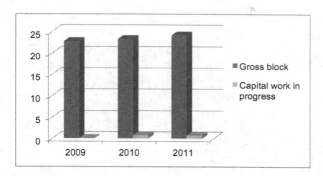

Figure 5.3 Long-term investment trend of Novartis India

Table 5.5 Composition of gross block of Novartis India (Rs crore)

Break up of gross block	2007	2008	2009	2010	2011
Buildings	3.47	3.47	3.47	3.47	3.47
Plant and machinery	14.06	14.22	13.52	13.78	15.09

Source: Novartis Annual Reports.

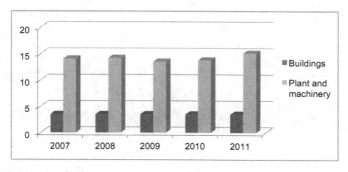

Figure 5.4 Gross block trend of Novartis India

Sources of fund: Analysing the balance sheet of the company, it can be easily inferred that there are no funds raised on short-term or long-term basis for long-term investment (Table 5.6). The company's efficiency in terms of asset turnover has been increasing over the past three years.

(c) Cipla Ltd

The investments of Cipla Ltd for the past three years are shown in Table 5.7 and Figure 5.5.

From this we can infer that, the investment in Cipla for the past three years has been around Rs 400 crore. The major source of financing for all these years were long-term loans with the exception for the year 2010 where there was proceed of about Rs 676 crore from

Table 5.6 Sources of funds of Novartis India (Rs crore)

	2009	2010	2011
Share capital	15.98	15.98	15.98
Reserves total	687.01	577.48	498.76
Secured loans	0	0	0
Unsecured loans	0.2	0.27	0.3

Source: Novartis Annual Reports.

Table 5.7 Long-term investment of Cipla (Rs crore)

	2009	2010	2011
Gross block	2,693.29	2,895.44	3929
Accumulated depreciation	700.8	884.27	1,060.98
Net block	1,992.49	2,011.17	2,868.02
Capital work in progress	366.32	684.24	253.07

	2009	2010	2011
Investments (Rs crore)	464.33	336.6	425.68

Source: Cipla Annual Reports.

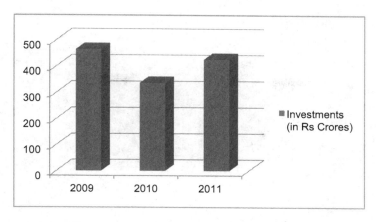

Figure 5.5 Long-term investment trend of Cipla

qualified institutional placements (QIP) issue. The investment is also seen on more or less on constant side due to pharmaceutical industry is one which is least impacted by any external economic shock.

2. Financial forecasting for capital investment

The future capital assets requirement has been determined with the help of 'financial forecasting technique'. As a practice, sales and expenditure have been forecasted with 10% increase in order to study the impact on PAT and determine the requirement of long-term assets proportionately. This helps the company to plan out their expansion better.

(a) Sun Pharmaceutical Industries Ltd

(I) SALES FORECASTING

From Table 5.8, it is found out that 10% increase in sales leads to 23.91% increase in PAT. So, it is moderately responsive.

(II) EXPENDITURE FORECASTING

It can be inferred from Table 5.9 that 10% increase in expenditure leads to 11.90% erosion of PAT.
So, PAT is more sensitive to change in sales.

Table 5.8 PAT impact to increased sales of Sun Pharma (Rs crore)

	2011	With 10% increase in sales
Income		
Sales turnover	3,157.36	3,473.10
Excise duty	52.66	52.66
Net sales	3,104.70	3,420.44
Other income	194.76	194.76
Total income	**3,297.47**	**3,615.20**
Expenditure		
Raw materials	894.94	894.94
Power and fuel cost	39.4	39.4
Employee cost	207.5	207.5
Other manufacturing expenses	107.61	107.61
Selling and administration expenses	504.87	504.87
Miscellaneous expenses	24.31	24.31
Total expenditure	**1,778.63**	**1,778.63**
Operating profit	1,518.84	1,836.57
Interest	0.59	0.59
Gross profit	1,518.25	1,835.98
Depreciation	64.23	64.23
Profit before tax (PBT)	1,454.02	1,771.75
Tax	57.04	57.04
Reported net profit	**1,383.80**	**1,714.71**

Table 5.9 PAT impact to increased expenditure of Sun Pharma (Rs crore)

	2011	With 10% increase in expenditure
Income		
Sales turnover	3,157.36	3,157.36
Excise duty	52.66	52.66
Net sales	3,104.70	3,104.70
Other income	194.76	194.76
Total income	**3,297.47**	**3,297.47**

Expenditure		
Raw materials	894.94	984.43
Power and fuel cost	39.4	43.34
Employee cost	207.5	228.25
Other manufacturing expenses	107.61	118.37
Selling and administration expenses	504.87	555.36
Miscellaneous expenses	24.31	26.74
Total expenditure	**1,778.63**	**1,956.49**
Operating profit	1,518.84	1,340.98
Interest	0.59	0.59
Gross profit	1,518.25	1,340.39
Depreciation	64.23	64.23
PBT	1,454.02	1,276.16
Tax	57.04	57.04
Reported net profit	**1,383.80**	**1,219.12**

(b) Novartis India Ltd

(I) SALES FORECASTING

(II) EXPENDITURE FORECASTING

As evident from Tables 5.10 and 5.11, it can be easily stated that a 10% increase in sales will result in a 31% increase in net profit, whereas 10% increase in expenditure will result in a 27% reduction in net profit.

So, here also PAT is more sensitive to sales.

(c) Cipla Ltd

(II) SALES FORECASTING

(ii) Expenditure forecasting

As can be seen from Tables 5.12 and 5.13, with a 10% increase in sales the net profit is about 54% so profits are highly leveraged, whereas with a 10% increase in expenditure the resultant decrease in profit is 46%.

PAT is sensitive to sales in this case also.

Table 5.10 PAT impact to increased sales of Novartis India (Rs crore)

	Original	With 10% increase in sales
Income		
Sales turnover	710.07	781.077
Excise duty	1.66	1.66
Net sales	708.41	779.417
Other income	100.59	100.59
Stock adjustments	2.84	2.84
Total income	811.84	882.847
Expenditure		
Raw materials	276.15	276.15
Power and fuel cost	2.5	2.5
Employee cost	104.89	104.89
Other manufacturing expenses	46.97	46.97
Selling and admin expenses	131.32	131.32
Miscellaneous expenses	28.44	28.44
Total expenditure	590.27	590.27
Operating profit	221.57	292.577
Interest	0.28	0.28
Gross profit	221.29	292.297
Depreciation	2.38	2.38
PBT	218.91	289.917
Tax	72.51	96.55
Fringe benefit tax	0	0
Deferred tax	–0.27	–0.27
Reported net profit	146.67	193.37

Table 5.11 PAT impact to increased expenditure of Novartis India (Rs crore)

	Original	With 10% increase in expenditure
Income		
Sales turnover	710.07	710.07
Excise duty	1.66	1.66
Net sales	708.41	708.41
Other income	100.59	100.59
Stock adjustments	2.84	2.84
Total income	811.84	811.84

Expenditure		
Raw materials	276.15	303.765
Power and fuel cost	2.5	2.75
Employee cost	104.89	115.379
Other manufacturing expenses	46.97	51.667
Selling and admin expenses	131.32	144.452
Miscellaneous expenses	28.44	31.284
Total expenditure	590.27	649.297
Operating profit	221.57	162.543
Interest	0.28	0.28
Gross profit	221.29	162.263
Depreciation	2.38	2.38
PBT	218.91	159.883
Tax	72.51	52.76
Fringe benefit tax	0	0
Deferred tax	−0.27	−0.27
Reported net profit	146.67	107.12

Table 5.12 PAT impact to increased sales of Cipla (Rs crore)

Year end	2011	With 10% increase in sales
Gross sales	6,183.87	6,802.257
Less: excise	48.71	48.71
Net sales	6,135.16	6,753.547
Expenditure		
Increase/decrease in stock	−125.74	−125.74
Raw materials consumed	2,986.17	2,986.17
Power and fuel cost	164.42	164.42
Employee cost	445.6	445.6
Other manufacturing expenses	798.63	798.63
General and administration expenses	267.71	267.71
Selling and distribution expenses	385.53	385.53
Miscellaneous expenses	120.44	120.44
Less: preoperative expenses capitalised	0	0

(*Continued*)

Table 5.12 (Continued)

Year end	2011	With 10% increase in sales
Total expenditure	5,042.76	5,042.76
Profit before depreciation, interest and tax (PBDIT) (excluding other income)	1092.4	1,710.787
Other income	298.72	298.72
Operating profit	1,391.12	2,009.507
Interest	10.87	10.87
Profit before depreciation and tax (PBDT)	1,380.25	1,998.637
Depreciation	228.86	228.86
Profit before taxation and exceptional items	1,151.39	1,769.777
Exceptional income/expenses	0	0
Profit before tax	1,151.39	1,769.777
Provision for tax	191	293.5820243
Profit after tax (PAT)	960.39	1,476.194976

Table 5.13 PAT impact to increased expenditure of Cipla (Rs crore)

Year end	2011	With 10% increase in expense
Gross sales	6,183.87	6183.87
Less: excise	48.71	53.581
Net sales	6,135.16	6,130.289
Expenditure		
Increase/decrease in stock	−125.74	−138.314
Raw materials consumed	2,986.17	3,284.787
Power and fuel cost	164.42	180.862
Employee cost	445.6	490.16
Other manufacturing expenses	798.63	878.493
General and administration expenses	267.71	294.481
Selling and distribution expenses	385.53	424.083
Miscellaneous expenses	120.44	132.484
Less: preoperative expenses capitalised	0	

Total expenditure	5,042.76	5,547.036
PBDIT (Excl OI)	1092.4	583.253
Other income	298.72	298.72
Operating profit	1,391.12	881.973
Interest	10.87	11.957
PBDT	1,380.25	870.016
Depreciation	228.86	251.746
PBT and exceptional items	1,151.39	618.27
Exceptional income/expenses	0	0
PBT	1,151.39	618.27
Provision for tax	191	102.5626156
PAT	960.39	515.7073844

Conclusion

It is evident from the foregoing discussion that among all the units, the major investments in Sun Pharma and Novartis have been in the buildings and the plant and machinery. The long-term assets are being financed by internal financing in Sun Pharma, whereas in Novartis there are no funds raised on short-term or long-term basis. Cipla's major source of financing for all these years was long-term loans. Regarding risk element, PAT has been found to be sensitive to sales in all the cases.

Discussion questions

1 Discuss the investment trend of Sun Pharma, Novartis and Cipla with regard to capital budgeting decision.
2 What are the sources of funds used by the above units for their capex decision?
3 Analyse the trend of gross block of the above units.
4 Evaluate the impact factor of the above units on profit with the help of forecasting analysis. How is it helpful in planning the capital investment requirements?
5 Comment upon the capital investment policy of the above units.

6

CAPITAL BUDGETING PRACTICES OF AUTOMOBILE SECTOR IN INDIA

Indian automobile industry

Following India's growing openness, the arrival of new and existing models, easy availability of finance at relatively low rates of interest and price discounts offered by the dealers and manufacturers all have stirred the demand for vehicles and a strong growth of the Indian automobile industry. The Indian automotive industry has emerged as a 'sunrise sector' in the Indian economy. India is emerging as one of the world's fastest-growing passenger car markets and second-largest two-wheeler manufacturer. It is also home for the largest motorcycle manufacturer and fifth-largest commercial vehicle manufacturer.

India is emerging as an export hub for sports utility vehicles (SUVs). The global automobile majors are looking to leverage India's cost-competitive manufacturing practices and are assessing opportunities to export SUVs to Europe, South Africa and South-East Asia. India can emerge as a supply hub to feed the world demand for SUVs.

India also has the largest base to export compact cars to Europe. Moreover, hybrid and electronic vehicles are new developments on the automobile canvas and India is one of the key markets for them. Global and Indian manufacturers are focussing their efforts to develop innovative products, technologies and supply chains.

The automotive plants of global automakers in India rank among the top across the world in terms of their productivity and quality. Top auto MNCs such as Hyundai, Toyota and Suzuki rank their Indian production facilities right on top of their global pecking order.

Key statistics

The amount of cumulative foreign direct investment (FDI) inflow into the automobile industry during April 2000 to January 2013 was worth US$7,653 million, amounting to 4% of the total FDI inflows (in terms of US dollars), as per data published by Department of Industrial Policy and Promotion, Ministry of Commerce.

The Indian small and light commercial vehicle (LCV) segment is expected to more than double by 2015–16 and grow at 18.5% CAGR for the next five years, according to a report titled 'Strategic Assessment of Small and Light Commercial Vehicles Market in India' by Frost and Sullivan.

The LCVs market – both passenger and goods carrier – is estimated to register a sales growth of around 20% during FY 2012–FY 2015, as per a RNCOS report titled, 'India LCV Market Outlook'.

India is the world's second-largest heavy commercial vehicle market. The RNCOS report, 'India MCV and HCV Market Outlook', observed that infrastructure boom and emergence of hub and spoke model, among other factors, have given a new dimension to the medium and heavy goods carrier commercial vehicles' sector in India. It is anticipated that the sales of medium and heavy commercial (M&HC) goods carriers will increase at a CAGR of more than 10.5% during 2011–12 to 2014–15.

In another RNCOS research report, 'Indian Automobile Sector Analysis', the production of passenger vehicle is forecast to grow at a CAGR of around 11% from 2009–10 to 2012–13, and domestic volume sales at a CAGR growth of around 12%.

Major developments and investments

- Yamaha Motor Co. has announced to set up its fifth global R&D centre at its Greater Noida facility.
- Honda Cars India Ltd (HCIL) plans to invest Rs 2,500 crore (US$462.11 million) at its Tapukara plant in Rajasthan. The company plans to set up a new assembly line for car with an installed annual capacity of 120,000 units.
- Isuzu Motors plans to set up its greenfield manufacturing facility in Andhra Pradesh, for pickup trucks or LCVs and SUVs, with an investment of Rs 1,500 crore (US$277.26 million) over five to seven years.

- Volvo plans to expand car operations in India. The company looks to drive in new models in the market apart from increasing its sales network.
- Global ultra-luxury car maker Rolls-Royce Motor Cars planned to launch exclusive 'India Edition' cars. The car maker would come up with a customised edition of its Phantom and Ghost models for Indian buyers.
- Escorts Ltd has inked a partnership with Italy-based BCS SpA to distribute and sell the speciality Ferrari brand of tractors in India.
- TVS Motor and BMW AG's motorcycle division have announced a deal to jointly develop bikes that would give the Indian automaker access to BMW technology. TVS Motor and BMW will develop motorcycles in the sub 500 cc segment.
- Bajaj Auto and Kawasaki Heavy Industries plan to take their partnership to Indonesia, under which select Bajaj products will be assembled at the Kawasaki facility and distributed through its network.
- Bajaj Auto also plans to become the first Indian automobile company to manufacture a street bike, with a 'Made in India' motorcycle tag, in the United States. The Indian company will manufacture this product for its partner KTM AG.

Government initiatives

The Government of India allows 100% FDI in the automotive industry through automatic route.

Some of the highlights of the Union Budget 2012–13 are as follows:

- The auto industry is encouraged by five years extension of 200% weighted deduction of R&D expenditure under Income Tax Act and also introduced the weighted deduction of 150% for expenditure on skills development. These measures will help the industry improve its products and performance.
- The increase in customs duty on cars and multi-utility vehicles (MUVs) valued above US$40,000 from 60% to 75% seems to be a step to encourage local manufacturing, value addition and employment.
- Also, the concessional import duty on specified parts of hybrid vehicles has been extended to lithium ion batteries and other parts of hybrid vehicles. This will help the industry to achieve better cost efficiency.

The Government of India plans to push the supply of vehicles powered by electricity over the next eight years. It is expected that there will be a demand of 5–7 million electricity-operated vehicles by 2020. The government also plans to introduce fuel-efficiency ratings for automobiles to encourage sale of cars that consume less petrol or diesel, as per Mr Veerappa Moily, Union Minister for Petroleum and Natural Gas.

The rapid improvement in infrastructure, huge domestic market, increasing purchasing power, established financial market and stable corporate governance framework have made the country a favourable destination for investment by global majors in the auto industry, as per Automotive Mission Plan (AMP) (2006–16). The AMP aims at doubling the contribution of automotive sector in GDP by taking the turnover to US$145 billion in 2016 with special emphasis on export of small cars, MUVs, two- and three-wheelers and auto components.

Road ahead

India is expected to become the eleventh-largest market for Renault by the end of 2013, as per Mr Carlos Ghosn, chairman and CEO, Renault. India is expected to be a critical global hub for the firm along with Brazil, Russia and, perhaps, another country in the Association of Southeast Asian Nations region. India is poised to become the second-largest economy in manufacturing by 2017, followed by Brazil as the third-ranked country, according to consulting major Deloitte.

Additionally, the vision of AMP 2006–2016 aims India 'to emerge as the destination of choice in the world for design and manufacture of automobiles and auto components with output reaching a level of US$145 billion accounting for more than 10 per cent of the GDP and providing additional employment to 25 million people by 2016'.

Moreover, the introduction of alternative fuels like hydrogen and biofuels needs to be promoted to ensure sustainability of the industry over the long term.

Also, manufacturing exports from India could increase from US$40 billion in 2002 to about US$300 billion in 2015, according to a report titled 'Made in India – the Next Big Manufacturing Export Story', jointly prepared by industry body CII and McKinsey. The report assesses that such an expansion would make India grab a share of approximately 3.5% of the world manufacturing trade (Table 6.1).

Exchange Rate Used: INR 1 = US$0.01849 as on 16 April 2013.

Table 6.1 Auto trend in India

Automobile domestic sales trends

Category	2005–6	2006–7	2007–8	2008–9	2009–10	2010–11	*Number of vehicles* 2011–12
Passenger vehicles	1,143,076	1,379,979	1,549,882	1,552,703	1,951,333	2,501,542	2,618,072
Commercial vehicles	351,041	467,765	490,494	384,194	532,721	684,905	809,532
Three-wheelers	359,920	403,910	364,781	349,727	440,392	526,024	513,251
Two-wheelers	7,052,391	7,872,334	7,249,278	7,437,619	9,370,951	11,768,910	13,435,769
Grand total	**8,906,428**	**10,123,988**	**9,654,435**	**9,724,243**	**12,295,397**	**15,481,381**	**17,376,624**

Source: Available at http://www.ibef.org/industry/india-automobiles.aspx (accessed on 18 June 2013).

Scope

Here, we analyse and compare the capital budgeting practices of three leading players in the automobile industry in India, namely, Tata Motors, Hero MotoCorp and Mahindra & Mahindra.

1. Tata Motors Ltd

Tata Motors Ltd is an Indian multinational automotive corporation headquartered in Mumbai, India. It is the eighteenth-largest motor vehicle manufacturing company in the world by volume. Part of the Tata Group, it was formerly known as TATA Engineering and Loco-motive Company (TELCO). Its products include passenger cars, trucks, vans and coaches. Tata Motors is South Asia's largest automobile company; it is the leader in commercial vehicles and among the top three in passenger vehicles.

2. Hero MotoCorp Ltd

Hero MotoCorp Ltd (formerly Hero Honda Motors Ltd) is the world's largest manufacturer of two-wheelers, based in India. In 2001, the company achieved the coveted position of being the largest two-wheeler manufacturing company in India and also the 'World No. 1' two-wheeler company in terms of unit volume sales in a calendar year. Hero MotoCorp Ltd continues to maintain this position till date.

3. Mahindra & Mahindra Ltd

Mahindra & Mahindra Ltd is an Indian multinational automaker headquartered in Mumbai, Maharashtra, India. It is one of the largest automobile manufacturers by production in India and a subsidiary of Mahindra Group conglomerate. The company was founded in 1945 in Ludhiana and changed its name to Mahindra & Mahindra in 1948.

Analysis and discussion

1. Financing and investment pattern of long-term assets

The financing and long-term investment trend of the units has been analysed to determine their growth pattern. It is further evaluated components' wise to determine the management approach for future expansion. Debt to equity ratio indicates the financing policy of the units for these assets.

(a) Tata Motors

Fixed assets additions during the year 2010–11 are Rs 2,292.92 crore, which included the Nano plant at Sanand, product development costs mainly for Winger Ambulance, Aria and other regulatory projects and other capex towards capacity for the new products, balancing equipments and the like. *Investments* increased marginally to Rs 22,624.21 crore as of 31 March 2011, as compared to Rs 22,336.90 crore as of 31 March 2010. An assembly plant in South Africa is being set up and is expected to start production next year. The net cash outflow from investing activity reduced during the current year to Rs 2,521.88 crore from Rs 11,848.29 crore for the previous year (Table 6.2).

During the past year, the company sold Rs 10,751.91 crore in subsidiary companies (mainly related to the acquisition of Jaguar Land Rover business) and joint ventures. The investment in fixed assets was Rs 2,381.65 crore during the year as against Rs 2,310.17 crore for the previous year.

(b) Hero MotoCorp

During 2011, the company incurred a capital expenditure of Rs 364.12 crore (Table 6.3). The funds went into *capacity expansion and replacements.*

Hero Honda has been a *debt-free* company for the past ten years. The unsecured loan of Rs 32.71 crore from the state government of

Table 6.2 Investment outlay of Tata Motors (Rs crore)

	2009	2010	2011	% growth
Debt to equity ratio (number of times)	1.08	1.11	0.79	
Net fixed assets	14,592.16	16,436.04	17,475.63	6.32
Depreciation	1,253.33	7,212.92	8,466.25	17.4
Gross fixed assets (including capital work in progress)	2,292.92	23,648.96	25,941.88	9.7
Investments	12,968.13	22,336.90	22,624.21	1.29

Source: Tata Annual Reports.

Haryana on account of sales tax deferment is interest-free and has no holding costs. Net interest payment by the company has been negative during the past few years (Table 6.3).

(c) Mahindra & Mahindra

The company acquired SYMC, a premier manufacturer of SUVs and recreational vehicles in Korea. The total cost of acquisition of SYMC was KRW 522,500,000,000 (approximately US$463 million) with KRW 427,095,235,000 (approximately US$378 million) payable for new stocks and KRW 9,5404,765,000 (approximately US$85 million) in corporate bonds for an equity stake of around 70% in SYMC (Table 6.4).

Table 6.3 Investment outlay of Hero MotoCorp (Rs crore)

	2009	2010	2011	Growth (%)
Debt to equity ratio (number of times)	0.02	0.02	0.50	
Net fixed assets	1,694	1,707	4,080.28	139
Depreciation	942.56	1,092.20	1,458.18	
Gross fixed assets (including capital work in progress)	1,694.25	1,706.92	4,205.42	146
Purchase of fixed assets (net)	(374.92)	(315.08)	(364.12)	
Investments	3,368.75	3,925.71	5,128.75	30.6

Source: Hero MotoCorp Annual Reports.

Table 6.4 Investment outlay of Mahindra & Mahindra (Rs crore)

	2009	2010	2011	Growth (%)
Debt to equity ratio (number of times)	0.56	0.37	0.23	
Net fixed assets	3,214	3,703	4,372	18
Depreciation	292	371	414	
Gross fixed assets (including capital work in progress)	5,541	6,240	7,214	15.6
Investments	5,786	6,398	9,325	45.75

Source: Mahindra Annual Reports.

The company is also seized of the global shift towards *sustainable mobility* driven by climate change concerns. Towards this objective, the company is investing in new alternate fuel technologies. The recent acquisition of Mahindra Reva Electric Vehicle Private Ltd is an important step towards remaining at the forefront of these developments. As of 31 March 2011, the gross block of fixed assets and capital work in progress was Rs 7,213.58 crore as compared to Rs 6,240.49 crore as of 31 March 2010.

During the year 2011, the company incurred capital expenditure of Rs 1,152.51 crore (previous year Rs 946.31 crore). The *major items of capital expenditure* were as follows:

- New Product Development.
- Capacity Enhancement.
- R&D including on the company's research facility in Chennai. This included purchase of intangible assets aggregating Rs 191.03 crore (previous year Rs 225.28 crore).

2. Operating risk (fixed assets versus net current assets)

Operating risk signifies the operational efficiency of business units. To measure the degree of operating risk, fixed to net current assets ratio has been used as it determines the resources' utilisation by a business and thus evaluates the operational efficiency.

(a) Tata Motors

Though net current assets are negative, indicating negative working capital during the past two years but at an absolute level, there has been an increase in current assets (Table 6.5). The increase is due to

Table 6.5 Assets composition of Tata Motors (Rs crore)

	2009	2010	2011	Growth (%)
Fixed assets	2,292.92	23,648.96	25,941.88 2,292.92	9.7
Current assets	2,584.00	11,506.61	14,090.61	22.5
Current liabilities	1,576.63	(14,609.16)	(13,032.53)	−10.8
Provisions	(459.28)	(2,763.43)	(3,222.71)	16.6
Net current assets	3,701.35	(5,865.98)	(2,164.63)	−63.1

Source: Tata Annual Reports.

(a) increased inventories on account of volumes and strategic inventory; and (b) increased receivables in respect of sales to various state transport undertakings wherein payments are received after sixty to ninety days of billing. Current liabilities are lower due to decrease in tenure from eighty-nine days to seventy-five days in respect of acceptances and reduction in redemption premium due to conversion of Foreign Currency Convertible Notes.

(b) Hero MotoCorp

Here, negative working capital picture is evident. It is a good sign as far as business proposition is concerned. At an absolute level also, there has been a decrease in current assets and increase in current liabilities during the period (Table 6.6).

(c) Mahindra & Mahindra

In the above case, unlike Tata Motors and Hero there has been a negative working capital only in 2011. In all other years, they have appositive working capital (Table 6.7).

Table 6.6 Assets composition of Hero MotoCorp (Rs crore)

	2009	2010	2011	Growth (%)
Fixed assets	1,694.25	1,706.92	4,205.42	146
Current assets	1,013.49	2,882.58	1,504.57	–48
Current liabilities	1,525.25	3,805.06	5,063.68	33
Provisions	526.97	1,026.35	1,081.07	5.36
Net current assets	(1,039.33)	(1,948.83)	(4,640.18)	138

Source: Hero Annual Reports.

Table 6.7 Assets composition of Mahindra & Mahindra (Rs crore)

	2009	2010	2011	Growth (%)
Fixed assets	5,541	6,240	7,214	15.6
Current assets	5,063	6,046	6,143	1.6
Current liabilities and provisions	4,798	5,197	6,768	30.2
Net current assets	265.17	849.97	(624.08)	

Source: Mahindra Annual Reports.

Conclusion

Among all the sample companies, major investment has been in case of Tata Motors. There have been fixed assets additions during the year 2010–11. All companies enjoy negative working capital benefits except Mahindra & Mahindra which has negative working capital only in 2011.

Discussion questions

1 What is the investment outlay of Tata Motors, Hero MotoCorp and Mahindra & Mahindra with respect to capital budgeting decision?
2 Discuss the financing policy of the above units for capital investments with the help of debt to equity ratio.
3 What type of depreciation policy is followed by the automobile companies?
4 Analyse the operating risk of the above units by studying comparative trend between fixed assets and current assets.
5 How do you rate the capital investment management of the above units?

7

CAPITAL BUDGETING PRACTICES OF POWER SECTOR IN INDIA

Power sector in India

India has the fifth-largest power generation capacity in the world with an installed capacity of 152 MW as of 30 September 2009 (Netscribes, 'Power Sector – India', March 2009). However, this is very low as compared to combined power consumption of the top four countries which is about 49% of the total power generated in the world. The average per capita consumption of electricity in India is estimated to be 704 kWh during 2008–9, which is fairly low when compared to that of some of the developed and emerging nations such United States (~15,000 kWh) and China (~1,800 kWh). The world average stands at 2,300 kWh (Central Electricity Authority).

Another part of power sector is transmission. India has only the capability to transmit 13% of the power it generates. With continuous plans of increasing the generation capacity of India, the transmission capacity is also expected to augment on the same lines.

The final part of the power sector is the distribution of power. One of the major problems faced by this segment is the high transmission and distribution losses (T&D losses) which are much higher than the benchmarks set by the other developing or developed countries. However, with separatisation of all segments of a power company, greater concentration has been given to the distribution of power and better efforts made to reduce the inefficiencies of the system.

Scope

Here, we will discuss two leading power units in India on comparative basis of public sector versus private sector.

1. *National Thermal Power Corporation Ltd*

India's largest power company, National Thermal Power Corporation (NTPC), was set up in 1975 to accelerate power development in India. NTPC is emerging as a diversified power major with presence in the entire value chain of the power generation business. Apart from power generation, which is the mainstay of the company, NTPC has already ventured into consultancy, power trading, ash utilisation and coal mining. NTPC became a Maharatna company in May 2010, one of the only four companies to be awarded this status.

2. *Suzlon*

The Suzlon Group is ranked as the world's fifth-largest wind turbine supplier, in terms of cumulative installed capacity, at the end of 2010. The company's global spread extends across Asia, Australia, Europe, Africa and North and South America with over 19,000 MW of wind energy capacity installed in twenty-eight countries, operations in thirty-two countries and a workforce of over 13,000.

The Suzlon Group offers one of the most comprehensive product portfolios – ranging from sub-megawatt onshore turbines at 600 KW, to the world's largest commercial 6.15 MW offshore turbine – built on a vertically integrated, low-cost, manufacturing base. The Suzlon Group – headquartered at Suzlon One Earth in Pune, India – comprises Suzlon Energy Ltd and its subsidiaries, including REpower Systems SE, a leader in offshore wind technology.

Analysis and discussion

1. NTPC

(a) Investment pattern of long-term assets

During the year 2010–11, the gross block of the company increased by around 9% than the previous year. This was on account of capitalisation of one unit of Korba-II (500 MW) Power Project and one unit of Dadri-II (490 MW) Power Project. However, net block increased by 13%. This was due to the fact that the company had revised its depreciation policy in line with the opinion expressed by the Comptroller and Auditor General of India. Due to the increase in construction activities the capital work in progress increased by 25% over the previous year (Table 7.1).

Table 7.1 Investment pattern of NTPC

	Growth (%)		
	Fixed assets	Net block	Total liabilities
2009–10	6.91	4.97	8.51
2010–11	8.88	12.99	9.90

Source: NTPC Annual Reports.

Table 7.2 Assets composition of NTPC (Rs crore)

	2008–9	2009–10	2010–11
Fixed assets	62,353.00	66,663.80	72,583.94
Net current assets	20,236.60	19,848.40	21,720.93

Source: NTPC Annual Reports.

The company has entered FY 2012 with an approved outlay for capital schemes of Rs 26,400 crore, which is 18% higher than the capital expenditure for FY 2011. The company aims at reducing cost while continuing to drive growth. Disciplined capital expenditure and prudent resource mobilisation strategies have been the abiding features of the company's management of finance. In fact, India's biggest bank, State Bank of India, has extended its largest-ever loan to any organisation in India or abroad by signing a loan agreement of Rs 10,000 crore with NTPC in July 2011. Environmental concerns underpin the company's growth strategy as the company strives to achieve a low carbon future. The approach includes increasing cycle efficiency of fossil fuel-based units, increasing the share of non-fossil fuel-based generation and research in CO_2 fixation technologies. Investment in technology is directly linked to creating value for the shareholders of NTPC (Table 7.2).

(b) Financing policy

The capacity addition programme will be financed with debt to equity ratio of 70:30 (Table 7.3). The directors believe that the internal

INVESTMENT DECISION

Table 7.3 Debt to equity ratio of NTPC

	2010–11	2009–10	2008–9
Debt:equity ratio	0.76	0.73	0.70

Source: NTPC Annual Reports.

accruals of the company will be substantial to finance the equity component for the new projects. Given its low gearing and strong credit ratings, the company is well positioned to raise the required borrowings.

The organisation is exploring domestic as well as international borrowing options including overseas development assistance provided by bilateral agencies to mobilise the debt required for the planned capacity expansion programme. During the year 2010–11, the company has tied up loans of Rs 3,479 crore including Rs 2,000 crore from HUDCO Ltd and Rs 1,000 crore from HDFC Bank Ltd for part-funding of debt requirement in respect of capital expenditure for the next three years.

The company has entered into a term loan agreement with State Bank of India on 7 July 2011 for Rs 10,000 crore for financing NTPC Ongoing Capital Expenditure for various power generation projects including renovation/modernisation of existing power plants.

Bonds amounting to Rs 720 crore were raised from the domestic market for financing the capital expenditure and refinancing the loans. The company also raised US$500 million senior unsecured fixed rate ten-year bonds under its US$1 billion medium term note (MTN) programme during the July 2011. The bonds carry a coupon rate of 5.625% per annum payable semi-annually and are due for maturity in July 2021.

2. Suzlon Energy Ltd

(a) Investment pattern of long-term assets

Fixed assets have shown a rise in value over the past three years while the net current assets have shown a decline over the past three years financial data (Table 7.4).

Table 7.4 Assets composition of Suzlon (Rs crore)

	2008–9	2009–10	2010–11
Fixed assets	915.83	1,355.74	1,439.52
Net current assets	5,943.53	4,685.39	4,725.42

Source: Suzlon Annual Reports.

Table 7.5 Debt to equity ratio of Suzlon

	2010–11	2009–10	2008–9
Debt:equity ratio	1.36	1.13	0.44

Source: Suzlon Annual Reports.

(b) Financing policy

Suzlon's strategy of expansion has been through inorganic growth. Inorganic growth is synonymous with growth that is fuelled through mergers and acquisitions. In order to fund this growth through the path of mergers and acquisitions, Suzlon has been exposed to considerable amount of debt. This is very evidently reflected in their debt to equity ratio (Table 7.5). The debt to equity has clearly grown at a pace over the past three years from 0.44 in 2008–9 to 1.36 in 2010–11.

Conclusion

NTPC's investment in fixed assets during the year 2010–11 is more than Suzlon's investments. Suzlon has been exposed to considerable amount of debt but NTPC has a much higher debt to equity ratio due to Central Electricity Regulatory Commission norms. So, NTPC's risk level is higher as compared to Suzlon.

Discussion questions

1   Discuss the investment trend of NTPC and Suzlon with respect to capital budgeting decision.
2   Critique the financing policy of the above units for capital investments with the help of debt–equity ratio.

3   Analyse the assets composition of the above units.
4   Comment on the capital investment management of the above units.
5   Discuss the regulatory perspective on capital investment in power
    sector in India.

Part III

FINANCING DECISION

8

CAPITAL STRUCTURE PLANNING AND POLICY

Introduction

The financing policy decision is deciding about the capital structure of the firm. A firm tries to have an optimum capital mix of debt and equity for shareholders' wealth maximisation. The weighted average cost of capital (WACC) is helpful in capital budgeting decisions. It is used as a discounting rate in calculating the NPV and IRR of a project and thus determines whether a company should go ahead with a project or not. Every firm tries to minimise its WACC by employing a suitable mix as a firm with lower WACC can more easily return profits to its owners.

The financing decision involves a consideration of three principal responsibilities of a finance manager. These are

(a) estimation of total financial requirements for the business enterprise;
(b) identification of sources of finance and determination of financing mix; and
(c) cultivating sources of finance and raising the required finance.

In other words, it covers two interrelated aspects, namely:

(a) determining an appropriate financial/capital structure; and
(b) raising the required amount of funds.

Capital structure defined

The assets of a company can be financed by increasing either the owners' claim or the creditors' claim. The owners' claim increases when the firm raises funds by issuing ordinary share or by retained earnings; the creditors' claim increases by borrowing. The various means of financing represent the financial structure of an enterprise. The left-hand side of the balance sheet (liability plus equity) represents the financial structure of a company. Traditionally, short-term borrowings are excluded from the list of methods of financing the firm's capital expenditure, and therefore, the long-term claims are said to form the capital structure of the enterprise.

Capital structure is the composition of debt and equity. Determination of an optimal capital structure has always been a topic of discussion among theoreticians for many decades. The financial or capital structure decision is a significant managerial decision. It influences the shareholder's return and risk. Consequently, the market value of the shares may be affected by the capital structure decision.

Theory of capital structure

Following are the basic four theories of capital structure.

1. Net income theory

Net income approach was presented by Durand. This theory states that the value of the firm can be changed by changing the capital mix, thereby decreasing the overall cost of capital. Debt is considered a cheaper source of finance on account of tax deductibility of interest and this ultimately decrease the WACC.

The overall cost of capital is measured in terms of WACC. It is the weighted average costs of equity and debts where the weights are the amount of capital raised from each source.

Assumptions of net income approach

- Increase in debt will not affect the confidence levels of the investors.
- The cost of debt is less than cost of equity.
- There are no taxes.

2. Net operating income theory

Net operating income theory is opposite to net income approach. This approach was also put forth by Durand. It states that the capital structure does not affect overall cost of capital and market value of firm. As per this approach, the WACC and total value of a company are independent of the capital structure decision or financial leverage of a company.

As per this approach, the market value is dependent on the operating income and the associated business risk of the firm. Both these factors cannot be impacted by the financial leverage.

Assumptions of net operating income approach

- The overall capitalisation rate remains constant irrespective of the degree of leverage.
- Value of equity is the difference between total firm value less value of debt, that is Value of Equity = Total Value of the Firm – Value of Debt.
- WACC remains constant.

3. Traditional theory/trade-off theory

This theory is mix of net income approach and net operating income approach. It suggests that there is an optimal debt to equity ratio where the overall cost of capital is the minimum and market value of the firm is the maximum. Before this point, the marginal cost of debt is less than cost of equity and after this point vice versa. So, beyond this point, changes in the financing mix can bring positive change to the value of the firm.

It has three stages:

(1) *First stage*: Initially, company should employ more debt in the capital structure for increasing the market value of firm.
(2) *Second stage*: Once the company attains optimal capital structure, where weighted cost of capital is least and market value of firm is maximum, it should not increase any debt further in capital structure.
(3) *Third stage*: If company goes for any amount of debt here, it can lose its market value because any increase in the amount of debt after the optimum level will increase the cost of debt and overall cost of capital.

Assumptions under traditional approach

- The rate of interest on debt remains constant for a certain period and thereafter with increase in leverage, it increases.
- The expected rate by equity shareholders remains constant till some point and then increases gradually.
- In result, the WACC first decreases and then increases. The lowest point on the curve is optimal capital structure.

4. Modigliani and Miller theory

Modigliani and Miller approach (MM theory) is fully opposite of traditional approach. This approach says that there is no relationship between capital structure and cost of capital. Value of firm and cost of capital are affected by investors' expectations. Investors' expectations are affected by large numbers of other factors.

Assumptions of Modigliani and Miller approach

- There are no taxes.
- Transaction cost for buying and selling securities as well as bankruptcy cost is nil.
- There is symmetry of information. This means that an investor will have access to same information that a corporate would and investors would behave rationally.
- The cost of borrowing is the same for investors as well as companies.
- Debt financing does not affect companies' earnings before interest and taxes (EBIT).

Modigliani and Miller approach indicates that, the value of a leveraged firm (firm which has a mix of debt and equity) is the same as the value of an unleveraged firm (firm which is wholly financed by equity), if the operating profits and future prospects are same.

5. Pecking order theory

Pecking order theory was popularised by Stewart C. Myers and it states that for raising capital, companies will prefer internal financing, debt and then issuance of new equity, respectively. Raising equity is viewed as a last resort. The rational is that companies will tend to take the course of least resistance, obtaining financing from sources that are readily available, and then steadily moving on to sources that may be more difficult to utilise.

Assumptions of pecking order theory

- New shares must be issued to outsiders.
- Even for rights issue, the firm will incur costs. So, equity is more subject to undervaluation than debt.

6. *Signalling theory*

This theory states that management has more information than an investor, which implies asymmetric information. Therefore, investors generally view all capital structure decisions as some sort of signal. So, choice of capital structure by the management can signal information to outsiders and change the value of the firm. This theory is also called the asymmetric information approach.

Assumptions of signalling theory

- Managers know more about the true value of the company's existing assets than shareholders (information asymmetry).
- Managers know more about the true value of the company's potential investment project.

7. *Market timing theory*

This theory states that companies time their equity issues in a way that they issue fresh stock when the stock prices are overvalued, and buy back shares when they are undervalued. As a result, variations in stock prices influence firm's capital structure. Companies do not usually care whether they finance with debt or equity; they simply pick the type of financing which, at that point in time, appears to be more valued by financial markets.

Factors affecting capital structure

There are various key factors which govern the capital structure decisions. They should be duly considered before taking any rational decision regarding capital structure. They are as follows.

1. *Profitability aspect*

It is logically the first step in the direction of designing a firm's capital structure. This analysis is based on EBIT–EPS relationship. EPS is a measure of a firm's performance; therefore, the EBIT/EPS analysis information can be extremely useful to the finance manager in arriving at an appropriate financing decision.

2. Liquidity aspect

The analysis of the liquidity of the firm is an important factor in capital structure planning in addition to profitability analysis. It is significant in the context of the risk of insolvency.

3. Nature of enterprise

The nature of the enterprise is one of the important factors affecting the capital structure of an enterprise. Business concerns with stable earning may raise funds by issues of debentures or preference shares because they will not feel the burden of fixed cost. On the other hand, the companies with fluctuating earnings rely more on equity share capital for raising their funds.

4. Control

The policy of control also determines the type of capital to be raised. If the management is not prepared for the dilution of control, it will prefer to raise capital through borrowings as the creditors cannot participate in the management of the company. If the management is prepared, it may go for the equity capital.

5. Flexibility of financial structure

Flexibility means the firm's ability to change its capital structure to the needs of the changing conditions. A capital structure is flexible if it is possible to acquire additional capital either through owned capital or through borrowed capital. So, if a company wants greater flexibility, it must have enough scope for addition to capital either through owned capital or borrowed capital.

6. Capital market conditions

Capital market conditions also affect the availability of a particular type of capital. In case of boom, people will like to invest in shares as they expect increasing profits, and during depression, they will like to invest in debentures so that they do get a given return on their investment.

7. Cost of rising capital

The cost of raising finance has an important influence on the capital mix. The cost of equity share capital is higher than that of debenture and preference share capital. Debentures are a cheaper source of finance because the interest payable on debentures entitles tax benefits to the company.

8. Legal requirements

State regulations regarding the issue of securities also have a bearing on the capital structure of a company. This is particularly true in the case of banking companies which are not allowed to issue any other type of security for raising funds except equity share capital on account of the Banking Regulation Act.

Concept of leverage

Leverage refers to any method or technique followed by a firm to multiply its gains. In other words, it is the employment of an asset or source of funds for which the firm has to pay a fixed cost or return. It is used by the company to maximise shareholders value.

The leverage can be either operating or financial. The use of fixed operating costs by a firm to magnify EBIT is called operating leverage. The use of fixed financing costs by a firm to magnify EPS is termed financing leverage.

Leverage ratio

This ratio is used to calculate the amount of fixed obligations involved in a company's structure and its ability to meet those obligations. As mentioned above, the leverage ratios are of two types: (a) *operating leverage ratio* and (b) *financial leverage ratio*.

Operating leverage ratio: It is the degree of fixed operating costs involved in a project. So, a firm with lower sales is a highly leveraged firm and a firm with higher sales is a low leveraged firm. It is calculated as

$$DOL = \frac{Percentage\ change\ in\ EBIT}{Percentage\ change\ in\ sales}.$$

Higher the degree of operating leverage, the greater is the operating risk and vice versa.

Financial leverage ratio: It is the degree of total debt involved in the financial structure of a firm. It is also called the debt to equity ratio. Its accepted norm is 2:1.

A high financial leverage ratio indicates risk of payment of interest and repayment of principal. It is calculated as

$$DFL = \frac{Percentage\ change\ in\ EPS}{Percentage\ change\ in\ EBIT}.$$

The higher the degree of financial leverage, the higher is the financial risk.

Box 8.1 Financial leverage and shareholder's wealth

The primary motive of a company in using financial leverage is to magnify the shareholder's returns, given the fact that the fixed financial cost is lower than the firm's rate of return (ROI). So, the difference between the earnings generated by assets financed by the fixed charges funds and costs of these funds is distributed to the shareholders as wealth in the form of higher EPS.

Measures of leverage: Ratios which measure how financially sound a company is to meet its long-term obligations are known as leverage or solvency ratios. It includes debt ratios which are based on balance sheet and coverage ratios based on income statement. There are three solvency ratios on the basis of which the analysis will be done further:

- Debt to equity ratio
- Interest coverage ratio (ICR)
- Debt service coverage ratio (DSCR)

Debt to equity ratio

It is a leverage ratio which indicates a company's financial leverage by comparing the total liabilities of the company to its net worth.

Debt to Equity Ratio = Long-Term Debt (Liabilities)/Net Worth.

This is a measurement of how much lenders, creditors and obligors have committed to the company versus what the shareholders have committed. In general, the lower the debt to equity ratio, the better it is. The ratio provides a general indication of a company's equity–liability relationship and is helpful to investors looking for a quick take on a company's leverage. A high debt to equity ratio generally means that a company has been aggressive in financing its growth with debt. The debt to equity ratio also depends on the industry in which the company operates. For example, airlines, manufacturing companies tend to have a debt to equity ratio above 2:1, while IT/IT-enabled service (ITES) companies have a negligible debt to equity ratio.

Interest coverage ratio

ICR is the ratio which gives an idea about a company's ability to pay interest on its overdue debt. ICR can be easily found out by the division of company's EBIT and the company's expenses on interest during the same period.

ICR = EBIT/Interest on Long-Term Loans.

The greater the ratio, the greater is the safety of the lender's interest as it shows its ability to pay its debt expenses. On the other hand, a lower ratio shows the company in poor light as it is going to struggle to pay its debt expenses. In general an ICR of 1.5 or below questions the company's ability to meet its debt expenses.

Debt service coverage ratio

It is the amount of cash flow available to meet annual interest and principal payments on debt, including sinking fund payments. This ratio should ideally be over 1. That would mean the property is generating enough income to pay its debt obligations.

DSCR is calculated by the following formulae:

DSCR = Cash Flow from Operating Activities after TAX/(Interest Payments + Instalments).

DSCR is an extension of ICR but it is a better ratio for solvency than ICR. It is calculated when a company takes loan from any bank/ financial institution.

A DSCR of less than 1 would mean a negative cash flow. For example, in the context of personal finance, this would mean that the borrower would have to delve into his or her personal funds every month to keep the project afloat. Generally, lenders frown on a negative cash flow, but some allow it if the borrower has strong outside income. Higher the ratio, the better it is.

A high DSCR assures the lenders a regular and periodical interest income, while a too low DSCR indicates insufficient earning capacity of the organisations to meet the obligations of long-term borrowings.

Capital structure analysis

The overall financial structure of an undertaking can be analysed from the point of view of:

(a) duration of time; and
(b) trading on equity.

Duration of time

The study of financial structure is done initially from the point of view of the length for which funds are needed with their respective ownership. As a matter of fact, an enterprise needs funds for financing long-term, medium-term and short-term requirements.

(i)   *Long-term finance* refers to that category of funds which are raised for a minimum period of ten years from shareholders, debenture holders, financial institutions and retained earnings. Such type of finance is used for investment in fixed assets, such as land, buildings, plants, machinery, furniture and fixtures and the like.

(ii) *Medium-term finance* is that category of finance which is raised for a period of more than one year but less than ten years from debenture holders, financial institutions, public deposits and commercial banks. It is used for investment in permanent working and for repayment of assets.

(iii) *Short-term finance* is that category of finance which is employed for a period of a year or less. It is raised from public deposits, trade credit and commercial banks and so represented by current liabilities and provisions. It is invested in current assets as a part of working capital.

A business firm can raise these funds from two main sources:

(i) owned funds; and
(ii) borrowed funds.

Owned funds refer to the funds provided by the owners. In a joint stock company, funds raised through the issue of shares and reinvestment of earnings are the owned funds. *Borrowed funds* refer to the borrowings of a business firm. In a company, borrowed funds consist of the funds raised from debenture holders, financial institutions, public deposits and commercial banks.

Discussion questions

1 Define capital structure. Discuss various theories of capital structure.
2 'Market timing theory is more practical than other theories of capital structure'. Explain.
3 'MM approach to capital structure is global in nature'. Discuss.
4 What are the factors which affect capital structure decision?
5 What is the concept of leverage?
6 Differentiate between operating leverage and financial leverage.
7 Discuss the measures of leverage.
8 How do you analyse the capital structure of a business?

9

FINANCING POLICY OF STEEL SECTOR IN INDIA

Given the capital budgeting decision, the firm has to decide the way in which the capital projects will be financed. Every time the firm makes an investment decision, it involves the financing decision. For example, a decision to build a new plant or to buy a new machine implies specific way of financing that project. Should a firm employ equity or debt or both? What are the implications of the debt–equity mix? What is an appropriate mix of debt and equity? In this financing discussion, an attempt has been made to explore the various aspects of the financial leverage in terms of deciding the capital structure of the firm and its impact on the shareholders' wealth. **Though 'financing approach' of few companies has been discussed in parts in the preceding chapters, in these chapters, it has been dealt in detail as a part of financing decision.**

Indian steel sector

The steel industry in India is over a century old, and India is among the top producers of steel globally. Availability of cheap labour, iron ore and strong domestic demand has led to the growth of the steel industry in India. The first steel plant in India was set up by Tata Iron and Steel Co. in 1907. The sector as a whole was freed from the license regime back in 1970 and has been expanding at an increased pace ever since. Not only the domestic companies but also the big international players have shown interest in setting up manufacturing facilities in India.

The steel industry has a number of players with large production capacities. Many companies are investing heavily in new manufacturing facilities to scale up production in near future. India is indeed a strategic producer of steel globally and companies in India are going for organic and inorganic growth to boost their production capacities. While Figure 9.1 indicates the annual steel production in India, Figure 9.2 shows the demand drivers for steel in India.

The market of India steel industry in 2011 was put at US$55.1 billion. The leading players in the Indian steel industry selected for the present study include:

(1) Steel Authority of India Ltd (SAIL);
(2) JSW Steel; and
(3) Tata Steel.

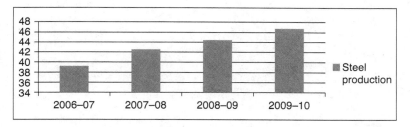

Figure 9.1 Annual production of steel
Source: Government of India, Ministry of Steel (http://steel.gov.in/).

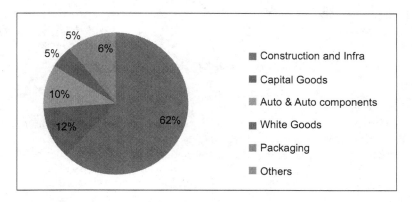

Figure 9.2 Demand drivers of steel
Source: Government of India, Ministry of Steel (http://steel.gov.in/).

Scope

In this section, we will be analysing following units.

1. Steel Authority of India Ltd

SAIL is an enterprise of the Indian government and has a market share of 20.1% in the Indian steel market. It has five integrated plants in India and is further looking to set up some more manufacturing facilities in India.

2. JSW Steel

JSW is an integrated steel manufacturer and is the largest steel producer in India in terms of installed capacity. It has a number of plants spread throughout India.

3. Tata Steel

Tata Steel has an annual crude steel production of 6.8 million tonnes. It has massive plans for expansion by setting up new plants.

Analysis and discussion

The *capital structure trend* of the units has been analysed with regard to constituents of capital mix and change in them during the period. *Financing policy* of the units has been examined by studying their debt to equity ratio of the units. *Degree of financial leverage* has been further calculated to measure the level of financial risk of the units.

1. Steel Authority of India Ltd

SAIL recorded an annual turnover of Rs 47,041 crore in 2010–11 – an increase of over 7% than the previous year. The net worth of the company increased from Rs 33,317 crore to Rs 37,069 crore in the past year. The company undertook a number of growth and expansion projects that resulted in a total capital expenditure of Rs 11,280 crore in 2010–11. In the past year, the company continued its process of debt restructuring to replace high-cost short-term loans with low-cost debts. The liquid assets of the company were Rs 20,165 as of 31 March 2011. The capital expenditure by the company was mainly financed through debt and there was no change in equity in the past year. Table 9.1 shows the financial performance of SAIL in the past ten years.

Table 9.1 Ten years at glance of SAIL

(₹crore)

Financials										
Year	2010–11	2009–10	2008–9	2007–8	2006–7	2005–6	2004–5	2003–4	2002–3	2001–2
Gross sales	47041	43935	48738	45555	39189	32280	31805	24178	19207	15502
Net sales	42719	40551	43204	39508	33923	27860	28523	21297	16837	13519
Earnings before interest, tax, depreciation and amortisation (EBITDA)	9155	11871	10946	12955	10966	7381	11097	4652	2165	1011
Depreciation	1486	1337	1288	1235	1211	1207	1127	1123	1147	1156
Interest and finance charges	475	402	259	251	332	468	605	901	1334	1562
PBT	7194	10132	9399	11469	9423	5706	9365	2628	–316	–1707
Provision for tax/income tax refund (–)	2290	3378	3228	3932	3221	1693	2548	116	–12	–
PAT	4905	6754	6170	7537	6202	4013	6817	2512	–304	–1707
Dividends	991	1363	1074	1528	1280	826	1363	–	–	–
Equity capital	4130	4130	4130	4130	4130	4130	4130	4130	4130	4130
Reserves and surplus	32939	29186	24018	18874	13054	8255	5881	529	–2141	–1878
Net worth (Equity capital and reserves and surplus)	37069	33317	28148	23004	17184	12386	10011	4659	1989	2252
Total loans	20165	16511	7563	3045	4181	4298	5770	8690	12928	14019
Net fixed assets	15083	13615	12305	11571	11598	12162	12485	13168	14036	14798
Capital work in progress	22226	14953	6550	2390	1199	758	366	382	361	556
Current assets (including short-term deposits)	38090	39154	34676	26318	20379	17384	14187	8075	7282	7107
Current liabilities and provisions	11496	11073	12277	9439	6500	8108	6608	6025	4777	4849
Working capital	26595	28081	22398	16879	13879	9276	7579	2050	2505	2258

(Continued)

Table 9.1 (Continued)

Financials										(₹ crore)
Year	2010–11	2009–10	2008–9	2007–8	2006–7	2005–6	2004–5	2003–4	2002–3	2001–2
(Current assets less current liabilities)										
Capital employed (net fixed assets + working capital)	41677	41696	34704	28450	25476	21438	20064	15218	16541	17056
Market price per share (in ₹) (As at the end of the year)	170	253	96	185	113	83	63	32	9	5
Key financial ratios										
EBIDTA to average capital employed (%)	21.70	31.11	34.66	48.05	46.41	35.28	62.91	29.30	12.89	5.72
PBT to net sales (%)	16.84	24.99	21.75	29.03	27.78	20.48	32.83	12.34	-1.88	-12.63
PBT to average capital employed (%)	17.26	26.56	29.77	42.54	39.88	27.27	53.09	16.55	-1.88	-9.66
Return on average net worth (%)	13.94	21.98	24.13	37.51	41.95	35.84	92.94	75.57	-14.35	-53.22
Net worth per share of ₹ 10 (₹)	89.75	80.66	68.15	55.69	41.60	29.99	24.24	11.28	4.82	5.45
EPS of ₹ 10 (₹)	11.87	16.35	14.94	18.25	15.02	9.72	16.50	6.08	-0.74	-4.13
Price–earnings ratio (times)	14.30	15.44	6.46	10.12	7.53	8.56	3.81	5.31	-11.94	-1.19
Dividend per share (DPS) of ₹ 10 (₹)	2.40	3.30	2.60	3.70	3.10	2.00	3.30	–	–	–
Effective dividend rate (%)	1.41	1.31	2.70	2.00	2.74	2.41	5.24	–	–	–
Debt–Equity (times)	0.54	0.50	0.27	0.13	0.24	0.35	0.58	1.87	6.50	6.23
Current ratio (times)	3.31	3.54	2.80	2.79	3.14	2.14	2.15	1.34	1.52	1.47
Capital employed to turnover ratio (times)	1.13	1.05	1.40	1.60	1.54	1.48	1.59	1.59	1.16	0.91
Working capital turnover ratio (times)	1.77	1.56	2.18	2.70	2.82	3.48	4.20	11.79	7.67	6.87
ICR (times)	7.08	14.44	29.00	46.39	29.29	13.07	16.43	3.88	0.76	-0.09

Source: Company Annual Report 2010–11.

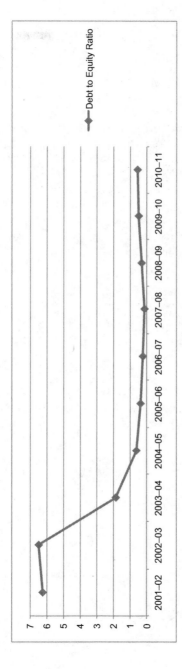

Figure 9.3 Debt to equity of SAIL

While studying the financial leverage of a company, it is important to study the debt to equity ratio of the company as it determines the mix of debt and equity in the financial mix of the company.

In the year 2010–11 high-cost short-term loans were replaced by low-cost debts. The deposits maintained by the company with the bank were of the tune of Rs 17,142 crore. The total debt taken by the company in the year increased by Rs 3,654 crore on account of borrowing of capital expenditure undertaken by the company. The capex in the year 2010–11 included modernisation and expansion projects to increase the production capacity to 23.46 million tonnes per annum (MTPA) from 13.82 MTPA.

A total amount of Rs 11,280 crore was funded through a mix of borrowings and internal accruals. No increase in equity was made in the year 2010–11. This resulted in increased leverage for the company as the amount of debt for the company increased whereas the equity remained constant (Tables 9.2 and 9.3).

2. JSW Steel

JSW Steel is the largest private steel manufacturing firm in India with a crude production of steel at 6.427 million tonnes. The production rose by 7% in the year 2010–11. The company has been growing at a CAGR of 29.87% in the past five years, with registered revenue of Rs 25,131 crore in 2010–11.

The global steel demand witnessed a downturn in the aftermath of the global meltdown, but with the global economy on a recovery path, the demand momentum is expected to pick up soon. The projected

Table 9.2 Increase in debt of SAIL (Rs crore)

		March 2011		March 2010	
Loan funds					
Secured loans	1.3	12854.59		8827.25	
Unsecured loans	1.4	8405.55	21260.14	8810.57	17637.82
Deferred tax liability (net)			1556.74		1430.13
Minority interest	1.16		1.20		1.02
			60434.27		52812.43

Source: Company Annual Report 2010–11.

Table 9.3 Change in equity of SAIL (Rs crore)

1.1: *Share capital*		
	As of 31 March 2011	As of 31 March 2010
Authorised		
5 billion equity shares of Rs 10 each	5000.00	5000.00
Issued, Subscribed and Paid-up		
4,13,04,00,545 equity shares of Rs 10 each fully paid.	4130.40	4130.40

Note: 1,24,43,82,900 equity shares of Rs 10 each (net of adjustments on reduction of capital) were allotted as fully paid up for consideration other than cash.

Source: Company Annual Report 2010–11.

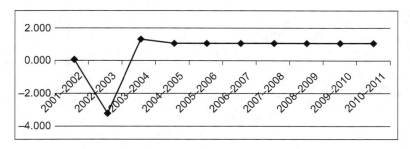

Figure 9.4 Degree of financial leverage of SAIL
Source: Company Annual Report 2010–11.

growth rate for 2012 is 2.6% in the developed economies, whereas the developing economies will drive the growth by 6.5%. Due to the expected growth, the global steel production in 2010 grew by 15% to 1,414 metric tonnes.

The Indian steel industry is placed fifth in terms of annual production at 63 million tonnes. Integrated steel contributes 55% of the total crude steel production in 2010–11 and 45% by secondary producers. The debt to equity ratio of JSW Steel is shown in Figure 9.5.

The net debt to equity ratio reached a peak value of 1.36 in FY 2008–9 and declined thereafter to 0.57 in 2010–11. The decline is

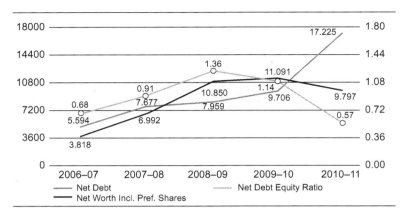

Figure 9.5 Debt to equity ratio of JSW

Table 9.4 Increase in debt of JSW (Rs crore)

Secured and unsecured loans

	2010–11	2009–10	Change	Change (%)
Secured loans	7,676	8,987	(1,311)	−15
Unsecured loans	4,276	2,598	1,678	65
Total	**11,952**	**11,585**	**367**	**3**

Source: Company Annual Report 2010–11.

attributed to the increase in net debt and a simultaneous increase in equity in 2010–11. Tables 9.4 and 9.5 depict the increase in debt and change in equity.

The company has been issuing a number of other instruments that will lead to dilution of EPS, that is, it will increase the number of shares outstanding in the market. The first one being *Foreign Currency Convertible Bonds* (FCCBs), the company had issued 3,350 FCCBs of US$100,000 each during FY 2007–8. Each bond is convertible into equity share of face value Rs 10 each at the conversion price of Rs 953.4. In 2007–8, only Deutsche Bank opted for the conversion of bonds into equity shares. The next are *equity warrants* issued by the company Sapphire Technologies Ltd, a promoter company. Each

Table 9.5 Increase in equity of JSW

		As of 31 March 2011	As of 31 March 2010
Schedule 1			
Share Capital			
Authorised			
2,00,00,00,000	Equity shares of Rs 10 each	2,000.00	2,000.00
1,00,00,00,000	Preference shares of Rs 10 each	1,000.00	1,000.00
		3,000.00	3,000.00
Issued and subscribed			
22,31,17,200 (18,70,48,682)	Equity shares of Rs 10 each fully paid-up	223.12	187.05
	Add: equity shares forfeited (amount originally paid-up)	61.03	61.03
27,90,34,907 (27,90,34,907)	10% cumulative redeemable preference shares of Rs 10 each fully paid-up	279.03	279.03
Total		563.18	527.11

Source: Company Annual Report 2010–11.

warrant entitles the holder to apply for and be allotted one equity share of the company at par value of Rs 10 each at a price of Rs 1,210 per share within eighteen months of the allotment date (within 15 December 2011). The next set of instruments include *Global Depository Receipts* (GDRs), 3,085,814 underlying shares of the company are outstanding as of 31 March 2011.

In February 2012, the finance committee of JSW Steel decided to avail of external commercial borrowings (ECBs) of US$275 million, at an interest rate of $ Libor plus 4% per annum. The term of the ECB is five years and one day from the date of drawdown. The company plans to use the money raised through ECBs for buying outstanding FCCBs, redemption of outstanding FCCBs and capital expenditure. The lenders will have the option of converting whole or part of the outstanding ECB into fully paid equity shares of face value of Rs 10 each, with full voting rights.

In another deal JSW Steel had taken over JSW Ispat in 2011 as it posted huge losses. JSW Ispat Steel Ltd had signed a deal to refinance its debt of the tune of US$1.4 billion.

From Figure 9.6 we can see that the degree of financial leverage at JSW Steel has been almost constant and moved slightly upwards in the past five years. The credit rating of the company was also upgraded from AA– to AA+ in FY 2010–11, the rating takes into account improved capacity utilisation, profitability margins and reduced leverage on account of improved cash flows. The company's total net debt gearing ratio decreased from 1.124 in FY 2009–10 to 0.57 in FY 2010–11. The weighted average cost of debt was also lower at 7.58% in FY 2010–11 as compared to 8.08% in FY 2009–10.

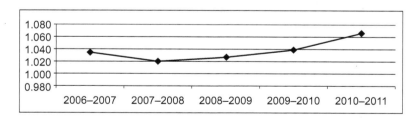

Figure 9.6 Degree of financial leverage of JSW
Source: Company Annual Report 2010–11.

3. Tata Steel

Tata Steel is part of the Tata Group headquartered in Mumbai. It is the tenth-largest producer of steel globally with an annual capacity of 23.5 million tonnes. Its largest plant is located in Jamshedpur, Jharkhand. The acquisition of Corus, UK-based steel maker in 2007 increased the capacity of Tata Steel and it is now the fifth-largest steel producer globally. It has its presence in over fifty countries and manufacturing operations in twenty-six countries.

In 2010–11, net cash inflow from financing activities stood at Rs 5,653 crore that included inflows of Rs 2.155 crore due to issue of equity and perpetual securities. The outflows were mainly due to interest and dividend payments of Rs 1,610 crore and Rs 708 crore, respectively. Regarding the debts, net debt witnessed an increase of Rs 3,062 crore due to non-convertible debentures and exchange rate fluctuations of Rs 833 crore.

A major portion of the debt taken by Tata was for Corus acquisition. To refinance it, new term loans were taken in September 2010, along with a £690 million revolving credit facility for working capital requirements. The facilities have maturities of between five and seven years along with minimising repayment obligations over the next five years.

The increase in equity was due to increase in authorised share capital of the company from Rs 8,000 crore to Rs 8,350 crore by creation of 350 million ordinary shares and alteration of the capital clause in the memorandum of association of the company (Table 9.6).

The debt rating of Tata Steel was upgraded by S&P from BB– to BB+ in August 2011, following strong cash flows and a good financial

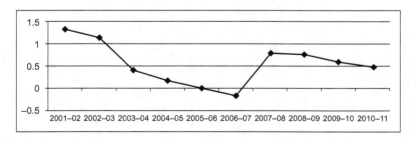

Figure 9.7 Debt to equity of Tata Steel
Source: Company Annual Report 2010–11.

Table 9.6 Increase in equity of Tata Steel

| | | Schedule A: Share capital | |
| | | *(Item No. 1(a), Page 134)* | |
		Rs crore	As of 31 March 2010 (Rs crore)
Authorised			
1,750,000,000	Ordinary shares of Rs 10 each		
	(31.03.2010: 1,750,000,000 ordinary shares of Rs 10 each)	1,750.00	*1,750.00*
350,000,000	'A' ordinary shares of Rs 10 each		
	(31.03.2010: Nil)	350.00	–
25,000,000	Cumulative redeemable preference shares of Rs 100 each		
	(31.03.2010: 25,000,000 shares of Rs 100 each)	250.00	*250.00*
600,000,000	Cumulative convertible preference shares of Rs 100 each		
	(31.03.2010: 600,000,000 shares of Rs 100 each)	6,000.00	*6,000.00*
		8,350.00	*8,000.00*
Issued			
960,126,020	Ordinary shares of Rs 10 each		
	(31.03.2010: 888,126,020 ordinary shares of Rs 10 each)	960.13	*888.13*
Subscribed			
959,214,450	Ordinary shares of Rs 10 each fully paid up		
	(31.03.2010: 887,214,196 ordinary shares of Rs 10 each)	959.21	*887.21*
	Add – amount paid up on 389,516 ordinary shares forfeited		
	(31.03.2010: 389,516 shares of Rs 10 each)	0.20	*0.20*
		959.41	*887.41*

Source: Company Annual Report 2010–11.

profile. In a bid to manage its funds effectively, the company focused on using portfolio investments and external financing for raising capital. The raised capital is being used by the company to rebalance the capital structure and finance the growth projects. Some of the financing measures taken by the company include raising Rs 10,822 crore (US$2.4 billion) of capital, through divestments of about Rs 3,121 crore (US$700 million), equity of around Rs 4,546 crore (US$1.02 billion), India's first rupee hybrid securities of around Rs 1,500 crore (US$336 million) and debt for the Jamshedpur expansion and working capital requirement of around Rs 1,655 crore (US$371 million). The above-mentioned financial measures helped the company to improve its financial ratios. The debt to equity ratio decreased from 0.78 in 2008–9 to 0.49 in 2010–11.The cash generated by the company also helped it to fund the Jamshedpur expansion programme through internal generations rather than drawing down the project debt that was tied up (Table 9.7).

The Tata Group took a huge amount of debt for funding its acquisition of Corus Steel. As of December 2011, the total debt of the company stood at Rs 50,528 crore that includes the loan taken to fund its acquisition of Corus. In 2011, Tata Group also raised Rs 4,977 crore through a follow-on public offer and bond issue. For the fiscal year 2011–12, the company is planning a capital expenditure of Rs 12,500 crore on various facilities and expansion plans.

Table 9.7 Debt of Tata Steel

Net debt			
	FY 2011	*FY 2010*	*Rs crore Change*
Secured loans	2,009	2,259	(250)
Unsecured loans	26,292	22,980	3,312
Total debt	28,301	25,239	3,062
Less: cash and bank balances	4,142	3,234	907
Less: Current investments	3,000	1,719	1,281
Net debt	21,160	20,286	874

Source: Company Annual Report 2010–11.

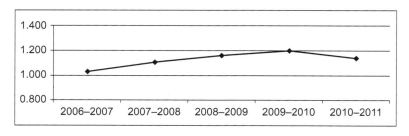

Figure 9.8 Degree of financial leverage of Tata Steel
Source: Company Annual Report 2010–11.

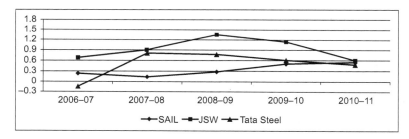

Figure 9.9 Debt to equity ratio of steel companies
Source: Company Annual Reports.

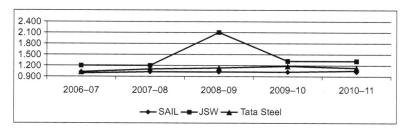

Figure 9.10 Degree of financial leverage of steel companies
Source: Company Annual Reports.

Conclusion

From Figure 9.9 we see that the debt to equity ratio of JSW is the highest among the three players, whereas that of SAIL is lowest. Owing to massive expansion plans of JSW, it has taken huge debts that have led to this high debt to equity ratio. On the other hand, SAIL has not taken high amounts of debts and hence has a low debt to equity ratio.

From Figure 9.10 we can see that JSW is highly leveraged owing to high amount of debts as compared to its equity. On the other hand, SAIL and Tata Steel both have low degree of financial leverage due to low amount of debts.

Discussion questions

1   Analyse the capital structure of SAIL, JSW and Tata Steel for their financing policies. Study debt to equity ratio for this.
2   Calculate and interpret the degree of financial leverage of the above units to examine the financial risk.
3   Comment upon the financing policy of these units.
4   What types of finances are used by the units in the present case?
5   What are the various capital structure theories which define the financing policy of business houses? Which theory of capital structure can be related to the above case?
6   Discuss the key factors which govern the capital structure decision.
7   'Leverage is employed for shareholders' wealth maximisation'. Explain
8   What are the types of leverage which form the basis of risk–return trade-off?
9   What are the various measures of financial leverage which are used by the businesses?

10

FINANCING POLICY OF DIVERSIFIED SECTOR IN INDIA

Diversification of Indian industry

Although the phenomenon of entering into multi-product/service activities has been noted increasingly in recent years, it has been there in the past. The type and direction of diversification depends upon the extent of area of specialisation available to a firm.

Diversification has been increasingly used by large corporations as a strategy for adapting to changes in the business environment. Prior to 1910, firms in the United States adapted to environmental changes through expansion, acquisition of firms and vertical integration. However, between 1910 and 1960, large firms diversified in a major way. As of 1970, 65% of the large firms in the United States had diversified into new fields, related or unrelated to their existing business. Likewise, firms in European countries also reveal a trend towards increasing diversification. As of 1970, 53% of the large firms in the United Kingdom, 455 in West Germany, 38% in France and 35% of the firms in Italy have diversified into other areas. Now, every other company is going diversified either to economise its resources or to tap markets well or to carve a niche in the market segment.

Scope

The present section analyses following key companies in the sector.

1. *Reliance Industries Ltd*

Reliance Industries Ltd (RIL) was set up by late Dhirubhai H. Ambani. It is India's largest private sector enterprise with annual revenue of more than US$58 billion. Its business activities range from exploration and production of oil and gas to petroleum refining and marketing to petrochemicals, textiles, retail and SEZs.

During its initial years following its inception, RIL mainly followed the organic growth strategy. During the late 1990s and early 2000s, Reliance went on to diversify into multitude of businesses including a diversified and integrated biotechnology initiative under Reliance Life Sciences; transportation, distribution, warehousing, logistics and supply chain services under Reliance Logistics; development and operation of cross-country pipelines for transporting petroleum products under Reliance Industrial Infrastructure Ltd and retails business under Reliance Fresh and Reliance Retail.

2. Adani Group

Adani Enterprises Ltd is an Indian conglomerate company, founded by Gautam Adani, the chairman of Adani Group. The core businesses of the group are commodities trading, edible oil-manufacturing, Mundra port operations and distribution of natural gas. It has more than fifty companies under its umbrella, like Adani Gas Ltd, Adani Enterprises, Adani Power, Adani Retail and Adani Mining.

3. Aditya Birla Nuvo Ltd

Aditya Birla Nuvo Ltd (ABNL) is a US$4 billion revenue conglomerate company. Having a market cap of approximately US$2 billion on 29 February 2012, ABNL is present across sectors such as financial services, telecom, fashion and lifestyle, IT-ITES and manufacturing businesses.

Analysis and discussion

The *financing pattern* of the units has been analysed with the help of debt to equity ratio. *Debt servicing* of the units has been determined by analysing ICR. This indicates the safety cushion for the lenders and company's interest-paying capacity.

1. Reliance Industries Ltd

A high debt to equity ratio implies that the company has an aggressive financing policy (Tables 10.1 and 10.2; Figures 10.1 and 10.2). Here the company seems to have got a pretty high debt to equity ratio in 2009 which shows that it had a bit lesser returns on the interests it had to pay on the loans taken.

Table 10.1 Debt to equity ratio of RIL

2007	2008	2009	2010	2011
0.45	0.46	0.65	0.49	0.46

Source: RIL Annual Reports.

Table 10.2 Long-term debt to equity ratio of RIL

2007	2008	2009	2010	2011
0.32	0.35	0.59	0.44	0.38

Source: RIL Annual Reports.

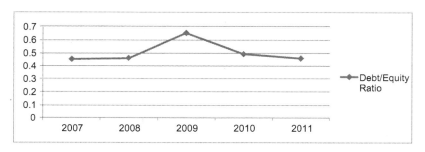

Figure 10.1 Debt to equity trend of RIL

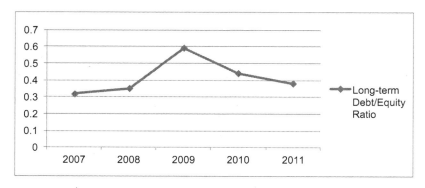

Figure 10.2 Long-term debt to equity trend of RIL

Table 10.3 ICR of RIL

2007	2008	2009	2010	2011
13.51	17.05	11.85	10.97	11.66

Source: RIL Annual Reports.

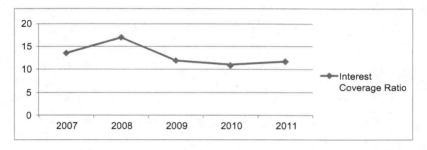

Figure 10.3 Interest coverage trend of RIL

The lower the ratio, the more the company is burdened by debt expense. The company has been performing better recently compare to that of 2007–8. But it has been decreasing as well in 2010–11 (Table 10.3 and Figure 10.3).

2. *Adani Group*

A high debt to equity ratio implies that the company has been adopting an aggressive financing policy by employing more debt. Here the continuously decreasing debt to equity ratio shows that there has been a consistent decline in the leveraged amount for the company (Table 10.4 and Figure 10.4).

The lower the ratio, the more the company is burdened by debt expense. The company has been performing better recently compare to that of 2007–8. And the ICR also appears to be increasing, showing there has been a decline in the leveraged amount in the capital (Tables 10.5 and 10.6; Figures 10.5 and 10.6).

Table 10.4 Debt to equity ratio of Adani

2007	2008	2009	2010	2011
2.9	2.29	1.95	1.76	0.06

Source: Adani Annual Reports.

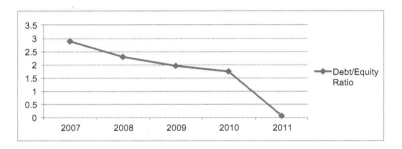

Figure 10.4 Debt to equity trend of Adani

Table 10.5 Long-term debt to equity ratio of Adani

2007	2008	2009	2010	2011
2.66	2.22	1.89	0.5	0.05

Source: Adani Annual Reports.

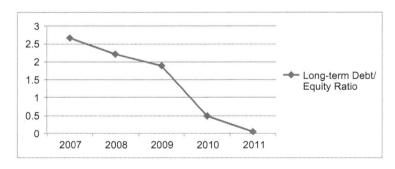

Figure 10.5 Long-term debt to equity trend of Adani

Table 10.6 ICR of Adani

2007	2008	2009	2010	2011
25.88	12.44	34.18	42.96	6.19

Source: Adani Annual Reports.

3. *Aditya Birla Nuvo Ltd*

Here also, a high debt to equity ratio indicates an aggressive financing mix by the company. The company seems to have got a pretty high debt to equity ratio in 2009, which shows that it had a bit lesser returns on the interests it had to pay on the loans taken. From 2009 to 2011 debt to equity ratio is decreasing, meaning its returns on the interests are increasing (Table 10.7 and Figure 10.7).

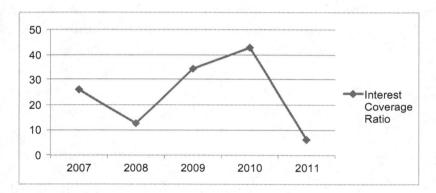

Figure 10.6 Interest coverage trend of Adani

Table 10.7 Debt to equity ratio of ABNL

2007	2008	2009	2010	2011
0.91	0.75	1.20	0.80	0.61

Source: Aditya Birla Annual Reports.

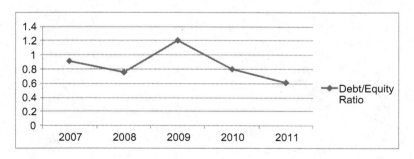

Figure 10.7 Debt to equity trend of ABNL

From 2009 to 2011 company has reduced its debt and has become less levered (Table 10.8 and Figure 10.8).

The lower the ratio, the more the company is burdened by debt expense. From 2009 to 2011 ICR increased and so company's burden by debt expense decreased (Table 10.9 and Figure 10.9).

Table 10.8 Long-term debt to equity ratio of ABNL

Year	2007	2008	2009	2010	2011
	0.53	0.50	0.71	0.60	0.40

Source: Aditya Birla Annual Reports.

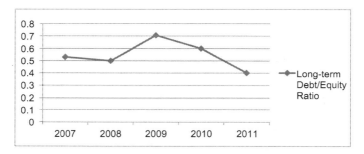

Figure 10.8 Long-term debt to equity trend of ABNL

Table 10.9 ICR of ABNL

2007	2008	2009	2010	2011
2.49	2.35	1.57	2.03	2.96

Source: Aditya Birla Annual Reports.

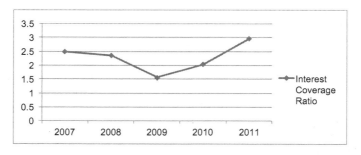

Figure 10.9 Interest coverage trend of ABNL

Table 10.10 Debt to equity ratio of diversified companies

Companies	Debt to equity ratio (2011)
Reliance	0.46
Adani Group	0.06
ABNL	0.61

Table 10.11 Long-term debt to equity ratio of diversified companies

Companies	Long-term debt to equity ratio (2011)
Reliance	0.38
Adani Group	0.05
ABNL	0.40

Table 10.12 ICR of diversified companies

Companies	ICR (2011)
Reliance	11.66
Adani Group	3.43
ABNL	2.96

Conclusion

It is clearly evident from the comparative analysis in Tables 10.10 to 10.12 also that Adani Group has a very low amount of leverage, but in terms of interest margin efficiency, Reliance emerges as a winner.

Discussion questions

1 Analyse the capital structure of RIL, Adani and ABNL for their financing policies. Examine debt to equity ratio for this.
2 Find out the interact coverage of these companies for long-term solvency.
3 Comment upon the financing policy of these units.
4 'Diversification diversifies the financing choices of business organisations for capital investments'. Explain in the present context.
5 What are the significant factors which have affected the capital structure decision of the above business units?
6 Which theory of capital structure can be related to the above case?

11

FINANCING POLICY OF CONSTRUCTION SECTOR IN INDIA

Construction industry in India

Today, India is the second fastest-growing economy in the world. The construction sector is an integral part of the Indian economy and the second-largest economic activity after agriculture. It has contributed an estimated Rs 384,282 crore to the national GDP in 2010–11 (a share of around 8%). The sector is highly labour-intensive and provides employment to more than 35 million people.

Since, the construction is the backbone of any industrial development; the Union Government has planned massive investment in this sector. The Planning Commission has estimated that investment requirement in infrastructure to the tune of about Rs 1,450,000 crore or US$320 billion during the Eleventh Five Year Plan period.

Scope

Following three construction companies are selected for the study.

1. Larsen & Toubro Ltd

Larsen & Toubro Ltd (L&T) is an engineering, procurement and construction company. It is one of the largest and most respected companies in India's private sector. L&T not only has a strong domestic presence but global standing as well, as evident in its international offices. Its overseas earnings have grown significantly in the past few years. It continues to grow its overseas manufacturing footprint, with facilities in China and Gulf region.

2. Punj Lloyd

Punj Lloyd is a design, engineering, procurement and construction company having strong presence in the energy and infrastructure sectors. With operations spread across the Middle East, Africa, the Caspian, Asia-Pacific and South Asia, Punj Lloyd provides EPC services in oil and gas, process, civil infrastructure and thermal power. It is today a diversified conglomerate with its successful venture into aviation, defence and upstream, through its subsidiaries and joint ventures.

3. Hindustan Construction Company Ltd

Hindustan Construction Company (HCC) is a construction company founded in 1926. HCC works in various sectors including transportation, power, marine, oil and gas pipeline construction, irrigation, utilities and urban infrastructure. It specialises in large-scale civil engineering, and developing construction technologies. It is considered as the pioneer in Indian infrastructure industry.

Analysis and discussion

1. Capital structure

Long-term funds' trend of the units has been analysed at each source level. This helps to find out the management financing approach.

Sources of long-term funds

The three companies studied used various sources to raise capital and to increase retained earnings by (options like employee stock option scheme). The various sources of funds used by these companies in past three FYs (i.e., 2008–9, 2009–10 and 2010–11) are shown in Table 11.1.

The contribution of various sources of funds as a percentage of total liabilities is shown in Tables 11.2 to 11.4.

It can be seen from the data presented in above tables that the share capitals form a very small percentage (i.e. around 1–2%) of the total capital of the construction companies in India, and they rely heavily on reserves and surplus, secured loans and unsecured loans for long-term capital.

Table 11.1 Long-term funds of construction companies

L&T	Punj Lloyd	HCC
Foreign currency loans	Unsecured loans	Unsecured loans
Secured redeemable non-convertible debentures	Secured loans	Secured loans
Unsecured redeemable non-convertible debentures	Redeemable non-convertible debentures	Employee stock option scheme
FCCBs	Employee stock option scheme	
Employee stock option scheme/bonus shares		

Source: Companies' Annual Reports.

Table 11.2 Percentage contribution of long-term funds of L&T

L&T	2010–11	2009–10	2008–9
Sources of funds			
Total share capital (%)	0.42	0.48	0.62
Equity share capital (%)	0.42	0.48	0.62
Share application money (%)	1.27	0.10	0.00
Preference share capital (%)	0.00	0.00	0.00
Reserves (%)	73.55	72.25	64.78
Revaluation reserves (%)	0.08	0.09	0.13
Net worth (%)	**75.31**	**72.92**	**65.52**
Secured loans (%)	3.66	3.81	5.80
Unsecured loans (%)	21.02	23.28	28.68
Total debt (%)	**24.69**	**27.08**	**34.48**
Total liabilities (%)	**100.00**	**100.00**	**100.00**

Source: L&T Annual Reports.

Table 11.3 Percentage contribution of long-term funds of Punj Lloyd

Punj Lloyd	2010–11	2009–10	2008–9
Sources of funds			
Total share capital (%)	0.97	0.94	1.09
Equity share capital (%)	0.97	0.94	1.09
Share application money (%)	0.00	0.00	0.00
Preference share capital (%)	0.00	0.00	0.00

Punj Lloyd	2010–11	2009–10	2008–9
Reserves (%)	50.80	49.52	45.85
Revaluation reserves (%)	0.06	0.07	0.09
Net worth (%)	51.83	50.52	47.04
Secured loans (%)	43.28	42.81	42.73
Unsecured loans (%)	4.90	6.67	10.24
Total debt (%)	48.17	49.48	52.96
Total liabilities (%)	100.00	100.00	100.00

Source: Punj Lloyd Annual Reports.

Table 11.4 Percentage contribution of long-term funds of HCC

HCC	2010–11	2009–10	2008–9
Sources of funds			
Total share capital (%)	1.21	0.75	0.77
Equity share capital (%)	1.21	0.75	0.77
Share application money (%)	0.00	0.00	0.46
Preference share capital (%)	0.00	0.00	0.00
Reserves (%)	29.27	36.88	28.98
Revaluation reserves (%)	0.00	0.00	0.00
Net worth (%)	30.48	37.63	30.21
Secured loans (%)	30.74	23.89	27.18
Unsecured loans (%)	38.77	38.49	42.62
Total debt (%)	69.52	62.37	69.79
Total liabilities (%)	100.00	100.00	100.00

Source: HCC Annual Reports.

2. Leverage and debt servicing

Debt to equity ratio has been analysed to determine the degree of financial leverage of the units. To measure the debt servicing of the units, ICR has been calculated and interpreted.

(a) Debt to equity ratio is a measure of a company's financial leverage. The long-term debt to equity ratio is shown in Figure 11.1

It can be seen from Figure 11.1 that the debt to equity ratio depends on the scale of operations of the construction company. As L&T has the largest scale of operation among the three, its long-term debt to equity ratio is the highest, whereas it is lower for HCC which is the

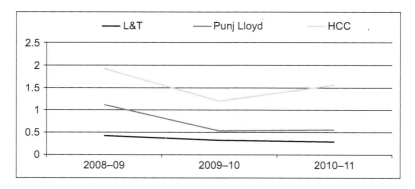

Figure 11.1 Long-term debt to equity ratio of construction companies
Source: Companies' Annual Reports.

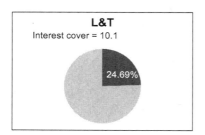

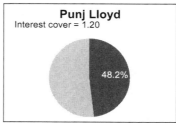

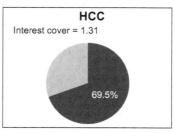

Figure 11.2 ICR of construction companies, 2010–11
Source: Companies' Annual Reports.

smallest among the three in term of scale of operations. This shows us that as a construction company grows its dependence on debt funding increases.

(b) ICR of the three companies is shown in Figure 11.2.

Figure 11.2 shows that the highly leveraged firm in the construction industry are also highly risky as they have a very low ICR. The high risk associated with these firms also increases the cost of debt capital, which in turn again reduces the interest cover making it even more risky.

3. Beta analysis

Beta is an indicator of the volatility of company's stock return to market return. Stocks with beta more than 1 indicate aggressive stocks, whereas stocks with beta less than 1 indicate conservative stocks. For the sample companies, beta values have been taken from SENSEX for 2010–11 to determine the risk factor of the stocks.

It is calculated as

$$\beta j = \frac{Covariance\ j\ m}{Variance\ m}$$

Here, j = company return
m = market return

Mathematically, it is expressed as

$$\beta_j = \frac{\text{Covar}_{j,\,m}}{\sigma_m^2}$$
$$= \frac{\sigma_j \sigma_m \text{Cor}_{j,\,m}}{\sigma_m \times \sigma_m} = \frac{\sigma_j}{\sigma_m} \times \text{Cor}_{j,\,m}$$

Beta values for the three companies are shown in Table 11.5.

Table 11.5 shows that the highly leveraged company is also the most volatile company in the share market. The high debt to equity ratio makes the investors more sceptical about the company and the volatility of the share price increases because of this un-surety about the performance of the firm.

Table 11.5 Beta analysis of construction companies, 2010–11

	Beta (Sensex)
L&T	1.21
Punj Lloyd	1.76
HCC	2.80

Source: BSE (www.bseindia.com).

Conclusion

It is evident from the above discussion that on an average, the construction companies in India rely very less on shareholders' funds, rather they rely more on internal financing, followed by leverage. Among three, L&T is the only company which is employing foreign currency loans. Therefore, their interest coverage is less which makes risk element on a higher side.

Discussion questions

1 Analyse the capital structure of L&T, Punj Lloyd and HCC for their financing policies. Use the contribution analysis of long-term funds for this.

2 Comment upon the financing policy of these units for:

(a) leverage using debt to equity ratio
(b) interest coverage using ICR.

3 Apply beta analysis to determine the volatility of these companies in stock market.

4 Discuss the sources of funds used by the business units in the present case.

5 Which theory of capital structure can be related to the above case?

12

FINANCING POLICY OF AUTOMOBILE SECTOR IN INDIA

The auto sector overview has already been given in the second section. Here, three leading Indian auto companies have been selected for studying the relationship between leverage and shareholders' wealth. These companies have not been discussed earlier.

Companies selected

Following companies in the auto sector are selected for the present discussion.

1   Ashok Leyland Ltd
2   Maruti Suzuki India Ltd
3   Bajaj Auto Ltd

Data analysis

We have followed followings steps to do the data analysis for all the chosen companies:

1   Debt to equity ratio of the units has been analysed to study their *financing policy.*
2   *Degree of financial leverage* has been further calculated to measure the level of financial risk of the units.
3   We have found the correlation between debt to equity ratio and return on equity (ROE) or return on net worth (RONW) (considering these two ratios as the main ratio for this analysis) to find the *impact of leverage on shareholder's wealth.*
4   If correlation is positive, then it is in line with the concept and no further analysis is required, but if correlation is found negative then additional analysis is required.

5. We have calculated the margin between ICR and EBIT margin, that is EBIT/net sales (MBIE) and margin between ROE and debt and equity (MBRD). If both MBIE and MBRD are increasing, they have positive correlation between them along with condition that MBIE is at least 50% more than MBRD. It implies that there is a positive impact of leverage on shareholder's wealth, that is, shareholder's wealth will increase with leverage.

1. Ashok Leyland Ltd

In case of Ashok Leyland we found that there is positive correlation between debt and equity and ROE and both are increasing for consecutive years (Table 12.1 and Figure 12.1). Hence it indicates that Ashok Leyland was able increase their shareholder's wealth by leveraging debt.

Table 12.1 Ashok Leyland's financing analysis

Types	Parameters	2008–9	2009–10	2010–11
Financial leverage ratios	Debt/equity	0.6700	0.9500	0.9700
	Debt/total asset	0.3605	0.3833	0.3886
	ICR	2.3000	6.3500	5.2400
Shareholder's wealth ratios	ROE or RONW	8.9700	19.0600	25.2900
	EPS	1.2600	2.9400	4.4200
Degree of financial leverage	EBIT	368.7700	646.6200	990.7200
	% change in EBIT		75.3451	53.2152
	EPS	1.2600	2.9400	4.4200
	% change in EPS		133.3333	50.3401
	Degree of financial leverage		1.7696	0.9460
Correlation	0.946614899	Positive correlation		
Margins	Interest	–	–	–
	Net sales	6,098.42	7,407.23	11,416.88
	Margin b/w ROE and D/E	8.3000	18.1100	24.3200
	Margin b/w ICR and EBIT/sales	2.239530239	6.262704209	5.153223227
Correlation	0.78702499	Positive correlation		

Source: Company Annual Reports.

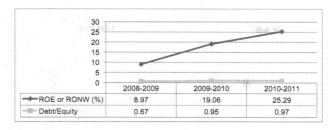

Figure 12.1 Ashok Leyland's financing trend

2. *Maruti Suzuki India Ltd*

In case of Maruti Suzuki India Ltd we found that there is negative correlation between debt and equity and ROE. Debt and equity is decreasing for consecutive years but, on other hand, ROE is fluctuating; first it increases sharply and in same fashion it falls sharply in next year. In this case, relation between ROE and debt and equity will not help us to find the impact of leverage on shareholder's wealth. Now in order to do further analyses we have calculated MBIE and MBRD. We have found that MBRD has increased in 2009–10 as compared to 2008–09 but it decreases in 2010–11, but, on other hand, MBIE is increasing for all consecutive years as compared to previous year. MBIE is also more than MBRD for all the three years with positive correlation between them. All this conditions help us to conclude that Maruti Suzuki India Ltd was able to maximise their shareholder's wealth by leveraging debt (Table 12.2 and Figure 12.2).

Table 12.2 Maruti's financing analysis

Types	Parameters	2008–9	2009–10	2010–11
Financial leverage ratios	Debt/equity	0.0900	0.0700	0.0400
	Debt/total asset	0.0696	0.0649	0.0215
	ICR	29.9100	108.2400	125.3500
Shareholder's wealth ratios	ROE or RONW	12.0800	23.5800	17.8100
	EPS	41.5700	85.4300	77.9800
Degree of financial leverage	EBIT	1,726.8000	3,626.0000	3,133.8000
	% change in EBIT		15.7062	–52.3773
	EPS	41.5700	85.4300	77.9800
	% change in EPS		9.5537	–51.3403
	Degree of financial leverage		0.6083	0.9802

(*Continued*)

Table 12.2 (Continued)

Types	Parameters	2008–9	2009–10	2010–11
Correlation	−0.395516082	Negative correlation		
Margins	Interest	51.0000	33.5000	25.0000
	Net sales	20,453.7000	29,098.9000	36,618.4000
	Margin b/w ROE and D/E	11.9900	23.5100	17.7700
	Margin b/w ICR and EBIT/sales	29.8256	108.1154	125.2644
Correlation	0.770653566	Positive correlation		

Source: Company Annual Reports.

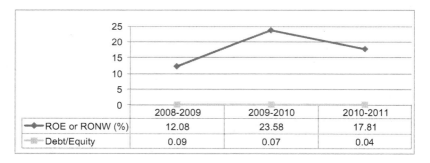

	2008-2009	2009-2010	2010-2011
ROE or RONW (%)	12.08	23.58	17.81
Debt/Equity	0.09	0.07	0.04

Figure 12.2 Maruti's financing trend

3. Bajaj Auto Ltd

In case of Bajaj Auto Ltd, we found that there is negative correlation between debt and equity and ROE. Debt and equity is decreasing for consecutive years, but, on other hand, ROE is fluctuating; first it increases sharply and falls slightly in the next year. In this case, relation between ROE and debt and equity will not help us to find the impact of leverage on shareholder's wealth. Now in order to do further analyses we have calculated MBIE and MBRD. We have found that MBRD has increased in 2009–10 as compared to 2008–9 but it decreases in 2010–11, but, on other hand, MBIE is increasing for all consecutive years as compared to previous year. MBIE is also more than MBRD for all the three years with positive correlation between them. All this conditions help us to conclude that Bajaj Auto Ltd was able to maximise their shareholder's wealth by leveraging debt (Table 12.3 and Figure 12.3).

Table 12.3 Bajaj's financing analysis

Types	Parameters	2008–9	2009–10	2010–11
Financial leverage ratios	Debt/equity	0.8400	0.6100	0.2100
	Debt/total asset	0.4564	0.3137	0.0585
	ICR	54.3200	403.6100	2,119.1900
Shareholder's wealth ratios	ROE or RONW	44.5000	70.9800	70.1600
	EPS	41.5000	111.0500	108.9200
Degree of financial leverage	EBIT	974.2200	2,413.5900	4,349.4400
	% change in EBIT		147.7459	80.2062
	EPS	41.5000	111.0500	108.9200
	% change in EPS		167.5904	−1.9181
	Degree of financial leverage		1.1343	−0.0239
Correlation	−0.761363723	Negative correlation		
Margins	Interest	21.0100	5.9800	1.6900
	Net sales	8,436.94	1,1508.5	16,398.23
	Margin b/w ROE and D/E	43.6600	70.3700	69.9500
	Margin b/w ICR and EBIT/sales	54.2045	403.4003	2,118.9248
Correlation	0.619829572	Positive correlation		

Source: Company Annual Reports.

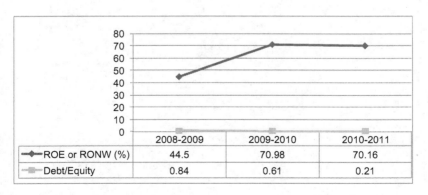

Figure 12.3 Bajaj's financing trend

Conclusion and suggestions

Financial leverage is a choice item and its practice depends on the trade-off between return and risk. It's better to choose equity option if EPS is higher at any value of EBIT; however, it is advisable to choose debt options, if EPS is higher at any value of EBIT.

Therefore we conclude that debt should be used for the impact on shareholder return, based upon the risk factor.

Discussion questions

1 Evaluate the financing policies of Ashok Leyland, Maruti Suzuki India Ltd and Bajaj Auto Ltd. Examine the financial leverage ratios for this.
2 Calculate and interpret the degree of financial leverage of these units for financial risk.
3 Determine the effect of financial leverage of the above units on shareholders' wealth, using correlation analysis.
4 Which theory of capital structure can be related to the above case?

13

FINANCING POLICY
OF IT SECTOR IN INDIA

Indian IT sector overview

IT is one of the most important industries in the Indian economy, being the backbone of industrial development. It has shown huge growth in recent years. In the past ten years, the IT industry in India has grown at an average annual rate of 30%. The liberalisation of the Indian economy in the early 1990s played a major role in the growth of the IT industry of India. Its importance arises from the fact that it is a service industry providing support services to every business and non-business organisation. It is a cash-rich industry with enough cash generated from its operations to meet its daily business expenditures. The billing of the man-hours based on the revenue recognition is the source of revenue. The companies in this sector follow both offshore and onshore model for its operations.

The IT industry in India has gained a brand identity as a knowledge economy due to its IT and ITES sector.

The IT–ITES industry has two major components:

- IT services; and
- Business process outsourcing (BPO).

The growth in the service sector in India has been led by the IT–ITES sector, contributing substantially to increase in GDP, employment and exports. The sector has increased its contribution to India's GDP from 1.2% in FY 1998 to 7.5% in FY 2012.

According to NASSCOM, the IT–BPO sector in India aggregated revenues of US$100 billion in FY 2012, where export and domestic revenue stood at US$69.1 billion and US$31.7 billion respectively, growing by over 9%. The major cities that account for about nearly

90% of this sectors exports are Bangalore, Chennai, Hyderabad, Delhi, Mumbai and Kolkata. Exports dominate the IT–ITES industry and constitute about 77% of the total industry revenue. Though the IT–ITES sector is export-driven, the domestic market is also significant with a robust revenue growth. The industry's share of total Indian exports (merchandise plus services) increased from less than 4% in FY 1998 to about 25% in FY 2012. According to Gartner, the 'Top Five Indian IT Services Providers' are Tata Consultancy Services, Infosys, Cognizant, Wipro and HCL Technologies.

This sector has also led to massive employment generation. The industry continues to be a net employment generator, providing direct employment to about 2.8 million, and indirectly employing 8.9 million people. However, the sector continues to face challenges of competitiveness in the globalised and modern world, particularly from countries like China and the Philippines.

Impact on India's growth

- About 58% of IT workforce come from tier II/III cities; 31% of them are women and 74% are below thirty years.
- Increasing adoption of technology and Telecom by consumers and focused government initiatives – leading to increased ICT adoption.
- Fast emerging as a growth story driven by a growing middle class, consumer spending and technology innovation.

Companies under study

Top five IT companies by revenues in India have been selected for the present study.

1. TCS

- Founded in 1968, TCS is an Indian multinational IT services, business solutions and consulting company headquartered in Mumbai, Maharashtra.
- Operates in 44 countries and has more than 199 branches across the world.
- Current revenue of $11.6 billion with an operating margin of 27% and net income at $2.6 billion; up 15.6% (fiscal year ending 31 March 2013).

- Major verticals are banking, financial and services industry (BFSI), telecom, energy and utility, manufacturing and so forth.

2. *Infosys*

- Incorporated in the year 1981, Infosys is an Indian multinational provider of business consulting, IT, software engineering and outsourcing services.
- Market capitalisation was $30.8 billion as of March 2013, making it India's sixth-largest publicly traded company.
- Current revenue of $7.39 billion with an operating margin of 23.51% (as on Q2 ending June 2013) and operating income at $1.9 billion.

3. *Wipro*

- Founded in 1945 by Azim Premji, WIPRO is an Indian multinational IT consulting and outsourcing service company located in Bangalore, Karnataka in India.
- Current revenue of $7.95 billion and an operating income of $1.28 billion.
- About 50% of revenue is from United States, 30% of revenue is from Europe and the rest from Asia Pacific (APAC) and emerging markets.
- Major verticals are BFSI, manufacturing, healthcare, retail and so forth.

4. *HCL*

- HCL is a leading global technology and IT enterprise with annual revenues of US$6.3 billion.
- HCL Enterprise comprises two companies listed in India, HCL Technologies and HCL Infosystems.
- HCL leverages an extensive global offshore infrastructure and network of offices in thirty-one countries to provide holistic, multiservice delivery in key industry verticals including financial services, manufacturing, consumer services, public services and healthcare.

5. *Mahindra*

- Founded in 1986 and part of the $12.5 billion Mahindra Group, Tech Mahindra Ltd is an Indian provider of IT, networking technology solutions and business support services (BPO) to the telecommunications industry.

- In partnership with British Telecommunications plc. (BT), focused primarily on the telecommunications industry.
- With a current revenue of $2.7 billion, BT is the largest client contributing 60% to its revenue.

On 25 June 2013, Tech Mahindra & Mahindra Satyam merging process completed and the name of the parent company was retained for the merged entity with a new logo and motto.

Analysis (financial + statistical for measuring impact and relationship)

As part of analysis, the financial statements of top five IT companies for the past three FYs have been analysed. The debt to equity ratio is calculated from the balance sheet and the coverage ratios are calculated from the profit and loss (P&L) statements.

Financial leverage of the units has been examined by studying their debt to equity ratio. *Debt servicing* of the units has been analysed with the help of their ICR. It has been further examined by studying debt–service coverage ratio.

Debt – Equity Ratio = Long-Term Debt (Liabilities)/Net Worth.

The long-term loans in debt to equity ratio are calculated by summing shareholders' funds and long-term borrowings, other long-term liabilities in non-current Liabilities. Provisions do not come under long-term loans. The net worth component is obtained from shareholders' funds.

The values thus obtained for top five IT companies in past three FYs are tabulated as shown in Table 13.1.

Key observations from Table 13.1

- The net worth of TCS is the highest of all Indian IT companies making it the No. 1 IT company in India.
- The long-term loans of Infosys are consistently zero which signifies the fact that it would prefer to fund its capital expenditure and working capital requirements from internal accruals.
- There is a drastic fall in long-term loans for both Wipro and Tech Mahindra in 2012–13 when compared to 2011–12. While the drop in case of Wipro is 96.83%, the drop in case of Tech Mahindra is 48.63%.

Table 13.1 Financing mix of the IT companies (Rs crore)

TCS	2010–11	2011–12	2012–13
Long-term loans	41.12	400.38	334.97
Net worth	19,579.49	29,579.23	32,562.25
Infosys			
Long-term loans	0	0	0
Net worth	24,501	29,757	36,059
WIPRO			
Long-term loans	2,201.3	2,237.7	70.8
Net worth	21,320.9	24,352.5	24,229.5
HCL Technologies			
Long-term loans	2,029.71	1,738.84	1,642.37
Net worth	7,651.99	9,835.09	8,644.09
Tech Mahindra			
Long-term loans	1,033	1,030.9	527
Net worth	3,384	3,443	4,183

Source: Annual reports published.

Table 13.2 Debt to equality ratio of the IT companies

Long-term debt to equity ratio

Company	2010–11	2011–12	2012–13
TCS	0.00	0.01	0.01
Infosys	0.00	0.00	0.00
Wipro	0.10	0.09	0.00
HCL	0.27	0.18	0.19
Tech Mahindra	0.31	0.30	0.13

The long-term debt to equity ratios are calculated and are tabulated in Table 13.2 and Figure 13.1.

From Figure 13.1 we notice that for industry giants, TCS and Infosys, it is on expected lines, that is, close to zero. Particularly, for Infosys, it is 0.00 in all three FYs. This is due to its zero-debt operating model.

Also, the debt to equity ratios for Wipro and Tech Mahindra have significantly dropped in 2012–13 when compared to 2011–12.

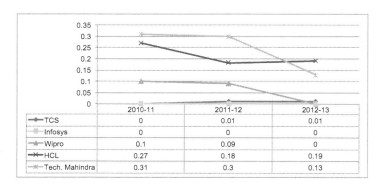

	2010-11	2011-12	2012-13
TCS	0	0.01	0.01
Infosys	0	0	0
Wipro	0.1	0.09	0
HCL	0.27	0.18	0.19
Tech. Mahindra	0.31	0.3	0.13

Figure 13.1 Debt/equality trend of the IT companies

In March 2013, Wipro underwent a demerger where it hived-off three non-IT business divisions, including consumer product segment, into a privately held company be named Wipro Enterprises Ltd.

Wipro to demerge non-IT businesses

To continue to be a publicly listed company with strong focus on IT, board to remain unchanged

IT giant Wipro today said it will demerge three non-IT business divisions, including consumer products segment, into a privately held company to be named Wipro Enterprises Ltd.

Press Trust of India, Mumbai, 1 November

This resulted in Wipro getting rid of all its non-IT loans. From Table 13.1, we can observe long-term loans going down by 96.83% from 2011–12 to 2012–13. As a result, its debt to equity ratio has fallen from 0.09 in 2011–12 to 0.01 in 2012–13.

On the other hand, for Tech Mahindra, the drop in debt to equity ratio is due to long-term loans coming down by 48.63% in 2013 when compared to that in 2012. Privately placed non-convertible debentures worth Rs 300 crore have been redeemed on 17 April 2013, which significantly brought its long-term loans down.

While ICR is used as an important indicator of solvency of a firm, it is not very relevant for an IT sector firm as they do not have much debt on their balance sheet, and hence their ICRs are astronomically high. Clearer picture emerges from DSCR (Box 13.1) as it evaluates the firm's solvency not merely on the basis of whether they can service their interests or not, but takes into account all the lease payments and principal payments incumbent upon the company apart from their interest costs.

Box 13.1 DSCR

DSCR is calculated by the following formulae:

Cash Flow from Operating Activities after TAX/(Interest Payments + Instalments)

Calculation of Cash Flow from Operating Activities after Tax

Cash Flow from Operating Activities after TAX = PAT + Depreciation + Interest.

All non-cash expenses are added to give a true picture of cash available which can be used to service debt payments, both principal and interest.

PAT, depreciation, interest can be directly obtained from the income statement of the firm.

Instalments

Instalments basically include the principal repayments and lease repayments of the borrowings which are due on the company.

Instalments cannot be accurately determined from the balance sheet of the firm or from the income statement, as principal and lease repayments are not reflected in the P&L statement. The only way to get instalments is from the *Cash Flow (from financing activities) statement* of the firm in which they are shown under the head 'Repayment of long term Borrowings'.

Significance of DSCR

- *DSCR* is used by banks and financial institutions giving long-term finance to organisations.
- This ratio is calculated to gauge the capability of the organisation to repay the dues arising as a result of long-term borrowings.
- A high debt service ratio assures the lenders a regular and periodical interest income.
- On the other hand, a too low DSCR indicates insufficient earning capacity of the organisations to meet the obligations of long-term borrowings.

As can be seen from the relevant dataset for each of the top five IT companies in Table 13.3 and Figure 13.2, DSCR for TCS and Infosys is extremely high, signifying the fact that these companies have very low debts. Actually, Infosys has no long-term debt at all.

Table 13.3 Debt servicing of the IT companies (Rs crore)

TCS	2010–11	2011–12	2012–13
PAT	7,569.99	10,975.98	12,786.34
Depreciation	537.82	688.17	802.86
Interest	20.01	16.4	30.62
Instalments	1.24	1.25	1.24
Infosys			
PAT	6,443.00	8,470.00	9,116.00
Depreciation	740	794	956
Interest	1	2	3
Instalments	0	0	0
WIPRO			
PAT	4,843.7	4,685.1	5,650.2
Depreciation	600.1	746.1	701.3
Interest	136	605.7	352.4
Instalments	8,252.20	6,867.10	8,253.20
HCL Technologies			
PAT	1,056.58	1,198.28	1,950.42
Depreciation	274.03	291.37	353.07
Interest	97.27	101.39	101.36
Instalments	108.35	0.76	3.74
Tech Mahindra			
PAT	696.7	460.6	652.5
Depreciation	138.3	150.5	157
Interest	111.3	102.5	109
Instalments	1,358.40	0	0
DSCR			
Company			
TCS	382.48565	661.78754	427.48964
Infosys	7,184	4,633	3,358.3333
Wipro	0.6651963	0.8078498	0.779016
HCL	6.9442661	15.575526	22.881541
Tech Mahindra	0.6438729	6.9619512	8.4266055

Source: Annual reports of companies.

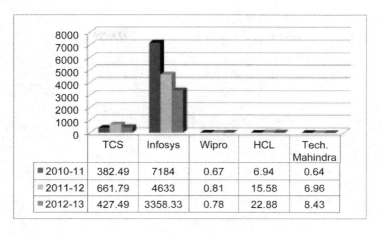

	TCS	Infosys	Wipro	HCL	Tech. Mahindra
2010-11	382.49	7184	0.67	6.94	0.64
2011-12	661.79	4633	0.81	15.58	6.96
2012-13	427.49	3358.33	0.78	22.88	8.43

Figure 13.2 DSCR trend of the IT companies

Wipro has DSCR value consistently less than one which means that cash flow from its operating activities after tax is not sufficient for servicing its own debts. The main reason behind this is due to the fact that both of its IT and non-IT businesses were merged in one unit. Hence, even though the IT business of Wipro did not have so much of debt, it was weighed down by the non-IT business which has not been going well. But since both businesses have been demerged now, there is a good chance that DSCR will come up for Wipro in coming Quarters.

For HCL, DSCR has been healthy and has been increasing on a year end-to-year end basis. But even then its DSCR is not as high as firms like TCS and Infosys. This is due to the fact that HCL is much smaller company in comparison to these companies and also that its long-term debt liabilities in comparison to its cash flow are a bit more.

Tech Mahindra is also in a similar situation like HCL. Being an even smaller company than HCL, obviously it does not generate much cash flow and has a bit of debt too on its balance sheet. In FY 2010–11, it had a very low DSCR (of 0.64) arising from its large instalments possibly obligation in its subsidiary 'Satyam' then. But after that Tech Mahindra has maintained a good DSCR with its cash flow from operating activities having now been able to cover its debts up to 8.43 times.

Recommendations

1   Going into the future, IT companies will have to recast their existing model in order to account for trends such as mobility, automation and the so-called Big Data or information deluge and disruptive technologies such as social media and cloud computing. As more and more employees are working less on desktop personal computers and more on laptops and tablets, and even smartphones and hence clients are and will be increasingly demanding newer service delivery technologies that can take account of these emerging trends such as mobility, social media and cloud computing – a method of delivery of IT services over a network, the internet in many cases for their employees.

2   The conventional model of our IT sector firms worked, since over 80% of the clients, who are based in the United States and the United Kingdom, outsourced and off-shored IT maintenance work to save money because labour in India was relatively cheaper; but that may no longer be the case with Indian IT workers getting 9–12% annual wage increases for years in a row. Also, with the United States and the United Kingdom economies seeing bad times, their governments are tightening work visa laws and want Indian IT firms to set up more local centres to create more jobs in their countries, which will increase labour and infrastructure costs. Only recommendation in this case can be to explore opportunities in other markets as well since IT requirement is slowly going to become unavoidable in all companies with scale be it in any market.

3   IT services firms should invest more in intellectual property-based offerings as these will experience accelerated growth in future with more and more clients focussing on outcomes rather than technologies or solutions from IT service providers.

Future outlook

Future outlook with respect to the financial health of the companies, which we have analysed with the help of solvency ratios like debt-equity, ICR and DSCR, seem to be in good shape. Though there seems to be no immediate or a short-term solvency problem for the IT companies which we have analysed particularly after IT and non-IT businesses of Wipro have been demerged, there is a chance that cash flows from operating activities may shrink in medium-long term, with the persisting slow growth in the global economy, and these macroeconomic factors leading to slowdown in demand. There also seems to be more competition from other South Asian countries on cheapness of IT services than before. And apart from these macroeconomic factors there is also a huge change going on in the type of technology solutions which are required as compared to before. If Indian IT companies are not able to adapt with time to the new realities, there is a good chance that they will not have as much cash inflows from their operational activities as they have today.

But this is also true that domestic Indian market will continue to drive growth due to new spectrum licensing, migration to direct-to-home platforms, broadband penetration, focus on value-added services and conducive regulatory environment. This will create opportunities for the software service providers who can assist operators in achieving their business objectives in these areas.

Discussion questions

1 Evaluate the financing policies of TCS, Infosys, Wipro, HCL and Mahindra. Examine the debt to equity ratios for this.
2 What types of finances are employed by the software companies for financing their long-term investments?
3 'Debt-service coverage indicator is the best measure for determining the margin of safety'. Justify.
4 Determine the debt servicing cushion of these companies by DSCR.
5 Which capital structure theory can be related to the above case?
6 'IT sector is low leveraged sector'. Comment.
7 What is the future outlook of the financial health of the software companies?

14

FINANCING POLICY OF BPO SECTOR IN INDIA

Indian BPO industry

Amidst speculation and uncertain global economic environment, the Indian IT BPO industry once again exhibited buoyancy and maturity with a spectacular rebound in FY 2011. Based on pent-up demand from the corporate sector and return of discretionary spending, there was a surge in customer IT spending across markets, both traditional and emerging.

The BPO segment has been growing at a CAGR of 31.4% since FY 2003. India has retained its position as the leading global sourcing destination with a 55% share in 2010 (up from 51% in 2009) and been able to increase its market share despite competition from emerging destinations. Indian companies have now over 400 delivery centres spread across 52 countries. Though United States remained the dominant market, higher growth was seen in European/Asian markets. The IT BPO industry has become one of the significant growth catalysts for Indian economy. It has helped India transform from a rural and agricultural-based economy to a knowledge-based economy.

The IT BPO industry is expected to grow to US$76 billion in revenues with exports accounting for US$59 billion. BPO segment is expected to grow by 14% overall in FY 2011. Domestic market is expected a healthy growth of 16% in FY 2011 and it is further expected to grow by 15–17% in FY 2012.

Companies for the study

*Following companies are selected in the sector
for the present study*

1. Allsec Technologies Ltd

Incorporated in 1998, Allsec Technologies Ltd is a BPO company. It has delivery centres in India and the Philippines. It provides service to varied sectors such as banking, financial services and insurance, telecommunication, retail, healthcare, energy and others. The company provides services such as data verification, processing of orders received through telephone calls, telemarketing, quality monitoring of calls by other call centres, customer services and human resource management and payroll processing.

2. NIIT Technologies Ltd

NIIT Technologies Ltd is a global IT solutions organisation, servicing customers in North America, Europe, Asia, Australia and the Middle East. It offers solutions focused around applications development and management, managed services, cloud computing, packaged implementation and BPO. The erstwhile software and services business of the NIIT Group, NIIT Technologies has an experience of over two-and-a-half decades in the software sector. It was spun off from the NIIT Group in 2004 and has been operating as a separate entity since then.

3. Tricom India Ltd

Tricom India Ltd (Tricom) is a leading IT and ITES provider offering unconventional experience, powered by a combination of domain expertise, process skills and superior technology to the clients. Tricom has been delivering services across the globe in BPO services, enterprise resource planning, business intelligence and data warehousing, emerging technologies and offshore software product development.

Tricom has presence in India, United Kingdom and United States and is listed on the BSE, NSE and Luxembourg Stock Exchange. Tricom is certified ISO 27001:2005, ISO 9001:2008 and Software Asset Management.

Analysis and discussion

The long-term funds' trend of the units has been analysed with regard to constituents of capital mix and change in them during the period. Financial leverage impact has been examined for interest factor on shareholders' return. Beta trend of the units (as explained in the Chapter 11) has been studied to determine the risk of these stocks.

1. Allsec Technologies Ltd

(a) Long-term funds used

Primarily the capital structure of company has almost remained constant. For long-term funds company has been dependent upon share capital and retained earnings (Table 14.1).

(I) SHARE CAPITAL

The equity capital of the company as of 31 March 2011 stands at Rs 152.38 million and has remained constant over the previous balance sheet date.

Table 14.1 Capital structure of Allsec (Rs crore)

Year	March 2011	March 2010	March 2009	March 2008	March 2007
Month	12	12	12	12	12
Sources of funds					
Total share capital	15.24	15.24	15.24	15.24	15.24
Equity share capital	15.24	15.24	15.24	15.24	15.24
Share application money	0	0	0	0	2.51
Preference share capital	0	0	0	0	0
Reserves	117.56	121.51	128.32	135.3	151.77
Revaluation reserves	0	0	0	0	0
Net worth	132.8	136.75	143.56	150.54	169.52
Secured loans	3.36	2.56	0.59	0.37	0.16
Unsecured loans	0	0	0	0	0
Total debt	3.36	2.56	0.59	0.37	0.16
Total liabilities	136.16	139.31	144.15	150.91	169.68

Source: Allsec Annual Reports.

Company has not issued any American depository receipts (ADR), GDR or warrants or any convertible instrument and hence have no impact on equity.

(II) RESERVES AND SURPLUS

The company's reserves and surplus as of 31 March 2011 stood at Rs 1,166 million represented by capital reserve at Rs 25 million (same as previous year), share premium on the equity shares amounting to Rs 1,202 million (same as previous year), Rs 131 million representing general reserve (Rs 0.74 million movement from stock options outstanding), Rs 193 million representing debit balance in the P&L account due to reasons mentioned above.

(III) SECURED LOANS

Secured loan balance of Rs 6 million represents balance payable towards hire purchase (HP) loans. This decreased by Rs 2.3 million during the year from Rs 8.3 million as of 31 March 2011 and this is primarily due to closure of HP loans due to completion/resignation of employees. There is an increase of Rs 10 million in bank overdraft.

(b) *Financial leverage and shareholders' return*

Although the company is reporting negative PAT, it is on account of very high depreciation, whereas the interest expense is almost constant every year equal to around Rs 4 million. Thus, due to negative PAT, the company need not pay any tax and thus no tax saving advantage, but negative PAT is eroding shareholders' value, revealed by firm's decreasing book value (Table 14.2).

(c) *Beta indices for company funds*

Beta indices for company funds: 1.09.

On account of continuous negative PAT, as well as negative operating cash flow, the company share has eroded its value from a peak of Rs 345 to Rs 10 now (Figure 14.1).

Thus, although market recovered to a great extent after 2008–9 crisis, the share of Allsec is currently trading at its low due to bleak future prospects on account of deteriorating global scenario as well as its inability to generate profits. But considering for the future, as the company is increasing its focus more on the domestic front and as it

Table 14.2 Financial performance of Allsec (Rs crore)

Year	March 2011	March 2010	March 2009	March 2008	March 2007
Months	12	12	12	12	12
Operating profit	**3.38**	**-2.61**	**-11.54**	**-7.37**	**32.63**
PBDIT	6.67	2.58	1.71	-2.57	36.41
Interest	0.47	0.37	0.38	0.26	0.39
PBDT	6.2	2.21	1.33	-2.83	36.02
Depreciation	10.34	10.14	8.45	8.39	7.94
Other written off	0	0	0	0	0
PBT	-4.14	-7.93	-7.12	-11.22	28.08
Extraordinary items	0.2	1.12	0.11	0.16	0
PBT (post extraordinary items)	-3.94	-6.81	-7.01	-11.06	28.08
Tax	0	0	0.21	2.49	-0.06
Reported net profit	**-3.95**	**-6.81**	**-7.23**	**-13.55**	**28.13**
Total value addition	138.17	124.68	108.04	106.38	80.66
Preference dividend	0	0	0	0	0
Equity dividend	0	0	0	0	7.62
Corporate dividend Tax	0	0	0	0	1.29
Per share data (annualised)					
Shares in issue (lakh)	152.38	152.38	152.38	152.38	152.38
EPS (Rs)	**-2.59**	**-4.47**	**-4.74**	**-8.89**	**18.46**
Equity dividend (%)	0	0	0	0	50
Book value (Rs)	87.15	89.74	94.21	98.79	109.6

Source: Allsec Annual Reports

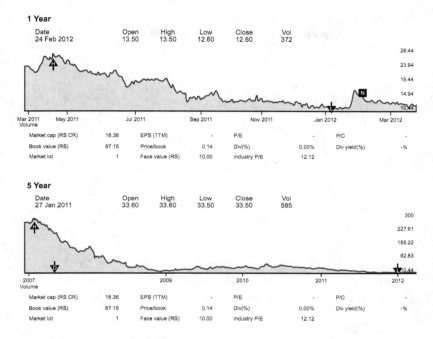

1 Year

Date	Open	High	Low	Close	Vol
24 Feb 2012	13.50	13.50	12.60	12.60	372

Market cap (RS CR)	18.36	EPS (TTM)	-	P/E	-	P/C	-
Book value (RS)	87.15	Price/book	0.14	Div(%)	0.00%	Div yield(%)	-%
Market lot	1	Face value (RS)	10.00	Industry P/E	12.12		

5 Year

Date	Open	High	Low	Close	Vol
27 Jan 2011	33.60	33.60	33.50	33.50	585

Market cap (RS CR)	18.36	EPS (TTM)	-	P/E	-	P/C	-
Book value (RS)	87.15	Price/book	0.14	Div(%)	0.00%	Div yield(%)	-%
Market lot	1	Face value (RS)	10.00	Industry P/E	12.12		

Figure 14.1 Beta trend of Allsec

Source: Moneycontrol (www.moneycontrol.com).

generated positive operating cash flow in year 2010, and hence in such favourable economic conditions, its share price can again rise to its highest of around 2010 levels.

2. NIIT Technologies Ltd

(a) Long-term funds used

Primarily the capital structure of the company has improved. For long-term funds, the company had been dependent upon secured loans but now it is dependent upon share capital and retained earnings. The share capital has increased over the years and net worth of the company has been improving (Table 14.3).

Table 14.3 Capital structure of NIIT (Rs crore)

Year	March 2011	March 2010	March 2009	March 2008	March 2007
Months	12	12	12	12	12
Sources of funds					
Total share capital	59.25	58.79	58.73	58.7	39.1
Equity share capital	59.25	58.79	58.73	58.7	39.1
Share application money	0.02	0.02	0	0	0.02
Preference share capital	0	0	0	0	0
Reserves	521.26	416.2	241.33	329.04	257.86
Revaluation reserves	0	0	0	0	0
Net worth	580.53	475.01	300.06	387.74	296.98
Secured loans	3.67	0.91	0.87	16.66	26.66
Unsecured loans	0	0	0	0	0
Total debt	3.67	0.91	0.87	16.66	26.66
Total liabilities	584.2	475.92	300.93	404.4	323.64

Source: NIIT Annual Reports.

(I) SHARE CAPITAL

The paid-up share capital of the company stands at Rs 593 million constituting 59,251,056 equity shares of Rs 10 each.

Company has not issued any ADR, GDR or warrants or any convertible instrument and hence have no impact on equity.

(II) RESERVES AND SURPLUS

The company's reserves and surplus as of 31 March 2011 stood at Rs 5,212 million represented by capital reserve at Rs 17 million (same as previous year), share premium on the equity shares amounting to Rs 60 million (increased from Rs 10 million), Rs 1,236 million representing general reserve, hedging reserve of Rs 17 million and Rs 3,882 million representing debit balance in the P&L account.

(III) SECURED LOANS

The company had secured loans amounting to Rs 37 million versus Rs 9 million in FY 2010.

(b) Financial leverage

The company reports positive PAT and enjoys tax-saving advantage. Thus, it is providing positive shareholders value. We can witness very low debt in overall liabilities composition. Debt accounts even less than 1% of total liabilities. Accordingly interest also comprises less than 1% of reported net profit.

So if we consider that the company would consist only of shareholders and zero debt, in that case its net profit would increase only marginally from Rs 123.25 to Rs 124 crore. So total dividend payment would increase from Rs 44.44 million to Rs 44.68 million (assuming that corporate income tax is 35% and dividend yield remains same). In that case the number of shareholders would increase by 5% and hence it results in reduced EPS as well as reduced shareholder wealth. Hence it points out that although the company is utilising very low debt and hence low risk, even this helps in increasing individual shareholder's wealth to a large extent (Table 14.4).

(c) Beta Indices for company funds

Beta indices for company funds: 1.34.

Thus, although market recovered to a great extent after 2008–9 crisis, the share of NIIT Technologies is currently trading lower than its highs of 2007 on account of deteriorating global scenario, but it is slowly recovering (Figure 14.2).

3. Tricom India Ltd

(a) Long-term funds used

Primarily the capital structure of company has almost remained constant. For long-term funds, the company has been dependent upon share capital, retained earnings and from loans. Secured and unsecured loans form a big part of the funds required by the company (Table 14.5).

(I) SHARE CAPITAL

The equity capital of the company as of 31 March 2010 stands at Rs 116.8 million constituting 58,400,450 equity shares of Rs 2 each and has remained constant over the previous balance sheet date.

The company has not issued any ADR, GDR or warrants or any convertible instrument and hence having no impact on equity.

Table 14.4 Financial performance of NIIT (Rs crore)

Year	March 2011	March 2010	March 2009	March 2008	March 2007
Months	12	12	12	12	12
Operating profit	**140.38**	**134.98**	**96.72**	**124.55**	**125.7**
PBDIT	158.4	125.78	128.47	173.68	137.83
Interest	1.03	0.43	0.81	1.49	2.19
PBDT	157.37	125.35	127.66	172.19	135.64
Depreciation	23.27	24.55	29.6	22.97	21.78
Other written off	0	0	0	0	0
PBT	134.1	100.8	98.06	149.22	113.86
Extraordinary items	−0.06	−0.02	0	0	0
PBT (post extraordinary items)	134.04	100.78	98.06	149.22	113.86
Tax	10.85	5.7	9.57	6.12	3.19
Reported net profit	**123.25**	**95.09**	**88.5**	**143.11**	**110.68**
Total value addition	467.22	355.7	402.03	316.29	167.35
Preference dividend	0	0	0	0	0
Equity dividend	44.44	41.15	38.17	38.16	25.42
Corporate dividend tax	5.25	6.24	1.3	0	4.32
Per share data (annualised)					
Shares in issue (lakhs)	592.51	587.88	587.27	586.98	391.01
EPS (Rs)	**20.8**	**16.17**	**15.07**	**24.38**	**28.31**
Equity dividend (%)	75	70	65	65	65
Book value (Rs)	97.97	80.8	51.09	66.06	75.95

Source: NIIT Annual Reports.

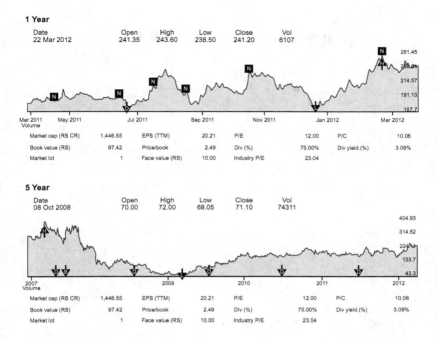

Figure 14.2 Beta trend of NIIT

Source: Moneycontrol.

Table 14.5 Capital structure of Tricom (Rs crore)

Year	March 2010	March 2009	March 2008	March 2007	March 2006
Months	12	12	12	12	12
Sources of funds					
Total share capital	11.68	11.68	11.66	11.62	4.52
Equity share capital	11.68	11.68	11.66	11.62	4.52
Share application money	0	0	0.01	0.05	0.33
Preference share capital	0	0	0	0	0
Reserves	79.84	63.65	54.4	41.15	13.81
Revaluation reserves	0	0	0	0	0
Net worth	91.52	75.33	66.07	52.82	18.66
Secured loans	54.53	45.13	28.52	7.03	6
Unsecured loans	15.89	20.5	0.02	0.81	2.13
Total debt	70.42	65.63	28.54	7.84	8.13
Total liabilities	161.94	140.96	94.61	60.66	26.79

Source: Tricom Annual Reports.

The company's reserves and surplus as of 31 March 2010 stood at Rs 798.4 million represented by capital reserve at Rs 31,995 (same as previous year), share premium on the equity shares amounting to Rs 220 million and Rs 47 million representing general reserve.

(III) SECURED LOANS

The company has taken secured loans from banks in the form of buyer's credit and term loans as well as working capital loans and vehicle loans which totally amount to Rs 545 million.

(b) Financial leverage

The company reports positive PAT and thus enjoys tax-saving advantage and provides positive shareholders value. We can witness that debt and equity are in the ratio of 7:9 in overall liabilities composition. Equity too is primarily represented by retained earnings and only around 15% of it is share capital. Accordingly, interest also comprises more than 60% of reported net profit.

So if we consider that company would consist only of shareholders and zero debt, in that case its net profit would increase from Rs 14.35 to Rs 20.41 crore. So total dividend payment would increase from Rs 12 million to Rs 20 million (assuming that corporate income tax is 35% and dividend yield remains same). But in that case the number of shareholders would also increase heavily by seven times thereby resulting in heavily reduced EPS as well as reduced shareholder wealth. Hence it points out that company is utilising highly leveraged capital and hence is in high risk, but this helps in increasing individual shareholder's wealth to a large extent (Table 14.6).

(c) Beta Indices for company funds

Beta indices for company funds: 0.93.

Currently, the company has not been performing well and its share prices have been going down. The price of its share has recovered from the shock in 2009 where the stock was worthless, but it still has to recover to its better days of 2007–8 (Figure 14.3).

Table 14.6 Financial performance of Tricom (Rs crore)

Year	March 2010	March 2009	March 2008	March 2007	March 2006
Months	12	12	12	12	12
Operating profit	**33.93**	**23.18**	**19.59**	**14.47**	**9.97**
PBDIT	27.67	23.46	23.04	17.39	11
Interest	9.32	6.14	2.51	1.33	0.97
PBDT	18.35	17.32	20.53	16.06	10.03
Depreciation	3.68	3.19	1.77	1.37	1.02
Other written off	0.07	0.07	0	0	0
PBT	14.6	14.06	18.76	14.69	9.01
Extraordinary items	0	0	−0.01	−0.02	−0.02
PBT (post extraordinary items)	14.6	14.06	18.75	14.67	8.99
Tax	0.26	−0.24	2.54	0.27	0.13
Reported net profit	**14.35**	**14.29**	**16.23**	**14.42**	**8.87**
Total value addition	20.77	22.48	22.13	16.04	13.78
Preference dividend	0	0	0	0	0
Equity dividend	1.4	1.17	2.68	2.44	1.16
Corporate dividend tax	0.24	0.2	0.46	0.41	0.16
Per share data (annualised)					
Shares in issue (lakh)	584	584	116.56	116.18	45.27
EPS (Rs)	**2.46**	**2.45**	**13.92**	**12.41**	**19.6**
Equity dividend (%)	12	10	23	21	20
Book value (Rs)	15.67	12.9	56.67	45.41	40.5

Source: Tricom Annual Reports.

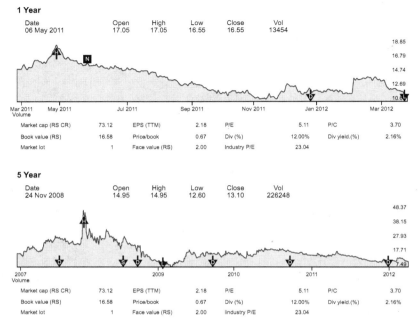

Figure 14.3 Beta trend of Tricom

Source: Moneycontrol

Conclusion

Indian BPO industry is one of the largest BPO industries of the world. It is a part of service industry and hence generally employs its total wealth primarily in the equity form with very low debt (Tricom is an exception and employs high debt). Low-leveraged equity provides that it very low risk but effectively it provides low growth opportunity to shareholders' wealth. It witnessed very high growth during precession period and generated returns for shareholders but subsequent to that it is facing irks of global recession and deteriorating global economic scenario has impacted companies' market capital standings. Allsec is currently trading low due to adverse global scenario as well as low profit generation. NIIT Technologies is also currently trading lower than its highs of 2007 due to same reason as Allsec but is slowly recovering.

Discussion questions

1 Analyse the capital structure of Allsec, NIIT and Tricom.
2 Evaluate the financial leverage of these companies.
3 Study the Beta trend of the above units to determine their market performance.
4 Which theory of capital structure can be related to the above case?
5 Discuss the sources of funds used by the above business units for their cost and risk.

15

SHAREHOLDERS' WEALTH MAXIMISATION IN FMCG SECTOR IN INDIA

After studying the financing policy of various companies in divergent sectors under financing section, the present chapter analyses the impact of financial leverage on shareholders' wealth with the help of DuPont model.

Overview of ten FMCG companies

The companies picked for the DuPont analysis are the top ten FMCG companies based on their market capitalisation (in crore) as of 10 June 2013.

- ITC Ltd: 151,078
- HUL: 67,858
- Nestle India: 39,819
- Dabur India: 18,632
- GCPL: 13,335
- Colgate-Palmolive: 12,764
- GlaxoSmithKline Consumer Healthcare: 9,842
- Procter & Gamble (P&G) Hygiene and Health Care Ltd: 9,777
- Marico: 9,078
- Emami: 6,836

ITC Ltd

ITC is an Indian diversified conglomerate with operations in four segments, namely, FMCG, agribusiness, paperboards, paper and packaging and hotels. It is the largest FMCG company in Indian market in terms of market capitalisation. Although primarily known for its vast cigarette and tobacco business, some of its major brands include

Mangaldeep, Goldflake, Sunfeast and Vivel, among others. ITC's net revenue grew by 17.2% in FY 2012 primarily driven by a 23.6% growth in the non-cigarette FMCG business. Its PAT increased by 22.4% and the net profits registered a growth of 23.6% in FY 2012. The EPS also went up to Rs 7.93 in FY 2012 compared to Rs 6.49 in FY 2011. Further, its return of capital employed improved substantially from 28.4% in FY 2011 to 45.4% in FY 2012 and total shareholder return grew at 25.7%. Major challenges were faced in the cigarette industry due to steep taxes being imposed in the current union budget. But the company has managed to pass on burden to customer as a result of which ROE shows consistent growth in the past three years.

Hindustan Unilever Ltd

More than 100 years old, HUL is a major FMCG company in India with brands like Dove, Lux, Lipton and Lifebuoy, among others. In 2010, the company was troubled by volatile and rapidly changing commodity markets but managed to pull through with a concerted focus on the rural market in India. It rolled out cross-category rural marketing efforts in FY 2010–11 through three major programmes, namely, Perfect Stores, Project Shaktimaan and Project Khushiyon ki Doli. By FY 2012, HUL's rural outlets accounted for almost 90% of HUL's turnover in retail outlets. Its customer base expanded to 25 million by FY 2011 giving HUL a renewed direction and footprint into the interiors of the country. FY 2011 saw the transfer of FMCG exports business division to wholly owned subsidiary, Unilever India Exports Ltd. Hence, the financial results of the demerged business undertaking do not form part of the company for the year ending 31 March 2012. This is probably why there was a major dip visible in the company's ROE.

Nestle India

The product line of the company includes Soups, Choco's, Baby Milk Powder, Maggi Masala, Munch, Polo, KitKat, Instant Coffee, Milkmaid and Tetra Pack Milk, among many others. Net sales increase in the year 2012 is 10.8% and net profit has increased by 11.1%. The cost of materials for goods sold in percentage of net sales has decreased to 45.5% from 48% in 2012. This is mainly due to high sales realisation, product and channel mix partly offset by the higher input costs.

Nestle is on an expanding spree in India; they have commissioned a new plant and upgraded their technology on many other plants. Nestle opened its first R&D centre in India in 2010. These activities have been financed by internal accruals and debt. In 2012, the total debt of the company was Rs 104,999.5 million.

Dabur India

The product line includes health and beauty products, personal care and packaged foods. The company ended 2012–13 with a strong 16.3% growth in net sales which touched Rs 6,146.4 crore. Net profit for the year recorded 18.4% growth to reach Rs 763.4 crore. The company has revamped the packaging of some of its products like Dabur Amla Hair oil to make it more attractive. The prime focus of this company in the coming years is penetration into rural markets.

Godrej Consumer Products Ltd

GCPL is involved in the manufacturing and marketing of FMCG. It operates in the segment of household and personal products. Apart from India, the company has its subsidiaries in the Netherlands, the United Kingdom, South Africa and Mauritius. The company operates in three major segments – home care, personal wash and hair care. Company is into Oleochemicals, which are used in a variety of applications including personal care (hair care, skin care, oral care and cosmetics), home care (laundry detergents) and pharmaceuticals. The growth in India's GDP per capita has led to a strong growth in the personal and home care market. Additionally, the significant size of the global personal and home care ingredients markets also represents a potential opportunity. The current environment has, however, seen fluctuating raw material costs (i.e., crude oil, palm and vegetable oil) which impact the Oleochemicals business.

Colgate-Palmolive

The company is active mainly in the oral and dental care category. The 2012 income statement shows an increasing sales trend year on year (YoY). The PBT is increasing YoY (Rs 485 crore to Rs 520 crore). The company invested 16.7% of its profit on brand-building activity. The PAT shows a decrease because of Rs 56 crore tax payment on the profit of its Baddi Manufacturing Facility. The company is currently focusing on creating medically proven superior toothpaste. In order to attract rural consumers, it is coming up with a small toothpaste pack costing Rs 10.

GlaxoSmithKline Consumer Healthcare

The company's portfolio includes Horlicks, Boost, Maltova, Viva, Crocin, Eno and Iodex. In 2012, the company achieved three key milestones – Rs 3,000 crore sales, Rs 3,000 share price Rs 100 EPS. The income statement shows 15% increase in sales and 23% increase in PAT during 2012 over the previous year. The company has achieved consistent double digit profitable growth for the eighth year in a row. Advertisement and promotion expenses during 2012 were 15.2% as a percentage of sales. The company has invested in capacity expansion project of a new manufacturing line using Vacuum Band Dryer technology, which involves extensive automation and controls. This is the world's largest vacuum band dryer line.

P&G Hygiene and Health Care Ltd

The company operates in a single reportable business and geographical segment. The company's core business is manufacturing, marketing and distribution of healthcare and feminine hygiene products. Under these businesses it has in its portfolio: VICKS – India's No. 1 Healthcare brand and WHISPER – India's leading feminine hygiene brand (in value terms). The focus of the company is now on rural Indian market. The income statement shows high advertising and raw material costs (approximately 80% of expenses). The company has reported no acquisitions or mergers.

Marico

Brands included in Marico are Parachute, Saffola, Hair & Care, Nihar, Medicare and Revive.

In 2012, the company achieved revenue from operations of Rs 4,008 crore, a growth of 28% over FY 2011. Volume growth underlying revenue growth was healthy at 17%.

ROE decreased by 12%. In February 2012, the company has executed agreements to purchase the personal care business of Paras Pharmaceuticals Ltd, from Reckitt Benckiser (Singapore) Pte Ltd for a consideration of Rs 740 crore to be paid in cash. This acquisition will give the company access to youth brands such as Setwet Zatak and Livon brands in male deodorants and hair gels category, respectively.

Emami

The company's core business is healthcare and beauty products. The income statement shows an increase in PAT by Rs 229 crore to Rs 259 crore (13.2% increase). Revenue growth is increased from Rs 1,247 crore to Rs 1,454 crore (16.6% increase). EBIDTA margin is kept 20% in spite of global slowdown. Emami managed to achieve this by passing on the costs to the consumer. The company faces issues related to high crude oil price and inflation and political unrest in Egypt, Libya, Algeria, Morocco and Kenya from where it sources its raw materials. The focus of the company is now on rural Indian market. The company is mainly promoting its recently acquired Zandu group of products in the market.

Shareholders' wealth maximisation: DuPont model

The ultimate objectives of the financial management in financing mix are 'maximisation of shareholders' and value'. Therefore, in this first section of capital mix, we have analysed the units in FMCG sector for shareholders' value.

DuPont Analysis is a method of performance analysis started by DuPont Corporation in the 1920s. DuPont analysis tells us the ROE effect, based on the following three variables:

- profitability, measured by net profit margin
- asset use efficiency, measured by total asset turnover and
- financial leverage, measured by the equity multiplier.

ROE = Profit Margin (Profit/Sales) × Total Asset Turnover (Sales/ Assets) × Equity Multiplier (Assets/Equity).

ROE is an indicator of how effectively a company's management uses investors' money – ROE shows the rate of return that the firm earns on stockholder's equity. If ROE is unsatisfactory, the DuPont analysis helps locate the part of the business that is underperforming.

DuPont analysis has been used here to find out whether these companies contribute to shareholders' wealth or not in Table 15.1.

Table 15.1 Competitive DuPont analysis of FMCG companies

Rank	Name	Amount (Rs crore)	TAT	NPM	EM	ROE
1	ITC Ltd	151,078	0.69	0.24	2.01	0.33
2	HUL	67,858	2.12	0.12	3.12	0.77
3	Nestle India	39,819	1.62	0.13	2.87	0.59
4	Dabur India	18,632	1.32	0.12	2.18	0.36
5	GCPL	13,335	0.87	0.19	1.42	0.24
6	CP*	12,764	2.42	0.16	2.59	1.03
7	GSKCH**	9,842	1.05	0.16	1.88	0.32
8	P&G	9,778	1.49	0.14	1.26	0.26
9	Marico	9,078	1.52	0.08	2.29	0.28
10	Emami	6,836	1.26	0.18	1.66	0.37

Note: *Colgate-Palmolive

** GlaxoSmithKline

The above data provides the net profit margin (NPM), total asset turnover (TAT) and equity multiplier (EM) data for the selected companies for 2012.

Source: Companies' Annual Reports.

Ranking and weight based on the DuPont scores

The companies were ranked on each of the four scores and a weight was assigned to them based on their ranking. The lowest weight indicates the highest rank

Rank as per market capitalisation	Company	Ranking as per total asset turnover	Ranking as per net profit margin	Ranking as per equity multiplier	Ranking as per ROE	Total score	Final ranking
1	ITC Ltd	10	1	6	6	23	5
2	HUL	2	9	1	1	14	2
3	Nestle	3	7	2	2	15	3
4	Dabur	6	8	5	5	24	6
5	GCPL	9	2	9	9	30	9
6	CP	1	5	3	3	10	1
7	GSKCH	8	4	7	7	26	7
8	P&G	5	6	10	10	30	10
9	Marico	4	10	4	4	26	8
10	Emami	7	3	8	8	22	4

Conclusion

The DuPont analysis was conducted for each of the companies to analyse their growth in the past three years. From the study of the various annual reports we have gathered the following information:

- FMCG companies are usually zero/low-debt companies with good dividend history and high reserve and surplus.
- They are considered a long-term investment by shareholders since they show steady growth.
- All these companies have a history. They have been in the market for a long period and hence are considered stable.
- They are considered an ideal investment during weak market and their market share prices are at an all-time high.

Based on our studies of the various ratios we deduce that Colgate-Palmolive although sixth in the ranking per market capitalisation ranks the highest in terms of shareholders' wealth maximisation.

Discussion questions

1   Evaluate the financial leverage of the following companies for shareholders' wealth maximisation using DuPont analysis:

   (a)   ITC Ltd
   (b)   HUL
   (c)   Nestle India
   (d)   Dabur India
   (e)   GCPL
   (f)   Colgate-Palmolive
   (g)   GlaxoSmithKline Consumer Healthcare
   (h)   P&G Hygiene and Health Care Ltd
   (i)   Marico
   (j)   Emami

2   'Leverage is employed for shareholders' wealth maximisation'. Explain in the present context.
3   'DuPont Analysis helps in determining the optimality of capital structure for shareholders' wealth maximisation'. Discuss.
4   Discuss the optimality of capital structure of the above business units. Which theory of capital structure can be related to the above case?

Part IV

INVESTMENT DECISION
Working capital management

16

WORKING CAPITAL MANAGEMENT
The conceptual framework

Introduction

The term 'working capital' has several meanings in business and economic development finance. From a financing perspective, working capital refers to the firm's investment in two types of assets. In one instance, working capital means a business's investment in short-term assets needed to operate over a normal business cycle. This meaning corresponds to the required investment in cash, accounts receivable, inventory and other items listed as current assets on the firm's balance sheet. In this context, working capital financing concerns how a firm finances its current assets. A second broader meaning of working capital is the company's overall non-fixed asset investments. Businesses often need to finance activities that do not involve assets measured on the balance sheet. For example, a firm may need funds to redesign its products or formulate a new marketing strategy, activities that require funds to hire personnel rather than acquiring accounting assets. When the returns for these 'soft costs' investments are not immediate but rather are reaped over time through increased sales or profits, then the company needs to finance them.

Meaning of working capital

In simple words working capital means the capital used to carry out the day-to-day operations of a business. This indicates whether a company has enough short-term assets to cover its short-term debt. Anything below 1 indicates negative working capital. While anything over 2 means that the company is not investing excess assets. Most believe that a ratio between 1.2 and 2.0 is sufficient.

Capital required for a business can be classified under two main categories:

- Fixed capital
- Working capital

Every business needs funds for two purposes, for its establishment and to carry on its day-to-day operations. Long-term funds are required to create production facilities through purchase of fixed assets such as plant and machinery, land, building, furniture and the like. Investment in these assets represents that part of firm capital that is blocked on a permanent or fixed basis called fixed capital. Funds are also needed for short-term purposes, that is, for the purchase of raw material, payment of wages and other day-to-day operations of business. These funds are known as working capital. In other words, working capital refers to that firm's capital, which is required for short-term assets or current assets. Funds thus invested in current assets keep revolving last and being constantly converted into cash and this cash flow is again converted into other current assets. Hence it is known as circulating or short-term capital.

The working capital requirement of any organisation is dependent on its working capital cycle or operating cycle as it is commonly referred to as shown in Figure 16.1. Shorter the length of the cycle, lower would be the working capital requirement and vice versa.

Operating cycle

Operating cycle is the number of days taken by a company to realise its inventories in cash. It is the sum of the time taken in selling inventories and the time taken in collecting cash from trade receivables. The length of the operating cycle determines the amount of investment required in working capital of an organisation.

Operating cycle is a measure of the operating efficiency and working capital management of a company. A short operating cycle is good as it indicates that the company's cash is tied up for a shorter period.

It is calculated as:

Operating Cycle = Inventory Conversion Period + Debtors Conversion Period.

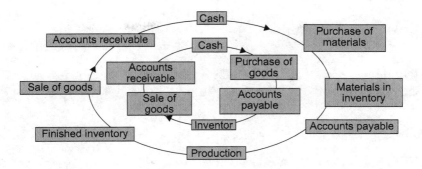

Figure 16.1 Operating cycle (working capital cycle)

Inventory conversion period is the average number of days taken by the company to sell its inventory. Debtors' conversion period is the time taken to realise receivables in cash.

Another useful measure used to assess the operating efficiency of a company is the cash cycle (also called the cash conversion cycle).

It is calculated as:

Cash Cycle = Operating Cycle – Payment Period to Suppliers.

Types of working capital policy

Following are the different type of working capital financing policy adopted by an organisation.

1. *Aggressive policy*

This is 'high risk, high return policy'. It involves keeping a low amount of current assets by the enterprise. It finances the current assets by short-term sources. Therefore, it is risky and results in 'negative working capital'.

Here, the strategy is to defer the payments to the suppliers the maximum possible extent and to collect from the customers sooner. So, business uses very little of its own cash, paying the creditors as late as it possibly can.

It is a high-risk arrangement because if the creditors ask for their payments and, for some reason, if the company does not have enough money to pay them off, then it might land up in trouble.

2. Conservative policy

This is the opposite of the aggressive approach. In this policy, you finance your current assets by long-term sources and keep safety net for future uncertainty. This results in positive working capital. So, this is the policy with the lowest risk, but it is less profitable as well as it reduces the money used in increasing the production.

3. Matching policy

This policy is an arrangement where the current assets of the business are used perfectly to match the current liabilities. It is a medium risk proposition. For example, if the creditor is due to be paid in five months, the company will ensure that there is enough cash to pay the creditor five months hence. It is also called 'hedging approach'.

Box 16.1 Negative working capital

Negative working capital occurs when current liabilities exceed current assets, which can lead to bankruptcy. In another scenario a negative working capital is a sign of managerial efficiency in a business with low inventory and accounts receivable (which means they operate on an almost strictly cash basis).

Negative working capital good or bad?

'Ordinarily, having negative anything is not a good thing, but with operating working capital it can be'.

Negative working capital is good if the following conditions are satisfied:

1   If payment of all short-term liabilities is on time
2   With good sales and profit margin
3   Proper inventory management

If the above conditions are fulfilled, the working capital is funded by cash profits generated from normal operating cycle and there is no strain on payment of liabilities.

Concept of working capital

1. Gross working capital

In simple words, working capital refers to the firm's investment in current assets so the total current assets of the firm are known as gross working capital.

2. Net working capital

It represents the difference between current assets and current liabilities. Net working capital may be positive or negative. Positive net working capital is that when current assets are more than current liabilities. But when current liabilities become more than current assets than it is negative working capital. It is calculated as

Working Capital = Current Assets – Current Liabilities.

How it works – example

Sample balance sheet of ABC Company is given in Figure 16.2.
Using the working capital formula and the information from Figure 16.2, we can see that ABC Company's working capital is

Rs 130,000 – Rs 1, 10,000 = Rs 20,000.

	Amount (Rs)		Amount (Rs)
Cash	60,000	Accounts payable	30,000
Marketable securities	10,000	Bank overdraft	50,000
Accounts receivable	20,000	Accrued expenses	10,000
Inventory	40,000	Cash credit	20,000
Total current assets	130,000	**Total current liabilities**	110,000

Figure 16.2 Balance sheet of ABC company

Constituents of working capital

Following are the working capital components.

These assets are reasonably expected to be converted into cash within one year in the normal course of business. They include **cash, accounts receivable, inventory, marketable securities, prepaid expenses** and other liquid assets that can be readily converted to cash.

1. Cash

Cash is an asset that is in money form. It typically includes bank accounts and money market funds. Marketable securities and treasury bills are easily converted into cash and are thus usually called 'cash equivalents'.

2. Accounts receivable

Accounts receivable are amounts owed by customers for goods and services a company allowed the customer to purchase on credit.

3. Inventory

Inventory includes raw material, semi-finished goods and finished goods lying unsold.

4. Marketable securities

Marketable securities are securities or debts that are to be sold or redeemed within a year. These are financial instruments that can be easily converted to cash such as common stock, government bonds or certificates of deposit.

5 Prepaid expense

It is a type of asset that arises on a balance sheet as a result of business making payments for goods and services to be received in the nearby future. While prepaid expenses are initially recorded as assets, their value is expensed over time as the benefit is received onto the income statement, because unlike conventional expenses, the business will receive something of value in the near future.

Current liabilities

These are the company's debts or obligations that are due within one year. Current liabilities appear on the company's balance sheet and include **short-term debt, accounts payable, accrued liabilities** and other debts.

1. Short-term debt

It comprises any debt incurred by a company that is due within one year. The debt in this account is usually made up of short-term bank loans taken out by a company.

2. Accounts payable

Accounts payable (A/P) are amounts owed to suppliers and other creditors for goods and services bought on credit.

3. Accrued liabilities

They are expense that a business has incurred but has not yet been paid. A company can accrue liability for any number of items, like a pension account that will pay retirees in the future. Accrued liabilities are recorded as either short- or long-term liabilities on a company's balance sheet.

Types of working capital

1. Permanent working capital

As the operating cycle is a continuous process, the need for working capital also arises continuously. But the magnitude of current assets needed is not always same; it increases and decreases over time. However, there is always a minimum level of current assets. This level is known as permanent or fixed working capital.

2. Temporary working capital

The extra working capital needed to support the changing production and sales activities, is called variable or functioning or temporary working capital. This can be shown in Figure 16.3.

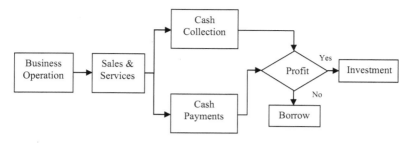

Figure 16.3 Process of cash management

Determinants of working capital

Followings are the main determinants of working capital.

1. Nature and size of business

The working capital of a firm basically depends upon nature of its business, for example public utility undertakings like electricity; water supply needs very less working capital because it offers only cash sales, whereas trading and financial firms have a very less investment in fixed assets but require a large sum of money invested in working capital.

The size of business also determines working capital requirement and it may be measured in terms of scale of operations. Greater the size of operation, larger will be requirement of working capital.

2. Manufacturing cycle

The manufacturing cycle also creates the need for working capital. Manufacturing cycle starts with the purchase and use of raw materials and completes with the production of finished goods. If the manufacturing cycle will be longer, more working capital will be required or vice versa.

3. Production policy

Production policy also determines the working capital level of a firm. If the firm has steady production policy, it may require continuous working capital. But if the firms adopt a fluctuating production policy means to produce more during the lead demand season, then more working capital may be required at that time but not in other periods during a FY. So the different productions policy gives rise to different types of need of working capital.

4. Firm's credit policy

The firm's credit policy directly affects the working capital requirement. If the firm has liberal credit policy, more credit period will be provided to the debtors thereby leading to more working capital requirement. With the liberal credit policy, operating cycle length increases and vice versa.

5. Sales growth

Working capital requirement is directly related with sales growth. If the sales are growing, more working capital will be needed due to the increasing need for more raw materials, finished goods and credit sales.

6. Business cycle

Business cycle refers to alternate expansion and contraction in general business. In a period of boom, larger amount of working capital is required, whereas in a period of depression lesser amount of working capital is required.

The importance of influence of these determinants on working capital may differ from firm to firm.

Working capital management

The management of working capital is concerned with two problems that arise in attempting to manage the current assets, current liabilities and the interrelationship that asserts between them.

The basic goal of working capital management is to manage current assets and current liabilities of a firm in such a way that a satisfactory optimum level of working capital is maintained, that is, it is neither inadequate nor excessive. This is so because both inadequate and excessive working capital position is bad for business.

Effective working capital management encompasses several aspects of short-term finance: maintaining adequate levels of cash; converting short-term assets (i.e., accounts receivable and inventory) into cash and controlling outgoing payments to vendors, employees, and others. To do this, successfully, companies invest short-term funds in working capital portfolios of short-dated, highly liquid securities, or they maintain credit reserves in the form of bank lines of credit or access to financing by issuing commercial paper of other money market instruments.

Effective execution requires managing and coordinating several tasks within the company, including managing short-term investments, granting credit to customers and collecting on this credit, managing inventory and managing payables. It also requires reliable cash forecasts, as well as current and accurate information on transactions and bank balances.

The scope of working capital management includes transactions, relations, analyses and focus:

- Transactions include payments for trade, financing and investment.
- Relations with financial institutions and trading partners must be maintained to ensure that the transactions work effectively.
- Analyses of working capital management activities are required so that appropriate strategies can be formulated and implemented.
- Focus requires that organisations of all sizes today must have a global viewpoint with strong emphasis on liquidity.

Significance of working capital management

Working capital is a common measure of a company's efficiency, liquidity and overall health. Positive working capital indicates that the company is able to pay off its short-term liabilities immediately, whereas negative working capital indicates that a company is unable to do so. This is why any decrease in working capital suggests that a company is becoming overleveraged and struggling to sustain.

Therefore, an efficient working capital management is of crucial importance. When not managed carefully, businesses can run out of liquidity in their current state. As a result, working capital shortage causes business to fail even though it may actually turn out to have profit.

It is important to understand the timing of payment, collection policies and asset purchases, the likelihood that a company will write off some past-due receivables for understanding working capital needs. Equally important is that working capital needs vary from industry to industry, especially considering how different industries depend on expensive equipments, use different revenue accounting methods and approach other industry-specific matters.

Cash management

Cash management is most important area of concern for any organisation which directly contributes in successfully achieving goals of the organisation if managed strategically, if not it will be one of the main reasons for revenue loss.

Cash management is an ongoing process of any organisation. It deals with controlling of the following:

1 *Cash inflows*: Efficiently handling of payment received from sales/ services or payment that will be received in near future once sales or service deal is finalised, in minimum possible time.
2 *Cash outflow*: Strategically dealing with vendors/suppliers to make payment in maximum possible time.
3 *Holding sufficient cash*: Efficiently managing sufficient cash in hand to assure that vendors/suppliers payments are done on time, day-to-day requirements of cash for operations is addressed and requirement of cash for new order or to start new project does not suffer due to insufficient cash.

Following points must be considered for successfully management cash:

- avoiding insolvency
- increasing collection rates
- selecting appropriate short-term investment vehicles
- increasing days with cash on hand.

Organisational need for cash is managed through

1 *Investment*: Short-term and long-term investment.
2 *Lending*: Borrow cash from bank and financial institutions for any big project (money intensive) or long duration projects that will finished in years.

Advantages of holding cash or near-cash are as follows:

1   It is essential that the firm have sufficient cash and near-cash assets to take trade discounts. Suppliers frequently offer customers discounts for early payment of bills. As the cost of not taking discounts is very high, firms should have enough cash to permit payment of bills in time to take discounts.
2   Adequate holdings of cash and near-cash assets can help the firm maintain its credit rating by keeping its current and acid test ratios in line with those of other firms in its industry. A strong credit rating enables the firm both to purchase goods from suppliers on favourable terms and to maintain an ample line of low-cost credit with its bank.
3   Cash and near-cash assets are useful for taking advantage of favourable business opportunities, such as special offers from suppliers or the chance to acquire another firm.
4   The firm should have sufficient cash and near-cash assets to meet such emergencies as strikes, fires or competitors' marketing campaigns, and to weather seasonal and cyclical downturns.

Discussion questions

1   Discuss the concept of working capital.
2   'Negative working capital is aggressive but desirable'. Justify.
3   What is operating cycle?
4   What are the different types of working capital?
5   'Positive working capital is safe by negative working capital is desirable'. Discuss various working capital financing policies in the context.
6   Discuss the various factors affecting working capital requirement.
7   'Working capital management is the most important part of the financial management of a business organisation'. Examine the significance of working capital management.
8   'Cash is the king'. Explain the importance of cash management in a business organisation.

17

OPERATING EFFICIENCY
OF AUTOMOBILE SECTOR
IN INDIA

Before analysing working capital management of the companies under study, it is better to appreciate the importance of operating efficiency of the units. The reason being is that working capital management is directly dependent upon the level of operational efficiency of an undertaking. Therefore, we are evaluating the operating efficiency of the Indian auto sector in this chapter.

The overview of Indian automotive industry has already been discussed in Part II.

Analysis

Working capital management is closely related to the operating efficiency level of the units. So, before analysing working capital in specific an attempt has been made to first evaluate operating efficiency in detail in order to appreciate working capital management better. We have taken auto sector for analysing the operating capacity.

Collection efficiency of the units is evaluated with regard to debtors' management and *inventory efficiency* of the units is measured with respect to inventory management. The analysis has been done for commercial automobile companies and passenger segment companies for a comparative evaluation.

Ratios

Following ratios are used for debtors' and inventory management of the units under study.

1. Debtors' management

- *Debtors turnover ratio (DTR) or accounts receivable turnover ratio:* It indicates the number of times average debtors (receivable) are turned over during a year.

  DTR = Net Sales/Average Trade Debtor.

- *Average collection period (ACP):* The approximate amount of time that it takes for a business to receive payments owed, in terms of receivables, from its customers and clients.

  ACP = 360 (No. of Working Days in an Year)/DTR.

2. Inventory management

- *Stock turnover ratio (STR):* It measures the velocity of conversion of stock into sales.

  STR = Net Sales/Average Inventory.

- *Average holding period (AHP):* It is the number of days, on average, a company is holding its stocks.

  AHP = 360 (No. of Working Days in an Year)/STR.

A Commercial vehicle manufacturers

1. Tata Motors
2. Ashok Leyland
3. Eicher Motors
4. Force Motors

1. Tata Motors

Tata Motors it is the leading commercial vehicle manufacturer in India. Tata Motors Ltd is an Indian multinational automotive corporation headquartered in Mumbai, India. It is the eighteenth-largest motor vehicle-manufacturing company in the world by volume. Part of the Tata Group, it was formerly known as TELCO. Its products include passenger cars, trucks, vans and coaches. Tata Motors is South Asia's largest automobile company; it is the leader in commercial vehicles and among the top three in passenger vehicles.

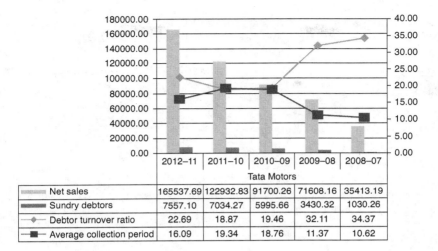

	2012–11	2011–10	2010–09	2009–08	2008–07
Net sales	165537.69	122932.83	91700.26	71608.16	35413.19
Sundry debtors	7557.10	7034.27	5995.66	3430.32	1030.26
Debtor turnover ratio	22.69	18.87	19.46	32.11	34.37
Average collection period	16.09	19.34	18.76	11.37	10.62

Figure 17.1 Debtors efficiency of Tata Motors

Note: Net sales are in Rs crore. ACP is in days.

Source: Company Annual Reports.

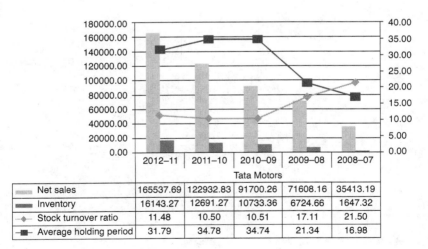

	2012–11	2011–10	2010–09	2009–08	2008–07
Net sales	165537.69	122932.83	91700.26	71608.16	35413.19
Inventory	16143.27	12691.27	10733.36	6724.66	1647.32
Stock turnover ratio	11.48	10.50	10.51	17.11	21.50
Average holding period	31.79	34.78	34.74	21.34	16.98

Figure 17.2 Stock efficiency of Tata Motors

Note: Net sales and inventory are in Rs crore. ACP is in days.

Source: Company Annual Reports

- DTR in 2008 had fallen 30% in 2009 as sales increased by two times but debtors have increased by three times in 2009. In 2010, 2011 and 2012 it has consistently increased.
- STR in 2008 is highest. It fell down to 17.11 in 2009 and by another 50% in 2010 to 10.51 times. This is due to increase in sales by twice.

2. Ashok Leyland

Founded in 1948, the company is one of India's leading manufacturers of commercial vehicles, such as trucks and buses, as well as emergency and military vehicles. Operating six plants, Ashok Leyland also makes spare parts and engines for industrial and marine applications. It sells about 60,000 vehicles and about 7,000 engines annually. It is the second-largest commercial vehicle company in India in the M&HC vehicle segment with a market share of 28% (2007–8). With passenger transportation options ranging from nineteen to eighty seaters, Ashok Leyland is a market leader in the bus segment. The company claims to carry over 60 million passengers a day, more people than the entire Indian rail network.

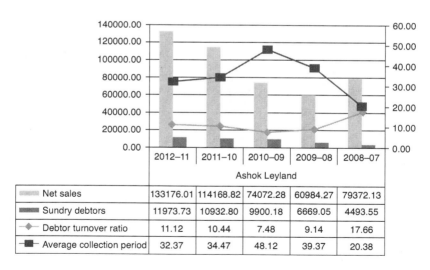

	2012–11	2011–10	2010–09	2009–08	2008–07
Net sales	133176.01	114168.82	74072.28	60984.27	79372.13
Sundry debtors	11973.73	10932.80	9900.18	6669.05	4493.55
Debtor turnover ratio	11.12	10.44	7.48	9.14	17.66
Average collection period	32.37	34.47	48.12	39.37	20.38

Figure 17.3 Debtors efficiency of Ashok Leyland

Note: Net sales are in Rs crore. ACP is in days.

Source: Company Annual Reports.

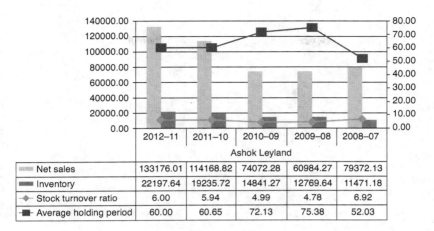

	2012–11	2011–10	2010–09	2009–08	2008–07
Net sales	133176.01	114168.82	74072.28	60984.27	79372.13
Inventory	22197.64	19235.72	14841.27	12769.64	11471.18
Stock turnover ratio	6.00	5.94	4.99	4.78	6.92
Average holding period	60.00	60.65	72.13	75.38	52.03

Figure 17.4 Stock efficiency of Ashok Leyland

Note: Net sales and inventory are in Rs crore. ACP is in days.

Source: Company Annual Reports.

The company has also maintained its profitable track record for sixty years. The annual turnover of the company was US$1.4 billion in 2008–9. Selling 54,431 medium and heavy vehicles in 2008–9, Ashok Leyland is India's largest exporter of medium and heavy duty trucks. Ashok Leyland is the largest supplier of logistics vehicles to the Indian Army. It has supplied over 60,000 of its Stallion vehicles which form the Army's logistics backbone.

- As sales fluctuate, sundry debtors consistently increase. This indicates that management strategies are becoming inefficient. The due impact is on low DTR which indicates management should focus on reducing the sundry debtors.

STR is also very low, indicating that it has to keep high stock; this is because Ashok Leyland is producing vehicles on order basis by keeping high inventory (or) it may be the stock on balance sheet preparation date in actual operations that is very low.

3. Eicher Motors

Eicher Motors is a commercial vehicle manufacturer in India. The company's origins date back to 1948, when Goodearth Company was established for the distribution and service of imported tractors. In 1959, the Eicher Tractor Corporation of India Private Ltd was established, jointly with the Eicher tractor company, a German tractor manufacturer. In 1960, the first tractor produced in India was put on

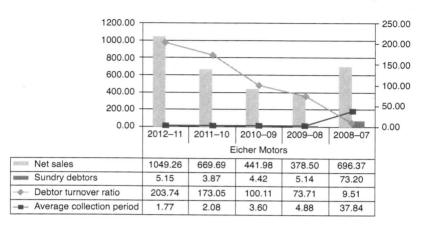

	2012–11	2011–10	2010–09	2009–08	2008–07
Net sales	1049.26	669.69	441.98	378.50	696.37
Sundry debtors	5.15	3.87	4.42	5.14	73.20
Debtor turnover ratio	203.74	173.05	100.11	73.71	9.51
Average collection period	1.77	2.08	3.60	4.88	37.84

Figure 17.5 Debtors efficiency of Eicher Motors
Note: Net sales are in Rs crore. ACP is in days.
Source: Company Annual Reports.

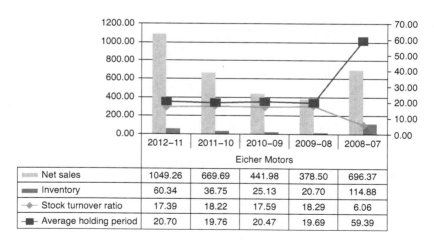

	2012–11	2011–10	2010–09	2009–08	2008–07
Net sales	1049.26	669.69	441.98	378.50	696.37
Inventory	60.34	36.75	25.13	20.70	114.88
Stock turnover ratio	17.39	18.22	17.59	18.29	6.06
Average holding period	20.70	19.76	20.47	19.69	59.39

Figure 17.6 Stock efficiency of Eicher Motors
Note: Net sales and inventory are in Rs crore. ACP is in days.
Source: Company Annual Reports.

the market. Since 1965 Eicher in India has been completely owned by Indian shareholders. The German Eicher tractor was partly owned by Massey-Ferguson from 1970, when they bought 30%. Massey-Ferguson bought out the German company in 1973.

In 2005, Eicher Motors Ltd sold their tractors and engines business to TAFE Tractors (Tractors and Farm Equipment Ltd) of Chennai, the Indian licensee of Massey-Ferguson tractors. The Eicher Group experienced a gross sales turnover of over Rs 1,900 crore (US$424 million) in 2005–6.

The Eicher Group has diversified business interests in design and development, manufacturing and local and international marketing of trucks, buses, motorcycles, automotive gears and components. VE Commercial Vehicles (VECV) Ltd is a 50:50 joint venture between the Volvo Group (Volvo) and Eicher Motors Ltd (EML).

- As sales fluctuate, sundry debtors consistently decrease .This indicates that management strategies are becoming efficient. The due impact is on high DTR which indicates that management does not to want increase the sundry debtors.
- STR is very consistent; Eicher management is strategically working on consistent STR.

4. Force Motors

The company is engaged in the manufacture of LCVs, small commercial vehicles, utility vehicles, agricultural tractors and other products related to automobile industry such as diesel engines. Formerly Bajaj Tempo, it was originally named Firodia Tempo Ltd and later after partial acquisition by Bajaj Auto as Bajaj Tempo Ltd.

The company was founded in 1958 by N. K.Firodia. Abhay N. Firodia is the chairman and Prasan Firodia is managing director. Force Motors started production of the Hanseat three-wheeler in collaboration with German Vidal & Sohn Tempo-Werke and went on to establish a presence in the LCVs field with the Matador, the proverbial LCV in India. Through the 1980s and 1990s, and especially in the past five years with a major product development effort, Force Motors has introduced new LCVs, a face-lifted series of Tempo Trax utility vehicles, new tractors and a new range of three-wheelers.

- As sales consistently increased, sundry debtors became consistent. This indicates that management strategically do not want to

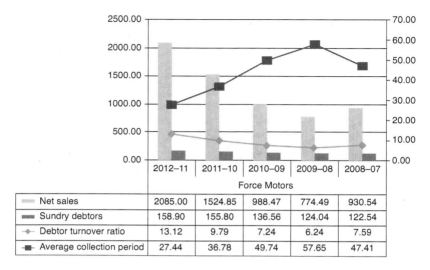

	2012–11	2011–10	2010–09	2009–08	2008–07
Net sales	2085.00	1524.85	988.47	774.49	930.54
Sundry debtors	158.90	155.80	136.56	124.04	122.54
Debtor turnover ratio	13.12	9.79	7.24	6.24	7.59
Average collection period	27.44	36.78	49.74	57.65	47.41

Figure 17.7 Debtors efficiency of Force Motors

Note: Net sales are in Rs crore. ACP is in days.

Source: Company Annual Reports.

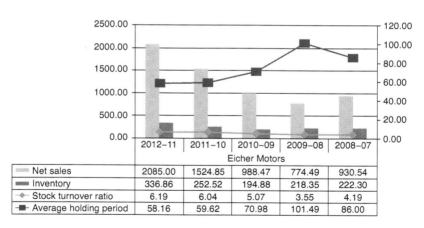

	2012–11	2011–10	2010–09	2009–08	2008–07
Net sales	2085.00	1524.85	988.47	774.49	930.54
Inventory	336.86	252.52	194.88	218.35	222.30
Stock turnover ratio	6.19	6.04	5.07	3.55	4.19
Average holding period	58.16	59.62	70.98	101.49	86.00

Figure 17.8 Stock efficiency of Force Motors

Note: Net sales and inventory are in Rs crore. ACP is in days.

Source: Company Annual Reports.

increase sundry debtors. The due impact is the consistent increase in DTR.

- STR is consistently increasing with sales and the AHP is consistently decreasing.

Conclusion for commercial section

The commercial vehicle manufacturer DTR and STR are consistently increasing with increase in sales; Tata Motors', Ashok Leyland's and Force Motors' DTR are below 25; however, Eicher Motor's DTR is above 100 (indicating that Eicher management is strategically making vehicles particularly after receiving order confirmation with advances in hand, e.g., ambulance).

B Passenger vehicle manufacturers

1 Hindustan Motors
2 Mahindra & Mahindra
3 Maruti Suzuki India Ltd
4 Honda
5 Hyundai

1. Hindustan Motors

Hindustan Motors Ltd, the flagship venture of the multibillion dollar CK Birla Group, was established during the pre-independence era at Port Okha in Gujarat. Operations were moved in 1948 to Uttarpara in district Hooghly, West Bengal, where the company began the production of the iconic Ambassador. Equipped with integrated facilities such as press shop, forge shop, foundry, machine shop, aggregate assembly units for engines, axles and the like and a strong R&D wing, the company currently manufactures the Ambassador (1,500 and 2,000 cc diesel, 1,800 cc petrol, CNG and LPG variants) in the passenger car segment and LCV one-tonne payload mini-truck HM-Shifeng Winner (1,500 cc diesel) at its Uttarpara plant.

The company was the largest car manufacturer in India before the rise of Maruti Udyog. It is the producer of the Ambassador car, widely used as a taxicab and as a government limousine. This car is based on the Morris Oxford, a British car that dates back to 1954.

One of the original three car manufacturers in India, founded in 1942 by Mr B. M. Birla, it was a leader in car sales until the 1980s, when the industry was opened up from protection. All through its history, the company has depended on government patronage for its sales and for survival by eliminating competition.

- HM encountered sudden downfall in YOY sales in 2012. Major contributor was reduced sales of Ambassador to 400 as compared

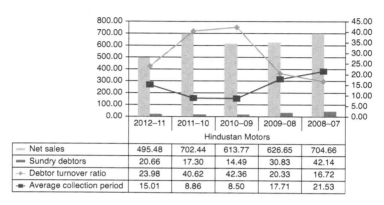

	2012–11	2011–10	2010–09	2009–08	2008–07
Net sales	495.48	702.44	613.77	626.65	704.66
Sundry debtors	20.66	17.30	14.49	30.83	42.14
Debtor turnover ratio	23.98	40.62	42.36	20.33	16.72
Average collection period	15.01	8.86	8.50	17.71	21.53

Figure 17.9 Debtors efficiency of Hindustan Motors

Note: Net sales are in Rs crore. ACP is in days.

Source: Company Annual Reports.

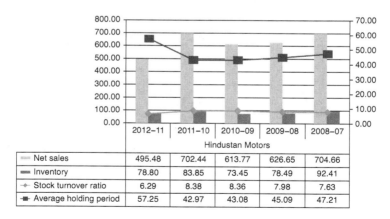

	2012–11	2011–10	2010–09	2009–08	2008–07
Net sales	495.48	702.44	613.77	626.65	704.66
Inventory	78.80	83.85	73.45	78.49	92.41
Stock turnover ratio	6.29	8.38	8.36	7.98	7.63
Average holding period	57.25	42.97	43.08	45.09	47.21

Figure 17.10 Stock efficiency of Hindustan Motors

Note: Net sales and inventory are in Rs crore. ACP is in days.

Source: Company Annual Reports

to 1,200 of 2011 (as it is not compliant to BS-IV norms for diesel engine cars).

- DTR has also reduced suddenly in 2012 which indicates that debtors became less liquid and accordingly, ACP has increased.
- AHP has encountered sudden increase in 2012 owing to reduced sales.

2. *Mahindra & Mahindra*

In 1945, two enterprising brothers named J. C. Mahindra and K. C. Mahindra joined forces with Ghulam Mohammed and started Mahindra & Mohammed as a steel company in Mumbai. Two years later, India won its independence, Ghulam Mohammed left the company to become Pakistan's first finance minister, and the Mahindra brothers ignited the company's enduring growth with their decision to manufacture Willys jeeps in Mumbai. The company's new name – Mahindra & Mahindra, of course. Soon established as the Jeep manufacturers of India, the company later commenced upon the task of expanding itself, choosing to utilise the manufacturing industry of LCVs and agricultural tractors. Today, Mahindra & Mahindra is a key game player in the utility vehicle manufacturing and branding sectors in the Indian automobile industry with its flagship UV Scorpio and swiftly exploits India's growing global market presence in both the automotive and farming industries to push its products in other countries.

Mahindra & Mahindra, branded on its products usually as 'Mahindra', produces SUVs, saloon cars, pickups, commercial vehicles and two-wheeled motorcycles and tractors. It owns assembly plants in Mainland China (People's Republic of China) and the United Kingdom, and has three assembly plants in the United States. Mahindra maintains business relations with foreign companies like Renault SA, France, and Navistar International, USA. Mahindra & Mahindra has a global presence and its products are exported to several countries. Its global subsidiaries include Mahindra Europe Srl. based in Italy, Mahindra USA Inc., Mahindra South Africa, and Mahindra (China) Tractor Co. Ltd.

- Mahindra & Mahindra has seen a steady year-on-year growth in terms of sales.
- Mahindra & Mahindra holds strong with the 30% and 20% plus growth in utility and van segments.

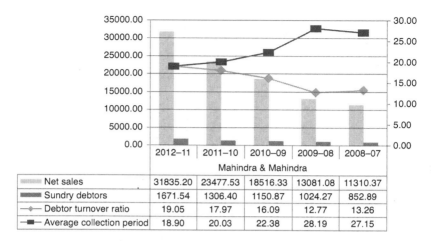

	2012–11	2011–10	2010–09	2009–08	2008–07
Net sales	31835.20	23477.53	18516.33	13081.08	11310.37
Sundry debtors	1671.54	1306.40	1150.87	1024.27	852.89
Debtor turnover ratio	19.05	17.97	16.09	12.77	13.26
Average collection period	18.90	20.03	22.38	28.19	27.15

Figure 17.11 Debtors efficiency of Mahindra & Mahindra

Note: Net sales are in Rs crore. ACP is in days.

Source: Company Annual Reports.

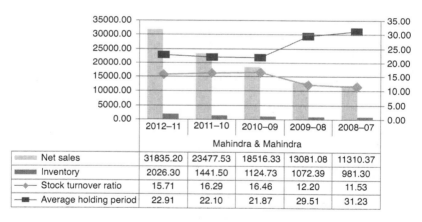

	2012–11	2011–10	2010–09	2009–08	2008–07
Net sales	31835.20	23477.53	18516.33	13081.08	11310.37
Inventory	2026.30	1441.50	1124.73	1072.39	981.30
Stock turnover ratio	15.71	16.29	16.46	12.20	11.53
Average holding period	22.91	22.10	21.87	29.51	31.23

Figure 17.12 Stock efficiency of Mahindra & Mahindra

Note: Net sales and inventory are in Rs crore. ACP is in days.

Source: Company Annual Reports.

- Mahindra & Mahindra has also worked on slowly but consistently improving on the ACP.
- With fast moving products, Mahindra & Mahindra's holding period is also low and second only to Maruti Suzuki India Ltd.

3. *Maruti Suzuki India Ltd*

Maruti Suzuki India Ltd commonly referred to as Maruti and formerly known as Maruti Udyog Ltd, is a subsidiary of Japanese automobile and motorcycle manufacturer Suzuki. As of November 2012, it had a market share of 37% of the Indian passenger car market. For more than a decade till Hyundai arrived, Maruti Suzuki had a complete dominance and monopoly over the passenger cars segment because TELCO and Mahindra & Mahindra were solely utility and commercial vehicle manufacturers. Maruti Suzuki manufactures and sells a complete range of cars from the entry level Alto, to hatchback Ritz, A-Star, Swift, Wagon R, Zen and sedans DZire, Kizashi and SX4, in the 'C' segment Eeco, Omni, multipurpose vehicle Suzuki Ertiga and SUV Grand Vitara.

Maruti Suzuki has 933 dealerships across 666 towns and cities in all states and union territories of India. It has 2,946 service stations, inclusive of dealer workshops and Maruti Authorised Service Stations in 1,395 towns and cities throughout India. It has thirty express service stations on thirty national highways across 1,314 cities in India.

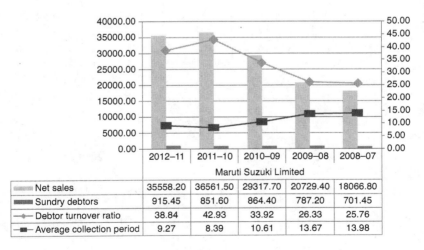

	2012–11	2011–10	2010–09	2009–08	2008–07
Net sales	35558.20	36561.50	29317.70	20729.40	18066.80
Sundry debtors	915.45	851.60	864.40	787.20	701.45
Debtor turnover ratio	38.84	42.93	33.92	26.33	25.76
Average collection period	9.27	8.39	10.61	13.67	13.98

Figure 17.13 Debtors efficiency of Maruti Suzuki

Note: Net sales are in Rs crore. ACP is in days.

Source: Company Annual Reports.

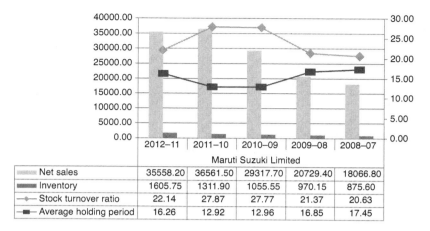

	2012–11	2011–10	2010–09	2009–08	2008–07
			Maruti Suzuki Limited		
Net sales	35558.20	36561.50	29317.70	20729.40	18066.80
Inventory	1605.75	1311.90	1055.55	970.15	875.60
Stock turnover ratio	22.14	27.87	27.77	21.37	20.63
Average holding period	16.26	12.92	12.96	16.85	17.45

Figure 17.14 Stock efficiency of Maruti Suzuki

Note: Net sales and inventory are in Rs crore. ACP is in days.

Source: Company Annual Reports.

- Maruti encountered a slight downfall in YOY sales in 2012 owing to overall downturn in the economy, reduced demand and elevated interest rates.
- DTR though showed upward trend till 2011 but suffered a little downfall in 2012 which indicates that debtors have become less liquid and accordingly, ACP has increased as compared to previous year.
- Though there is decrease in sales, STR and AHP show quite consistent trend.

4. Honda

HCIL is a subsidiary of the Honda of Japan for the production, marketing and export of passenger cars in India. Formerly known as Honda Siel Cars India Ltd, it began operations in December 1995 as a joint venture between Honda Motor Company and Usha International of Siddharth Shriram Group. In August, 2012, Honda bought out Usha International's entire 3.16% stake for Rs 1.8 billion in the joint venture. The company officially changed its name to HCIL and became a 100% subsidiary of Honda.

The company's product range includes Honda Brio, Honda Amaze, Honda City, Honda Accord and Honda CR-V, which are produced

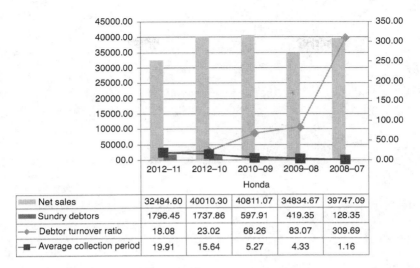

	2012–11	2012–10	2010–09	2009–08	2008–07
Net sales	32484.60	40010.30	40811.07	34834.67	39747.09
Sundry debtors	1796.45	1737.86	597.91	419.35	128.35
Debtor turnover ratio	18.08	23.02	68.26	83.07	309.69
Average collection period	19.91	15.64	5.27	4.33	1.16

Figure 17.15 Debtors efficiency of Honda

Note: Net sales are in Rs crore. ACP is in days.

Source: Company Annual Reports.

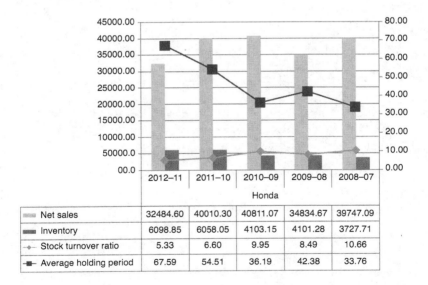

	2012–11	2011–10	2010–09	2009–08	2008–07
Net sales	32484.60	40010.30	40811.07	34834.67	39747.09
Inventory	6098.85	6058.05	4103.15	4101.28	3727.71
Stock turnover ratio	5.33	6.60	9.95	8.49	10.66
Average holding period	67.59	54.51	36.19	42.38	33.76

Figure 17.16 Stock efficiency of Honda

Note: Net sales and inventory are in Rs crore. ACP is in days.

Source: Company Annual Reports.

at the Greater Noida facility. Honda's models are strongly associated with advanced design and technology, apart from the established qualities of durability, reliability and fuel-efficiency.

- Company's lack of diesel engine had added to its problems. In domestic market past year 2011–12 its sales drop by 8.5%. In 2012, Honda Siel a JV declared the company sick under Sick Industrial Companies Act.
- Honda has announced to change its corporate name of its wholly owned Indian car subsidiary to HCIL.

5. Hyundai

Hyundai Motor India Ltd is a wholly owned subsidiary of the Hyundai Motor Company in India. It is the second-largest automobile manufacturer in India. Hyundai Motor India Ltd was formed on 6 May 1996 by the Hyundai Motor Company of South Korea. For more than a decade till Hyundai arrived, Maruti Suzuki had a complete dominance and monopoly over the passenger cars segment because TELCO and Mahindra & Mahindra were solely utility and commercial vehicle manufacturers.

Hyundai Motor India Ltd's first car, the Hyundai Santro was launched on 23 September 1998 and was a runaway success. Within a few months of its inception Hyundai Motor India Ltd became the second-largest automobile manufacturer and the largest automobile exporter in India.

Hyundai Motor India Ltd presently markets six models of passenger cars across segments. The A2 segment includes the Santro, i10, eon and the i20, the A3 segment includes the Accent and the fluidic Verna and the fluidic Elantra, the A5 segment includes the Sonata Transform and the SUV segment includes the Santa Fe.

- Hyundai Motor India became the country's second-largest car manufacturer and it offers seven cars in India including three hatchbacks, three sedans and one SUV. It recorded a 4.7% jump in domestic sales, 3.1% in exports and the cumulative sales stood at 4.1% in calendar year January to December 2012.
- In the year 2012, in difficult market conditions, the company refreshed i20, launched Sonata and Elantra which resulted in strong volumes and consolidated its leadership position.

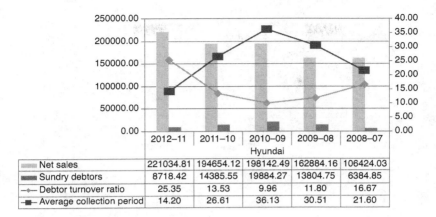

	2012–11	2011–10	2010–09	2009–08	2008–07
Net sales	221034.81	194654.12	198142.49	162884.16	106424.03
Sundry debtors	8718.42	14385.55	19884.27	13804.75	6384.85
Debtor turnover ratio	25.35	13.53	9.96	11.80	16.67
Average collection period	14.20	26.61	36.13	30.51	21.60

Figure 17.17 Debtors efficiency of Hyundai

Note: Net sales are in Rs crore. ACP is in days.

Source: Company Annual Reports.

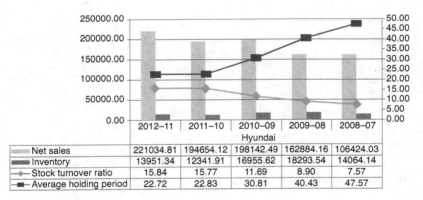

	2012–11	2011–10	2010–09	2009–08	2008–07
Net sales	221034.81	194654.12	198142.49	162884.16	106424.03
Inventory	13951.34	12341.91	16955.62	18293.54	14064.14
Stock turnover ratio	15.84	15.77	11.69	8.90	7.57
Average holding period	22.72	22.83	30.81	40.43	47.57

Figure 17.18 Stock efficiency of Hyundai

Note: Net sales and inventory are in Rs crore. ACP is in days.

Source: Company Annual Reports.

Conclusion for passenger section

- Debtor ratio : 20–25
- STR : 20–22
- All companies have shown an improving trend in DTR except for Honda which indicates poor efficiency of collection.

175

- Honda's STR is also reflecting large amount of stocks being held with poor sales. The numbers are also significantly higher than industry averages.

Discussion questions

1 What are the constituents of working capital of the above business units, (i) commercial segment and (ii) passenger segment?
2 Discuss the use of following ratios for working capital management:

   (a) DTR and ACP.
   (b) STR and AHP.

5 Analyse the debtors' efficiency and stock efficiency of commercial segment and passenger segment.
6 What is meant by working capital cycle? What role it plays in determining the working capital requirement of a business? Explain in the present case.
7 Comment on the working capital management of the above units.
8 What are the types of working capital approaches followed by the business organisations internationally? Which approach is cited in the present case?

18

WORKING CAPITAL ANALYSIS OF CORPORATE INDIA

We start the working capital analysis by reviewing the working capital trend of the Indian companies for the period from 2009–10 to 2011–12 in this chapter. The analysis is twofold:

1 *Standalone*: This involves analysis of an individual company in an industry.
2 *Sector*: This involves sectoral analyses of two companies in the sector on comparative basis.

The companies and sectors have been selected to have a wider representation. Most of these companies are major conglomerates or top companies in their sector. Some companies have very high working capital but less PAT. This shows that they are not using their funds effectively. An attempt has been made to study the trend in working capital of the companies over the years for finding out their approach towards working capital management. A correlation analysis has also been done to find out the relationship between working capital and profitability of companies.

Sectors which generally have high working capital are

- aluminium and aluminium products
- cement and construction material
- construction real estate
- diamond and jewellery
- finance – non-banking financial company (NBFC)
- pharmaceuticals
- power generation/distribution and so forth.

A Standalone analysis

Following is the analysis of the working capital trend of the select companies, sector wise.

1. IT sector

Infosys Ltd

- Infosys follows no debt policy.
- IT sector traditionally keep many employees on hold for sudden projects.
- It requires huge working capital.
- Human capital is the main capital of IT sector; therefore, there is a less chance of having huge debts.
- **Correlation Coefficient = 0.9867**

Infosys has a very high correlation coefficient between WC and PAT, meaning that both WC and PAT go hand in hand (Table 18.1 and Figure 18.1).

Table 18.1 Working capital picture of Infosys (Rs crore)

	Working capital	PAT	Current ratio (in times)
2011–12	22,457.64	7,986	4.72
2010–11	17,528.4	6,443	5.05
2009–10	16,635.2	5,755	5.38

Source: Annual Report of Infosys.

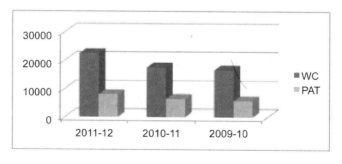

Figure 18.1 Working capital trend of Infosys

Table 18.2 Working capital picture of NTPC (Rs crore)

	Working capital	PAT	Current ratio (in times)
2011–12	21,699.4	9,223.7	1.84
2010–11	22,061.1	9,102.6	2.04
2009–10	22,076.8	8,728.2	2.24

Source: Annual Report of NTPC.

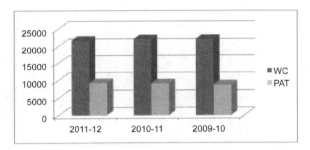

Figure 18.2 Working capital trend of NTPC

2. Power sector

NTPC Ltd

- NTPC almost maintains the same working capital as Infosys.
- Reduction in current ratio shows that the liabilities have increased more than assets.
- Also PAT has slightly increased.
- This shows a low expansion in operations of the company.
- **Correlation Coefficient = –0.7152**

The increase in WC would decrease the PAT and vice versa (Table 18.2 and Figure 18.2).

3. Engineering sector

Bharat Heavy Electricals Ltd

- Bharat Heavy Electricals Ltd (BHEL) is expanding rapidly.
- The WC had almost doubled in three years.
- **Correlation Coefficient = 0.9762**

179

Table 18.3 Working capital picture of BHEL (Rs crore)

	Working capital	*PAT*	*Current ratio (in times)*
2011–12	20,106.1	7,039.9	1.70
2010–11	18,454.6	6,011.2	1.74
2009–10	10,641.3	4,310.6	1.29

Source: Annual Report of BHEL.

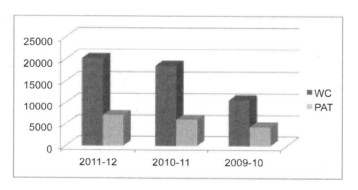

Figure 18.3 Working capital trend of BHEL

It has a very high correlation coefficient between WC and PAT. This can be attributed to the expansion plans laid down two years ago (Table 18.3 and Figure 18.3).

4. Coal sector

Coal India Ltd

- Coal India Ltd (CIL) is country's largest coal producer and supplier.
- It has a high current ratio which it should try to reduce.
- It has maintained the same working capital with reducing current ratio, meaning increasing scale of operations from 2009 onwards.
- That was the reason for increased PAT since 2009.
- **Correlation Coefficient = 0.7742**

It has a positive correlation between WC and PAT (Table 18.4 and Figure 18.4).

Table 18.4 Working capital picture of CIL (Rs crore)

	Working capital	PAT	Current ratio (in times)
2011–12	13196.4	8065.1	2.68
2010–11	11123.8	4696.1	2.61
2009–10	12083.3	3779.9	3.22

Source: Annual Report of CIL.

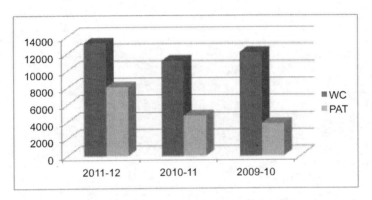

Figure 18.4 Working capital trend of CIL

B Sector analysis

Here, we have taken top two companies of select sectors and analyse them on comparative basis to know the industry trend of working capital.

1. Aluminium

Hindalco versus NALCO

- These companies have very low or negative correlation between working capital and PAT.
- The working capital involved is huge, due to high inventory cycle time.
- Hindalco had reduced the current ratio to below 2, after which their profits have increased, signifying better utilisation of funds.

181

- National Aluminium Company seems to have problems in managing WC investment as they have consistently high CR and profits are not increasing year on year like Hindalco (Figure 18.5).

2. Cement

Ambuja versus UltraTech

- UltraTech Cement had a reducing current ratio but the value of working capital increased and so did PAT showing their increase in scale.
- Ambuja Cements Ltd (ACL) on the other hand increased their working capital with a meagre increase in PAT.
- Both these companies have a very high positive correlation between working capital and PAT (Figure 18.6).

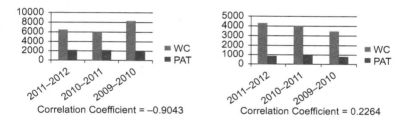

Figure 18.5 Working capital trend of aluminium industry (Rs crore)

Note: Current ratio is in times.

Source: Annual Reports of Companies.

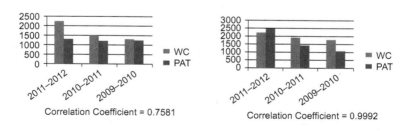

Figure 18.6 Working capital trend of cement industry (Rs crore)

Note: Current ratio is in times.

Source: Annual Reports of Companies.

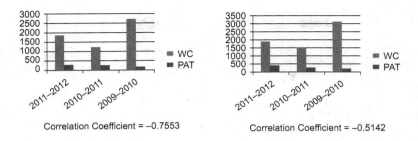

Correlation Coefficient = -0.7553   Correlation Coefficient = -0.5142

Figure 18.7 Working capital trend of diamond and jewellery industry (Rs crore)
Note: Current ratio is in times.
Source: Annual Reports of Companies.

3. Diamond and jewellery

Gitanjali versus Rajesh exports

- This industry needs to have a high working capital to reduce risk as market demand depends on various external factors like season, government policies, exchange rates and so forth.
- Both the companies have a negative correlation between working capital and PAT.
- Both the companies reduced their Working capital while increasing their PAT showing better utilisation of funds (Figure 18.7).

4. NBFC

Muthoot versus Shriram

- Both the companies have almost same positive correlation between working capital and PAT.
- Both the companies reduced their current ratio while increasing their PAT showing better utilisation of funds.
- After 2009, the current ratio of Muthoot Finance Ltd reduced drastically, while increasing the working capital and PAT, showing the growth in the company and their increase in operations.
- Shriram had reduced its working capital drastically after 2009 achieving almost 50% increase in PAT in the next year.
- These companies should plan out strategies to dealing with bad debts (Figure 18.8).

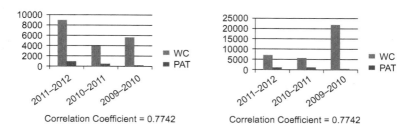

Figure 18.8 Working capital trend of NBFC industry (Rs crore)

Note: Current ratio is in times.

Source: Annual Reports of Companies.

Conclusion

- Working capital is one of the critical inputs for the operation of an organisation.
- Working capital *has a strong effect on the PAT of a company.*
- There are two kinds of strategies decided by profitability versus risk:
    - Risk Free – Positive Working Capital
    - Aggressive – Negative Working Capital.

- The more positive working capital, the more stagnation of money; as a result less utilisation of resources.
- After 2009 many companies have increased their scale of operations increasing both current assets and current liabilities but reducing the current ratio below; as a result more PAT is seen than previous years.

Discussion questions

1 Is working capital requirement sector-based? Explain in the present case.
2 'Permanent working capital is required for continuing operations, whereas temporary working capital is required for urgent needs'. Explain with specific sector.
3 Analyse the working capital trend for the following companies in different sectors with the help of 'Current Ratio' and also find out

the interrelationship between working capital and PAT for studying the impact on profitability:

(a) Infosys in IT sector
(b) NTPC in power sector
(c) BHEL in engineering sector
(d) CIL in coal sector.

4 Evaluate the industry trend of working capital on the parameters used in Q1 for the following sectors:

(a) Aluminium sector
(b) Cement sector
(c) Diamond and jewellery sector
(d) NBFC sector.

5 Comment on the working capital management of the units with regard to strategies adopted by them.

6 'Cash management is vital for every sector but it is highly essential for service sector'. Argue.

19

WORKING CAPITAL ANALYSIS OF TEXTILE SECTOR IN INDIA

Textile industry in India

Indian textile industry is one of the leading textile industries in the world. It used to be unorganised a few years back, but since economic liberalisation of Indian economy in 1991, the picture has changed considerably. It is much organised and reformed in terms of global challenges. India earns about 27% of its total foreign exchange through textile exports. Further, the textile industry of India also contributes nearly 14% of the total industrial production of the country. It is also one of the largest employment providers in the country. It not only generates jobs in its own industry but also creates jobs for the other ancillary sectors. Indian textile industry can be divided into the various segments, like Cotton Textiles, Silk Textiles, Woollen Textiles, Readymade Garments, Hand-Crafted Textiles and Jute and Coir.

Companies for study

The three companies selected for the present study are Bombay Dyeing and Manufacturing Company, Raymond Ltd and DCM Shriram Ltd (DSIL).

1. Bombay Dyeing

The Bombay Dyeing and Manufacturing Company Ltd was set up in 1879. It is one of India's largest producers of textiles. The company's product range includes linens, towels, home furnishings, kids wear, and the like, which are available at more than 2,000 stores across the country.

2. Raymond Ltd

The Raymond Group was incorporated in 1925 and within a period of a few years, it expanded from an Indian textile major to a global conglomerate. Today, the Raymond Group is vertically and horizontally integrated to provide customers total textile solutions.

3. DCM Shriram Ltd

DSIL is the flagship company of the DCM Shriram Group. Its portfolio comprises sugar, alcohol, fine chemicals, rayon and textiles. The group has a strong emphasis on technology and quality.

Analysis and discussion

Working capital financing of the units is analysed with regard to sources used for working capital requirements. *Profitability and liquidity interrelationship* has been tested with the help of relevant ratios. *Inventory and credit management* has been examined in the light of inventory holding period and debtors' collection period. Working capital efficiency is ultimately dependent on cash. Therefore, *cash management* has been evaluated for paying and collection efficiency.

1. Bombay Dyeing

(a) Working capital financing

During the year, total borrowings of the company were brought down from Rs 1,775 crore as of 31 March 2010 to Rs 1,237 crore as of 31 March 2011. Despite increase in the interest rates by RBI to the extent of 200 basis points, the company managed to reduce its average interest cost by 50 basis points through judicious borrowing arrangements. The average working capital in textile and polyester staple fibre (PSF) division increased commensurate with the increase in the scale of business as also operationally to take advantage of rising commodity prices. In the real estate business, the receivables were reduced on account of realisation of sale proceeds of commercial building. The company continued to fund its working capital from consortium of banks led by State Bank of India.

Bombay Dyeing has effectively managed its net working capital over the past few years; the company is following a conservative approach

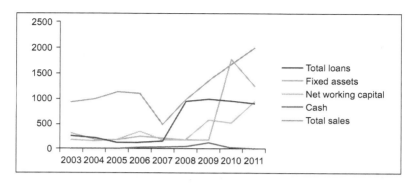

Figure 19.1 Working capital policy of Bombay Dyeing (Rs crore)
Source: Bombay Dyeing Annual Reports.

by decreasing it dependence on short term loans. As per annual report 2010–11, the company's short-term loans have decreased by 48% from Rs 163 crore in 2010 to Rs 90 crore in 2011.

The performance of the company during the year was good, as it continued its initiative on improvement in productivity, quality and control on costs, working capital and better capacity utilisation through effective implementation of theory of constraints (TOC) model.

As evident Figure 19.1, the net working capital of the company has increased as the sales of the company have increased, and therefore proportion is consistent. Moreover the cash with the company is declining which is a good sign as they are invested to generate more benefits.

Note: Material costs are valued on the basis of the average consumption rates at the yearend in order to reflect the fair picture of the costs incurred. Conversion and other costs are determined on the basis of standard costs. Cost of inventory at retail outlets is determined on a 'retail method', by reducing the gross margin percentage from the sales value of the inventory. Cost of ready finished cloth is determined by a combination of specific identification plus weighted average method.

(b) Relationship between profitability and liquidity

Profitability and liquidity of the company are inversely correlated as we can see that with decreasing EBIT margins the quick ratio has declined. The current ratio though has increased on the back of reduction in current liabilities.

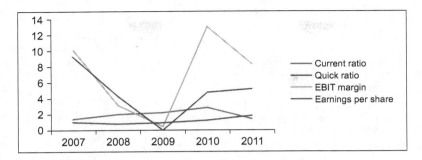

Figure 19.2 Profitability and liquidity of Bombay Dyeing
Source: Bombay Dyeing Annual Reports.

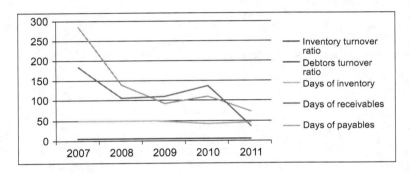

Figure 19.3 Inventory and credit management of Bombay Dyeing
Source: Bombay Dyeing Annual Reports.

(c) Inventory and credit management

Efficient management of credit systems has led to decrease in days receivable and payables and other ratios have maintained constant over the years; days of inventory has reduced slightly from fifty days initially in FY 2007 to forty-six days in FY 2011.

(d) Cash management

The company is following a more efficient cash management policy with sundry debtor decreases even with sales increasing continuously. The cash in hand is also managed better and are invested in long-term investments. The creditors are constant even with rising sales so

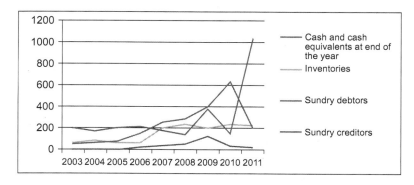

Figure 19.4 Cash management of Bombay Dyeing (Rs crore)
Source: Bombay Dyeing Annual Reports.

company is following a conservative policy for managing its net working capital.

2. Raymond Ltd

(a) Working capital financing

The performance of the company during the year was good, as it continued its initiative on improvement in productivity, quality and control on costs, working capital and better capacity utilisation through effective implementation of TOC model.

The TOC adopts the common idiom, 'A chain is no stronger than its weakest link' as a new management paradigm. This means that processes, organisations and the like are vulnerable because the weakest person or part can always damage or break them or at least adversely affect the outcome.

The analytic approach with TOC comes from the contention that any manageable system is limited in achieving more of its goals by a very small number of constraints, and that there is always at least one constraint. Hence the TOC process seeks to identify the constraint and restructure the rest of the organisation around it.

As per data from annual report the working capital loans have increased and are in the form of secured loans. Short-term unsecured loans are also issued by the company in the form of commercial papers. The sales of the company have been continuously increasing but the

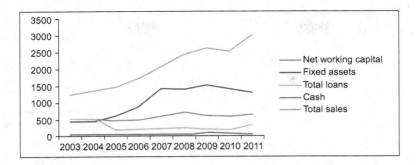

Figure 19.5 Working capital policy of Raymond (Rs crore)
Source: Raymond Annual Reports.

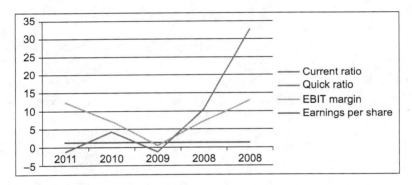

Figure 19.6 Profitability and liquidity of Raymond
Source: Raymond Annual Reports.

cash and networking capital have been continuously decreasing which entails a better working capital management initiatives.

(b) Relationship between profitability and liquidity

The company is faced negative EPS in FY 2011 due to loss on the account of exceptional items and high interest charges, but current ratios have been increasing as result of inventory.

The days payable have increased and days receivables have decreased, thereby helps in reducing operating cycle of the company which has increased the efficiency and decreased the net working capital requirement. Inventory turnover ratio has increased recently due to uncertain economic conditions in the year 2008–10.

(c) Cash management

All the values except cash and cash equivalents are positively correlated with increasing sales which shows that company has not been able to reduce significantly liabilities and the amount has grown with the rise in sales. But as the profitability of the company has reduced, the cash in hand has gone down and as a result the company has taken additional loan for working capital of the amount Rs 45 crore in FY 2010–11.

3. DCM Shriram Ltd

(a) Working capital financing

The majority of working capital is financed with long-term loans which is a conservative and a low-risk approach. The company does not use any of its short-term borrowings and therefore the firm has sufficient short-term borrowing capacity to cover unexpected financial needs and avoid technical solvency. The strategy adopted by DCM Shriram is low profit and low risk.

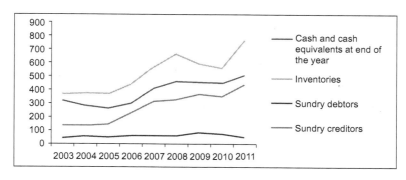

Figure 19.7 Cash management of Raymond (Rs crore)
Source: Raymond Annual Reports.

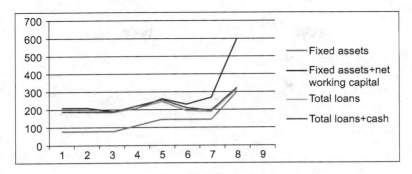

Figure 19.8 Working capital policy of DCM (Rs crore)
Source: DCM Annual Reports.

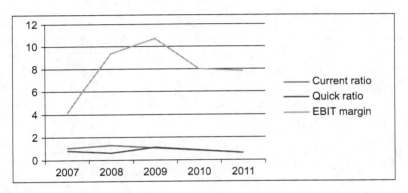

Figure 19.9 Liquidity and profitability of DCM
Source: DCM Annual Reports.

(b) Liquidity and profitability

Here we can see that there is indeed a negative relationship, that is, there is no relationship as such between liquidity and profitability in case of DCM Shriram. However, the current ratio has generally deteriorated over the years. The decrease in current ratio is primarily due to days of inventory and the days of receivables which are swiftly converted into cash and hence the current ratio has deteriorated, that is, the decrease in current assets is due to aggressive working capital management.

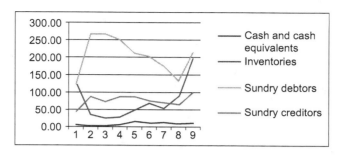

Figure 19.10 Cash management of DCM (Rs crore)
Source: DCM Annual Reports.

(c) Cash management

The cash management strategies are intended to minimise the operating cash balance requirement. So we can see from Figure 19.10 that the cash position has been maintained having a trade between inventories and account receivables.

Conclusion

Financing policy of working capital

- DCM Shriram follows a conservative approach of working capital management as it finances part working capital loans from long-term loans.
- Aggressive working capital management by Raymond Ltd.
- Aggressive working capital management by Bombay Dyeing Ltd.

Operating cycle

- The payable period has increased, signifying that the credit policies have significantly improved. However, days of inventory and receivables have marginally increased as well for DCM Shriram.
- For Bombay Dyeing, the net operating cycle has decreased .But there has been significant increase in days of inventory and days of receivable which signifies that the operating efficiency has decreased.
- Number of days in working capital or net operating cycle has decreased which signifies that the company has become more efficient.

- The operating cycle is shortest for Bombay Dyeing in most of the years to its aggressive inventory management.

Liquidity and profitability

- In DCM Shriram, the negative relationship between liquidity and profitability is not emphasised. It can be due to the reason because the liquidity position is maintained at more or less the constant level.
- In Bombay Dyeing, as we can see, there is a discernible negative relationship between liquidity and profitability as evident in Figure 19.2.
- In Raymond Ltd, the company has been in the red and as a result its liquidity ratio has been on the higher side. There is no discernible relation that emerges here.
- Comparatively Bombay Dyeing has the highest liquidity ratios and that is reflected in its profitability as well.

Discussion questions

1 Discuss the financing policy of working capital of Bombay Dyeing, Raymond and DCM Shriram.
2 What sources of funds are used by the business units for meeting their working capital requirements, both permanent and temporary, in the present case?
3 Analyse the interrelationship between profitability and liquidity of the above units with the help of relevant ratios for working capital efficiency.
4 How important inventory management is for working capital management?
5 Critique the inventory and credit management of the above units with the help of efficiency ratios.
6 Comment upon the cash management of the above units.
7 What is the significance of credit management for improving cash management?
8 Discuss the operating cycle efficiency of the above units.

20

WORKING CAPITAL ANALYSIS OF CEMENT SECTOR IN INDIA

Indian cement industry

The cement industry is one of the most energy-intensive sectors of the Indian economy. A historical examination of productivity growth of Indian industrial sector reveals that much-needed growth and development of Indian industry is not possible without the cement sector. The Indian cement industry is the second-largest market after China. It had a total capacity of about 300 million tonnes as of FY ended 2010–11. The industry is mainly divided into five main regions, namely, north, south, west, east and the central region. Looking at the high potential for growth, a lot of foreign players have displayed their interest in the Indian markets.

Scope

Following leading cement companies are analysed here.

1. ACC Ltd

ACC Ltd is India's foremost cement manufacturer with a countrywide network of factories and marketing offices. It was set up in 1936 and has been a pioneer and trendsetter in cement and concrete technology. It is also one of the initial companies in India to include commitment to environment protection as a corporate objective.

2. Ambuja Cements Ltd

ACL is also one of the leading cement manufacturing companies in India. The company, initially called Gujarat Ambuja Cements Ltd, was founded in 1983 and commenced cement production in 1986.

The global cement major Holcim acquired management control of ACL in 2006. The company is currently known as Ambuja Cements Ltd or ACL. It has a cement capacity is about 25 million tonnes.

3. UltraTech Cements Ltd

UltraTech Cement Ltd is among the top ten producers of cement globally. It is the largest manufacturer of White Cement in India. The company manufactures and markets Ordinary Portland Cement, Portland Slag Cement and Portland Pozzalana Cement, Ready Mix Concrete, White Cement and Building Products.

Analysis and discussion

Liquidity trend of the units has been examined with the help of liquidity ratios. *Operating efficiency aspect* has been analysed with regard to inventory and debtors' efficiency in specific and working capital turnover in total. Sources of funds have been studied to find out the *working capital financing. Profitability and its impact on liquidity* has been tested at company level and also at industry level. *Inventory management* is judged in terms of holding period. *Cash management* trend has been evaluated component-wise for the cash sufficiency. *Credit management* is evaluated for the collection efficiency.

1. ACC Ltd

(a) Liquidity

The liquidity ratios show an improving trend for the three years under consideration. The company is comfortable in terms of its current assets covering its current liabilities (Table 20.1).

Table 20.1 Liquidity analysis of ACC

Ratio/year	December 2011	December 2010	December 2009
Current ratio	0.99	0.79	0.72
Quick ratio	0.77	0.59	0.47
Absolute liquidity ratio	0.633	0.436	0.441

Source: ACC Annual Reports.

(b) Operating efficiency

Inventory turnover ratio shows that inventory is rapidly turning into receivables. A ratio of around 10 shows a comfortable position in this regard. Thus, company does not need much working capital as very small amount is blocked in inventory due to high turnover (Table 20.2).

DTR is also improving every year. Thus ACC is able to manage its debtors very efficiently. It means that the credit policy is quite strict and thus contributes to low requirement of working capital.

Negative working capital ratio is in general considered bad as the company does not have sufficient current assets to cover the current liabilities. But in case of ACC, it is a beneficial thing as here the company is utilising the credit facility of its suppliers to extend credit to its customers. Thus, instead of using its own money, it is enjoying at the expense of its suppliers. Thus with working capital turnover ratio is negative.

(c) Financing policy of working capital

Company's cash and cash equivalents as of 31 December 2010 were Rs 2,388 crore. The company's debt programme continues to enjoy a 'AAA' rating from CRISIL. During the year under review, the consortium arrangement for meeting working capital requirement was discontinued and the company opted for multiple banking arrangements (Table 20.3).

Table 20.2 Operating efficiency of ACC

Ratio/year	December 2011	December 2010	December 2009
Inventory turnover ratio	10.40	10.11	11.10
DTR	47.77	44.84	33.96
Working capital turnover ratio	−1.86388	−1.36535	−2.02112

Source: ACC Annual Reports.

Table 20.3 Working capital financing of ACC (Rs crore)

Loans	2011	2010	2009
Secured loans	500	509.93	550.00
Unsecured loans	10.73	13.89	16.92

Source: ACC Annual Reports.

There is marginal decrease in loan funds on account of repayment of loans from 2010 to 2011. From 2009 to 2010, there is a decrease in secured loans primarily on account of repayment of rupee term loan of Rs 50 crore during the current year. Also, there is marginal decrease in unsecured loan.

(d) Relationship between profitability and liquidity

Interest for the year was lower at Rs 92.91 crore compared to Rs 103.91 crore in the previous year (2010) on account of accessing of low cost funds and better working capital management. Net interest costs were contained and reduced by 6% as a result of effective financial and working capital management.

The average industry current ratio is around 2.10. Comparing ACC's current ratio (around 1.0) with the industry average, we see that the liquidity position of the company is not as comfortable as other companies. But its efficient management of working capital covers up for the risk that low liquidity throws up (Table 20.4).

Profitability of the company is more than the industry average for 2011. Thus we see that due to efficient management of working capital, ACC is able to extract higher profits at the same time keeping lesser reserves of working capital.

(e) Inventory management

We can see that ACC is very strict when it comes to the customer paying up their dues. At the same time, it pays its suppliers after a considerable gap. Thus in this gap period, ACC enjoys on the expense of its suppliers' money. Thus it is very efficient in its working capital management (Table 20.5a).

Table 20.4 Profitability and liquidity of ACC

PAT growth (%)	2011	2010	2009
Industry	−28.94	10.49	−3.99
ACC	18.33	−30.29	32.48

Source: ACC Annual Reports.

199

Table 20.5a Collection and payables analysis of ACC

	2011		2010		2009	
	ACC	Industry	ACC	Industry	ACC	Industry
Receivable days	7.64	14.54	8.14	15.06	10.75	15.20
Payable days	86.00	55.42	92.46	62.93	97.91	64.07

Source: ACC Annual Reports.

Table 20.5b Inventory analysis of ACC

	2011		2010		2009	
	ACC	Industry	ACC	Industry	ACC	Industry
Inventory days	35.09	44.46	36.10	41.57	32.89	40.64

Source: ACC Annual Reports.

ACC has better processes to handle its inventory as compared to other firms in the industry. The less the inventory number of days, the less is the capital blocked in inventory. It is another example of efficient working capital management. The management conducts physical verification of inventory at reasonable intervals during the year. The company maintains proper records of inventory and no material discrepancies were noticed on physical verification. The company did not carry any inventory of raw materials and stock of traded finished goods at the end of the year. All these showcase the efficient inventory management techniques of ACC (Table 20.5b).

(f) Cash position

There is increase in investments by 15.38% from 2009 to 2010 due to following reasons:

- Increase in the investment of mutual funds as compared to previous year. As of 31 December 2010, the company invested Rs 1,307.56 crore (previous year it invested Rs 1,129.47 crore) in mutual funds of its surplus cash.
- About 100% investment in Encore Cement and Additives Private Ltd, a company engaged in manufacturing and supply of ground slag.

- About 45% investment in Asian Concretes and Cements Private Ltd, a company engaged in cement grinding.

But there is decrease in investments from 2010 to 2011 on account of following:

- Decrease in current investment by Rs 127.71 crore as compared to previous year.
- During the current year, the company has subscribed Rs 50 crore to equity share capital of its wholly owned subsidiary, ACC Concrete Ltd.

Thus the company is investing its surplus cash in mutual funds. Some part of this surplus cash can be attributed to efficient working capital management (Table 20.6).

(g) Credit management

Here are the steps ACC normally takes if a client does not pay their invoice by the due date:

- Review the client's file.
- Contact the client by phone to arrange suitable payment.
- Send a reminder letter to the client.
- Review the client's file a second time.
- Send the client's invoice to a collection agency.
- Provide the collection agency with additional copies of invoice and cessation forms, and send levy adjustment forms to the client if required.

If the payment remains unpaid sixty-two days after the invoice date, the following penalties will apply:

- Interest will be charged at 1% per month compounding.
- An extra 10% penalty (in addition to interest) for every six months from the due date on the total balance outstanding.

Table 20.6 Cash management of ACC (Rs crore)

ACC	2011	2010	2009
Cash and cash equivalents	1,652.56	2,388	1,876
Investments	1,624.95	1,702.67	1,475.64

Source: ACC Annual Reports.

- The total of penalties and interest cannot be more than three times the amount of the unpaid levy.

Thus, ACC has very good working capital management practices within the industry. While most other companies have a positive working capital, ACC follows the aggressive strategy and has a negative working capital. It is more risky but by disciplined management, ACC is reaping the rewards in terms of high profitability (Table 20.7).

2. Ambuja Cements Ltd

(a) Liquidity

The liquidity ratios show an increasing trend, which means increase in current assets with respect to increase in current liabilities. The company is becoming more comfortable in terms of meeting current obligations, but at the same time it is keeping more money idle in the form of current assets (Table 20.8).

(b) Operating efficiency

Inventory turnover ratio shows that inventory is rapidly turning into receivables. A ratio of around 10 shows a comfortable position in this

Table 20.7 Credit management of ACC

	2011		2010		2009	
	ACC	Industry	ACC	Industry	ACC	Industry
Receivable days	7.64	14.54	8.14	15.06	10.75	15.20

Source: ACC Annual Reports.

Table 20.8 Liquidity analysis of Ambuja

Ratio/year	December 2011	December 2010	December 2009
Current ratio	1.14	1.07	0.89
Quick ratio	0.84	0.74	0.59

Source: Ambuja Annual Reports.

regard. This shows the efficiency in managing inventories, which leads to a great deal of reduction in current assets (Table 20.9).

DTR is also improving every year. Thus, ACL is able to manage its debtors very efficiently. This shows the efficiency of management in extract the payment quickly, leading to a savings in working capital investment.

There is no particular trend shown in the working capital turnover ratio. In 2008, it was negative, whereas in 2009, it suddenly rose 26.5. It is an indication of piling up net working capital investment in 2009 compared to 2008. But in 2010, reduction in the ratio to 13.5 against 26.5 in previous fiscal year shows an improvement.

(c) Financing policy of working capital

Company's cash and cash equivalents as of 31 December 2011 were Rs 2071 crore. The company's debt programme continues to enjoy a 'AAA' rating from CRISIL. Current liabilities include mainly two items, creditors of goods and trade and other deposits. Creditors form almost 50% of total current liabilities including provisions.

There was a repayment of secured loan in 2009. Even, unsecured loans fund has been reduced from Rs 65 crore in 2009 to Rs 49 crore in past two years. This indicates that the company is having a low-geared capital structure and a conservative approach (Table 20.10).

Table 20.9 Operating efficiency of Ambuja

Ratio/year	December 2011	December 2010	December 2009
Inventory turnover ratio	10.38	9.19	11.36
DTR	52.58	37.60	33.39
Working capital turnover ratio	13.48	26.51	–21.09

Source: Ambuja Annual Reports.

Table 20.10 Working capital financing of Ambuja (Rs crore)

Loans	2011	2010	2009
Secured loans	0	0	100.00
Unsecured loans	49	49	65

Source: Ambuja Annual Reports.

(d) Relationship between profitability and liquidity

Interest for the year was lower at Rs 52 crore compared to Rs 48 crore in the previous year (2010) on account of accessing of low cost funds and better working capital management. Net interest costs were maintained at nearly the same level as a result of effective financial and working capital management.

The average industry current ratio is around 2.10. Comparing ACL's current ratio (around 1.14) with the industry average, we see that the liquidity position of the company is not as comfortable as other companies. But its efficient management of working capital covers up for the risk that low liquidity throws up. The company is operating at low working capital, their saving financial costs relative to others (Table 20.11).

Although ACL had shown a negative growth in 2011, its performance has been much better than that of the whole industry. Thus, we see that due to efficient management of working capital, ACL is able to extract higher profits at the same time keeping lesser reserves of working capital.

(e) Inventory management

We can see that Ambuja is very strict when it comes to the customer paying up their dues. At the same time, it pays its suppliers after a considerable gap. Thus, in this gap period, ACL enjoys on the expense of its suppliers' money. Thus, it is very efficient in its working capital management (Table 20.12a).

Table 20.11 Profitability and liquidity of Ambuja

PAT growth (%)	2011	2010	2009
Ambuja	–2.43	5.34	–14.48

Source: Ambuja Annual Reports.

Table 20.12a Collection analysis of Ambuja

	2011	2010	2009
	Ambuja	Ambuja	Ambuja
Receivable days	7.64	8.14	10.75

Source: Ambuja Annual Reports.

Ambuja has better processes to handle its inventory as compared to the industry as a whole. The less the inventory number of days, the less is the capital blocked in inventory. It is another example of efficient working capital management. The management conducts physical inventory verification such as cycle count to ensure that inventories are accurately maintained and no sales are lost due to operational inefficiency. The company was carrying raw material inventory of Rs 557 crore and finished goods of around Rs 350 crore during the end of FY. This shows some form of inefficiency on the parts of management (Table 20.12b).

(f) Cash position

There is an increase in investments by 30% from 2010 to 2011. The company's cash position has also increased from 2010 to 2011. The company is maintaining more liquidity in recent years (Table 20.13).

(g) Credit management

ACL are quite strict as far as receivables are concerned. Thereby, it is able to manage good relationship with debtors, at the same time taking advantage of low debtors' days (Table 20.14).

Table 20.12b Inventory analysis of Ambuja

	2011	2010	2009
	Ambuja	Ambuja	Ambuja
Inventory days	34.69	39.10	31.69

Source: Ambuja Annual Reports.

Table 20.13 Cash management of Ambuja (Rs crore)

ACL	2011	2010	2009
Cash and cash equivalents	2,071	1,648	881
Investments	591	457	263

Source: Ambuja Annual Reports.

3. UltraTech Cement Ltd

(a) Liquidity

The liquidity position has been stable over the past three years. Both current ratio and quick ratio has been stable at around 0.65 and 0.30 levels, respectively, over the past three years. The company is highly leveraged in terms with regard to working capital and operating at a negative working capital. Going forward, we will discuss in details what contributes to the same (Table 20.15).

(b) Operating efficiency

Inventory turnover ratio shows that inventory is rapidly turning into receivables. A ratio of around 10 shows a comfortable position in this regard. Thus, the company does not need much working capital, as very small amount is blocked in inventory due to high turnover (Table 20.16).

Table 20.14 Credit management of Ambuja

	2011		2010		2009	
	ACC	Industry	ACC	Industry	ACC	Industry
Receivable days	6.92	14.54	6.10	15.06	8.78	15.20

Source: Ambuja Annual Reports.

Table 20.15 Liquidity analysis of UltraTech

Ratio/year	December 2011	December 2010	December 2009
Current ratio	0.69	0.64	0.62
Quick ratio	0.34	0.30	0.34

Source: UltraTech Annual Reports.

Table 20.16 Operating efficiency of UltraTech

Ratio/year	December 2011	December 2010	December 2009
Inventory turnover ratio	10.70	10.21	11.00
DTR	36.37	37.74	34.86
Working capital turnover ratio	−7.51	−7.53	−7.78

Source: UltraTech Annual Reports.

DTR is also stable at around 36 level. UltraTech is able to manage its debtors very efficiently. It means that the credit policy is quite strict and thus contributes to low requirement of working capital.

Negative working capital ratio is in general considered bad as the company does not have sufficient current assets to cover the current liabilities. But in case of UltraTech, it is a beneficial thing as here the company is utilising the credit facility of its suppliers to extend credit to its customers. Thus, instead of using its own money, it is enjoying at the expense of its suppliers. Thus with working capital turnover ratio is negative.

(c) Financing policy of working capital

Company's cash and cash equivalents as of 31 December 2010 were Rs 1200 crore. The company's debt programme continues to enjoy a 'AAA' rating from CRISIL. The firm is utilising the credits from suppliers to finance major parts of its working capital.

The company is standing at huge loans as of 31 December 2011. The secured loans have been increased to Rs 2,790 crore from Rs 854 crore a year ago. Similarly unsecured loans have also seen a sharp rise in 2011 compared to that of 2010 (Table 20.17).

(d) Relationship between profitability and liquidity

Interest for the year was high at Rs 288 crore compared to Rs 124 crore a year ago in the previous year (2010) due to the huge loan funds, both secured and unsecured, that the company took during the year.

The average industry current ratio is around 2.10. Comparing UltraTech's current ratio (around 1.0) with the industry average, we see that the liquidity position of the company is not as comfortable as other companies. But its efficient management of working capital covers up for the risk that low liquidity throws up.

Profitability of the company is more than the industry average for 2011. Thus we see that due to efficient management of working

Table 20.17 Working capital financing of UltraTech (Rs crore)

Loans	2011	2010	2009
Secured loans	2,790	854	1,176
Unsecured loans	1,355	750	966

Source: UltraTech Annual Reports.

capital, UltraTech is able to extract higher profits at the same time keeping lesser reserves of working capital (Table 20.18a).

(e) Inventory management

We can see that UltraTech is very strict when it comes to the customer paying up their dues. At the same time, it pays its suppliers after a considerable gap. Thus, in this gap period, UltraTech enjoys on the expense of its suppliers' money. Thus, it is very efficient in its working capital management (Table 20.18b).

UltraTech has better processes to handle its inventory as compared to other firms in the industry. The less the inventory number of days, the less is the capital blocked in inventory. It is another example of efficient working capital management. The management conducts physical verification of inventory at reasonable intervals during the year. The company maintains proper records of inventory and no material discrepancies were noticed on physical verification (Table 20.18c).

Table 20.18a Profitability and liquidity of UltraTech

PAT growth (%)	2011	2010	2009
Ultra Tech	30.13	10.29	–3.48

Source: UltraTech Annual Reports.

Table 20.18b Collection analysis of UltraTech

	2011	2010	2009
	UltraTech	UltraTech	UltraTech
Receivable days	9.94	9.54	10.35

Source: UltraTech Annual Reports.

Table 20.18c Inventory analysis of UltraTech

	2011	2010	2009
	UltraTech	UltraTech	UltraTech
Inventory days	33.6	35.3	32.7

Source: UltraTech Annual Reports.

Table 20.19 Cash management of UltraTech (Rs crore)

UltraTech	2011	2010	2009
Cash and cash equivalents	145	84	105
Investments	1,055	351	381

Source: UltraTech Annual Reports.

(f) Cash position

There is increase in investments by almost 200% (Table 20.19).

- Huge loans, both secured and unsecured, were taken by the company during the year.
- The revenue of the company almost doubled from 2010 to 2011.

Conclusion

After analysing the three companies as well as with the industry, we have observed that UltraTech Cements Ltd is more efficient in managing receivable days, payable days and inventory days. UltraTech is able to operate at a negative working capital and with a huge negative working capital ratio of around 7. Although operating with such a negative working capital is not an easy task, huge growth over past few years, especially almost 85% growth in previous year is supporting it.

It has also been seen that ACL is more conservatively operated than ACC and UltraTech Ltd, thereby failing to take the advantage of low working capital investment. ACL is seen as low-geared companies, whereas UltraTech's loan book is huge. It has taken huge loans, both secured and unsecured, to support its huge growth.

In terms of contribution to profitability, it is seen that ACC and UltraTech are able show better financial performance than that of the whole industry as well as ACL due to efficient management of working capital and other operations. UltraTech is able to obtain a better credit terms due to its growing scale of business and efficiency of management.

UltraTech has shown tremendous growth past year compared to its earlier years but it raises the question whether it is sustainable. Whether it will be able to show the same kind of credit terms from suppliers and efficient working capital management is the biggest challenge. But, on the other hand, ACC has shown consistently good performance in terms of inventory management, payables and receivables and the like.

Discussion questions

1 Analyse the liquidity position of ACC, Ambuja and UltraTech with the help of liquidity ratios.
2 What is the level of operating efficiency of the above units? Discuss with the help of efficiency ratios.
3 Discuss the working capital financing policy of the above units.
4 Analyse the interrelationship between profitability and liquidity of the above units in the industry for working capital efficiency.
5 Comment upon the inventory management of the above units with the help of inventory ratios.
6 Evaluate the cash position of the above units. What are the techniques used by business houses to improve cash management?
7 Discuss the operating cycle efficiency of the above units.
8 What is the credit policy of the above units? Is it liberal or conservative?

21

WORKING CAPITAL ANALYSIS OF IT SECTOR IN INDIA

The IT industry overview and the companies' profile have already been discussed in Part III.

Scope

Following IT companies are analysed in the present chapter:

1. Infosys Ltd
2. TCS Ltd

Analysis and discussion

Liquidity trend of the units has been analysed with the help of liquidity ratios. *Receivables management* is evaluated with regard to the collection efficiency. 'Ageing schedule of debtors' has also been examined to find out their recovery status. *Cash management* has been evaluated for each component regarding their adequacy.

1. Infosys

(a) Liquidity

The liquidity ratios trend in Figure 21.1 shows that all the ratios are above 2 indicating the high liquidity position in the Infosys operations and therefore less cash tied up in its operations. The company continues to be debt-free and maintains sufficient cash to meet its strategic objectives. During fiscal 2010–11, internal cash flows have more than adequately covered working capital requirements, capital expenditure, investment in subsidiaries and dividend payments. At 31 March

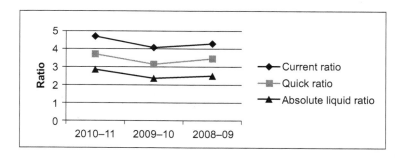

Figure 21.1 Liquidity trend of Infosys
Source: Infosys Annual Reports.

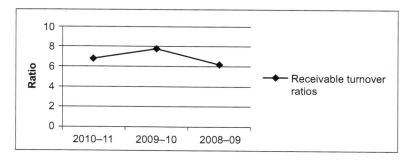

Figure 21.2 Receivables trend of Infosys
Source: Infosys Annual Reports.

2011 the company was sitting on huge cash balance of Rs 15,095 crore. These funds are deposited in banks, financial institutions and liquid mutual funds. The growth of the company is financed mainly through the cash generated from the operations. The company rarely needed to look for the outside debt.

(b) Receivables management

The receivable turnover trend in Figure 21.2 shows that the DSO (days sales outstanding) for the company has always been in the range from forty-seven to fifty-nine days which suggests that credit policy of the company has been very good at helping it to maintain its liquidity.

Provisions are made for all debtors outstanding for more than 180 days depending on the management perceptions of the risk. The need for provisions is based on various factors including collectability of specific dues, risk perceptions of the industry in which client operates and general economic factors affecting client's ability to settle. Provisions for bad and doubtful debts as a percentage of revenue are 0.01% of revenue (Table 21.1).

2. TCS

(a) Liquidity

The liquidity ratios over the period from 2009 to 2011 value ranged from 0.5 to 3 as evident from Figure 21.3. It shows that the most liquid assets of the company, that is, cash and bank balances are not

Table 21.1 Debtors' analysis of Infosys

Days	2011 (%)	2010 (%)
0–30	58.3	61.7
31–60	33	31.9
61–90	4.3	3.8
Above 91	4.4	3.6
Total (%)	100	100

Source: Infosys Annual Reports.

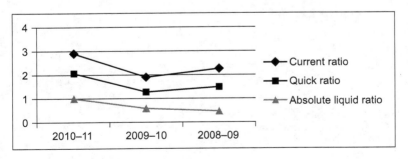

Figure 21.3 Liquidity trend of TCS
Source: TCS Annual Reports.

enough to meet the current liabilities when compared to the ratios of the Infosys. Therefore, the liquidity position of the company is not as strong as that of Infosys.

(b) Receivables management

The receivable turnover ratio of the company has been approximately around 4.8 to 5.4 which is less as compared to the Infosys as seen above. It shows that TCS has more liberal credit policy compared to Infosys and its DSO ranged from sixty-seven days to as high as seventy-five days. The DSO for Infosys was less than sixty days over the same period. Therefore, TCS seems to have gone for profitability more over liquidity as compared to Infosys.

SUNDRY DEBTORS

Sundry debtors of the company were at 21.97% of revenues on 31 March 2011, as compared to 19.50% on 31 March 2010. It shows the liberal credit policy followed by TCS as compared to Infosys which had 15–16% sundry debtors as percentage of revenues.

(c) Cash management

The amount held in fixed deposits with banks in India increased from Rs 3,531 crore on 31 March 2010 to Rs 6,061.17 crore on 31 March 2011, which is the company's cash management strategies (Table 21.2).

The company's growth has largely been financed by cash generated from operations. The company has sufficient cash generated

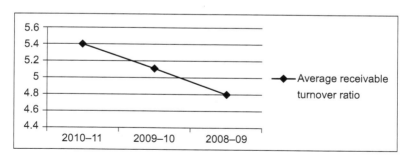

Figure 21.4 Receivables trend of TCS

Source: TCS Annual Reports.

Table 21.2 Cash management of TCS (Rs crore)

	As of 31 March 2011	As of 31 March 2010
Fixed deposit with banks in India	6,061.70	3,531.31
Deposits with banks overseas	527.22	538.61
Current bank accounts – India	108.73	116.34
Current bank accounts – overseas	616.27	417.69
Cheques in hand, remittances in transit and cash	64.17	114.64
Total	7,378.09	4,718.59

Source: TCS Annual Reports.

from operations for meeting its working capital requirements as well as capital expenditure requirements. As of 31 March 2011, the company had available lines of credit with multiple bankers aggregating Rs 2104 crore interchangeable between fund-based and non-fund-based limits.

Conclusion

The IT industry's working capital scenario on the basis of above discussion is presented as follows:

- DSO range from fifty to seventy-five days;
- sundry debtors from 16 to 22% of the revenue;
- no inventory management as it is a service-based industry;
- high liquidity as liquidity ratios are above 1;
- less cash tied in operations compared to manufacturing industries;
- bad and doubtful debts form 0.01% of revenue; and
- cash management mainly from investments in liquid mutual funds.

Infosys has been found to have higher amount of liquidity as compared to TCS. Though it is good, in a way, it also leads to blockage of funds, so can be checked upon by Infosys.

Discussion questions

1 Analyse the liquidity position of Infosys and TCS with the help of liquidity ratios.
2 Discuss their receivables' management with the help of relevant ratios.
3 Evaluate their sundry debtors' profile for collection efficiency with the help of 'ageing' schedule.
4 Comment upon the cash management of the above units.
5 'The IT sector is regarded as the cash cow for working capital management'. Explain.

22

POSITIVE AND NEGATIVE WORKING CAPITAL IMPACT IN CORPORATE SECTOR IN INDIA

Focus

The analysis has been done on following parameters:

• Working capital approach

Working capital has both the shades – positive and negative. In this chapter, working capital analysis of comparative companies in various sectors is done to have an insight into the trend of positive and negative working capitals and their 'impact on profitability'.

1. Telecom sector

Idea Cellular and Reliance Communication

On seeing the number of days in working capital we see that Idea is able to recover the money from its debtors in 12 days with working capital of 55.36 days and Reliance in 59 days with working capital of 59 days, which shows that Idea is using the money of suppliers for 55.36 days whereas Reliance is arranging funds from other sources for 81 days which is increasing the finance cost for Reliance Communications by 3% which is clear from the comparison of difference between PBDIT and PBDT of both the companies which clearly shows a difference of 3% in finance cost of both the companies. If Reliance is able to rotate its debtor more efficiently, it can lower its finance cost and would increase its profitability (Table 22.1 and Figure 22.1).

Table 22.1 Telecom: working capital position

Details of Idea Cellular (negative working capital)

	March 2012	March 2011	March 2010	March 2009	March 2008
Net current assets	–2,963.97	–2,410.30	–161.11	1,400.27	–1,117.66
PBDIT%	25	24	31	36	40
PBDT%	17	18	22	23	29
Difference B/T PBDT and PBDIT (%)	8	6	8	12	10
Current ratio	0.53	0.49	0.96	0.98	0.43
Quick ratio	0.55	0.52	0.86	1.31	0.55
Inventory turnover ratio	364.1	293.64	253.76	230.69	243.35
DTR	30.38	34.4	31.2	37.32	38.28
Average raw material holding	–	–	–	–	–
Average finished goods held	–	–	–	–	0
Number of days in debtors	12	11	12	10	10
Number of days in working capital	–55.36	–56.59	–4.89	51.14	–59.88

Details of Reliance Communications (positive working capital)

	March 2012	March 2011	March 2010	March 2009	March 2008
Net current assets	2,731.00	8,746.53	10,782.57	16,177.55	7,277.13
PBDIT%	35	21	34	62	45
PBDT%	24	14	25	55	39
Difference B/T PBDT and PBDIT (%)	11	7	9	7	6
Current ratio	0.77	0.96	1.37	1.45	0.95
Quick ratio	1.19	1.81	2.14	2.7	1.63
Inventory turnover ratio	36.88	–	–	–	–
DTR	6.22	7.18	8.42	11.72	15.61
Average raw material holding	–	–	–	–	–
Average finished goods held	–	–	–	–	–
Number of days in debtors	59	51	43	31	23
Number of days in working capital	81.02	236.59	286.38	386.03	177.11

Source: Annual Reports of Companies.

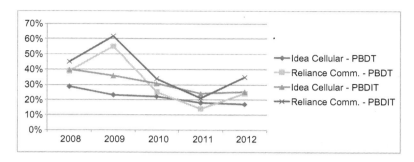

Figure 22.1 Telecom: PBDT and PBDIT analysis

Note: Idea is with negative WC and Reliance Communications is with positive WC.

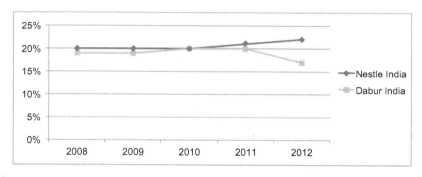

Figure 22.2 FMCG: PBDT analysis

Note: Nestle is with negative WC and Dabur is with positive WC.

2. FMCG

Nestle and Dabur

Despite negative WC, profitability is higher in Nestle.

In this case Nestle with negative working capital is more profitable than Dabur with positive working capital. But on comparing the current ratio of both the companies we find that current ratio of Nestle is less than 1 which means that it is more risky for the creditors as compare to Dabur whose CR is approximately near 1 (Table 22.2 and Figure 22.2).

Table 22.2 FMCG: working capital position

Details of Nestle India (negative working capital)

	December 2012	December 2011	December 2010	December 2009	December 2008
Net current assets	−1065	−884	−657	−598	−423
Net sales	8327	7491	6260	5142	4329
PBDT%	22	21	20	20	20
Current ratio	0.54	0.42	0.62	0.6	0.66
Quick ratio	0.22	0.24	0.27	0.24	0.29
Inventory turnover ratio	11.55	11.6	12.33	11.61	11.39
DTR	82.04	83.83	98.22	93.68	87.37
Average raw material holding	–	29.98	21.98	30.95	25.19
Average finished goods held	–	22.14	22.77	22.17	26.46
Number of days in working capital	−46.03	−42.48	−37.78	−41.86	−35.17

(Continued)

Table 22.2 (Continued)

Details of Dabur India (positive working capital)

	March 2012	March 2011	March 2010	March 2009	March 2008
Net current assets	360	243	30	276	-34
Net sales	3759	3274	2867	2408	2094
PBDT%	17	20	20	19	19
Current ratio	1.15	0.99	0.93	1.19	0.91
Quick ratio	0.85	0.78	0.68	0.99	0.58
Inventory turnover ratio	7.19	8.65	11.31	10.94	12.52
DTR	17.62	19.67	23.62	22.63	25.94
Average raw material holding	86.17	63.26	52.96	45.18	45.68
Average finished goods held	28.16	29.32	22.08	21.28	20.13
Number of days in working capital	34.43	26.7	3.76	41.32	-5.8

Source: Annual Reports of Companies.

3. Automobile

Bajaj Auto and Hero MotoCorp

Negative working capital is decreasing profits (highly negative in Hero MotoCorp).

In this case we first consider the percentage of WC to sales turnover and as it is clear from the figures that Hero MotoCorp is highly negative as compared to Bajaj in the initial and later years. Initially Hero was more profitable but in year 2009 and 2010 we see that the difference in profits of both the companies is 4% and 2%, respectively (in 2009, difference in WC is also 1%) In 2011, Hero has the highest negative working capital with a difference of 17% in WC and 13% in profits and this difference again decreases in 2012 with an increase in working capital. This clearly states that though Hero (fifty-five days) is able to hold its creditor for a longer period then Bajaj (thirty-four days), the cost of sales of Hero is more than Bajaj and thus effecting its profitability (Table 22.3 and Figure 22.3).

4. Cement

ACC and Ambuja

In 2009, both the companies had negative working capital and ACC performed better comparatively. ACC is able to manage the creditors efficiently (Table 22.4 and Figure 22.4).

5. Airlines

Kingfisher and Jet Airways

Conclusion

- Negative working capital can result in profitability.
- Managers have to play smart.
- By managing the operating cycle efficiently, one can improve the profit percentage without infusing own capital and using the suppliers' money.

Table 22.3 Automobile: working capital position

Balance sheet of Bajaj Auto

	March 2012	March 2011	March 2010	March 2009	March 2008
Net current assets	-599.02	-1,191.88	-1,355.03	-200.9	-238.56
Sales turnover	20,475.74	17,386.51	12,420.95	9,310.24	9,856.66
WC/sales (%)	-3	-7	-11	-2	-2
PBDT%	21	27	21	12	14
Current ratio	0.88	0.8	0.69	0.84	0.88
Quick ratio	0.72	0.71	0.55	0.73	0.64
Inventory turnover ratio	30.97	32.8	28.87	28.64	29.33
DTR	49.66	51.77	37.41	27.45	21.93
Average raw material holding	6	6	8	6	5
Average finished goods held	9	9	9	10	11
Average debtors held	7	7	10	13	17
Average creditors held	34	48	68	38	42
Number of days in working capital	-11	-26	-41	-8	-10

Balance sheet of Hero MotoCorp

	March '12	March 2011	March 2010	March 2009	March 2008
Net current assets	-2,659.04	-4,886.95	-2,101.58	-1,183.76	-1,013.33
Sales turnover	25,252.98	20,787.27	16,856.43	13,553.23	12,048.30
	-11%	-24%	-12%	-9%	-8%
	17%	14%	19%	16%	15%
Current ratio	0.42	0.24	0.58	0.46	0.48
Quick ratio	0.28	0.15	0.49	0.31	0.32
Inventory turnover ratio	40.84	43.88	42.8	47.53	42.82
DTR	117.09	162.08	122.63	55.1	32.7
Average raw material holding	9	10	11	8	11
Average finished goods held	3	2	1	2	2
Average debtors held	3	2	3	7	11
Average creditors held	55	104	63	52	59
Number of days in working capital	-41	-91	-48	-35	-35

Source: Annual Reports of Companies.

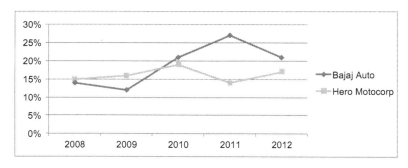

Figure 22.3 Automobile: PBT analysis

Note: Both the companies are having negative WC.

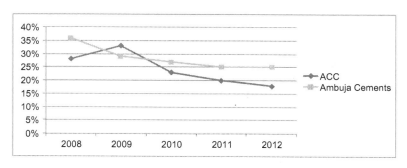

Figure 22.4 Cement: PBT analysis

Note: ACC is with negative WC and Ambuja is with positive WC.

But the following drawbacks of negative working capital should be kept in mind:

Drawbacks of negative WC

- Current ratio for companies with negative working capital is always less than 1.
- Any disturbance in the operating cycle may have a negative impact on the firm's profitability and may lead to bankruptcy.
- High dependency on suppliers.

Table 22.4 Cement: working capital position

Details of ACC

	December 2012	December 2011	December 2010	December 2009	December 2008
Net current assets	-1,261	-565	-1,355	-1,207	-342
Net sales	11,358	9,348	7,648	8,022	7,230
PBDIT%	19	22	24	34	28
PBDT%	18	20	23	33	28
Current ratio	0.72	0.87	0.68	0.67	0.89
Quick ratio	0.46	0.58	0.43	0.42	0.61
Inventory turnover ratio	11.15	18.59	19.04	25.22	27.51
DTR	40.29	42.62	40.04	31.22	24.12
Average raw material holding	0	39.41	44.39	37.17	33.05
Average finished goods held	0	7.09	8.05	7.01	6.45
Number of days in debtor	9	9	9	12	15
Number of days in creditor	49	77	125	110	72
Number of days in working capital	-39.96	-21.75	-63.76	-54.17	-17.02

(Continued)

Table 22.4 (Continued)

Details of ACL

	December 2012	December 2011	December 2010	December 2009	December 2008
Net current assets	801	490	210	–248	485
Net sales	9,730	8,473	7,372	7,083	6,182
PBDIT%	26	26	28	30	36
PBDT%	25	25	27	29	36
Current ratio	1.22	1.14	1.07	0.89	1.26
Quick ratio	0.95	0.85	0.75	0.57	0.74
Inventory turnover ratio	11.17	10.38	9.19	11.36	7.54
DTR	42.84	45.92	52.58	37.6	33.39
Average raw material holding	0	15.54	19.91	14.69	36.96
Average finished goods held	0	5.97	6.05	4.58	8.01
Number of days in debtor	9	8	7	10	11
Number of days in creditor	–21	9	23	42	28
Number of days in working capital	29.65	20.84	10.27	–12.58	28.24

Source: Annual Reports of Companies.

Table 22.5 Airlines: working capital position

Balance sheet of Kingfisher Airlines

	March 2012	March 2011	March 2010	March 2009	March 2008
Net current assets	1,504.55	1,734.76	1,343.35	329.19	491.59
PBDT%	-57	-21	-45	-38	-44
Net PBT	-3446.09	-1520.78	-2417.92	-2155.21	-682.59
Current ratio	0.81	1.22	0.78	0.64	0.97
Quick ratio	0.55	0.62	0.58	0.52	0.88
Inventory turnover ratio	26.83	4,185.44	4,659.30	5,738.39	–
DTR	17.49	16.34	18.35	41.01	46.67
Number of days in working capital	98.6	100.19	95.42	22.49	91.14

Balance sheet of Jet Airways

	March 2012	March 2011	March 2010	March 2009	March 2008
Net current assets	-3,621.85	394.92	64.44	890.37	-216.11
PBDT%	1	7	5	-4	4
Net PBT	-1255.33	46.63	-467.55	-469.62	-412.59
Current ratio	0.39	0.64	0.34	0.37	0.61
Quick ratio	0.5	0.77	0.86	1.09	0.77
Inventory turnover ratio	3,051.04	2,778.81	4,349.40	7,370.16	2,143.82
DTR	13.64	14.39	13.53	11.31	9.19
Number of days in working capital	-85.64	11.12	2.22	27.7	-8.83

Source: Annual Reports of Companies.

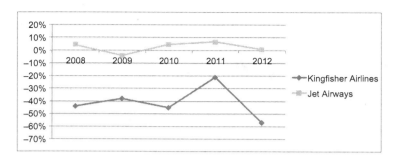

Figure 22.5 Airlines: PBT analysis

Note: Jet Airways is with negative WC and Kingfisher is with positive WC.

Discussion questions

1 What are the constituents of working capital of the above business units?

2 Analyse the working capital approach on comparative basis in the following sectors, using relevant ratios:

   (a) Telecom sector.
   (b) FMCG sector.
   (c) Automobile sector.
   (d) Cement sector.
   (e) Airlines sector.

3 What type of working capital policy is desirable – positive or negative? Discuss in the above context.

4 Discuss the various factors affecting working capital requirement with regard to the present case.

Part V

DIVIDEND DECISION

23

DIVIDEND POLICY
An overview

Introduction

Shareholder value maximisation implies increase in the wealth of shareholders by the company in the form of high returns. Returns comprise both dividend yield and capital yield. Dividend yield arises when company regularly pays dividend to shareholders in relation to the surplus. Capital gain arises when company shows high business performance which is reflected in the stock market by increase in the market price. So, it is a planned strategy by the management to magnify the returns to shareholders by outperforming the accepted benchmarks. Dividend policy plays an important role in this. Here, the importance of an adequate dividend policy is stressed upon.

Dividend policy

It is the decision of the management with regard to the profits to be distributed as cash dividends and part to be reinvested for future growth. It also involves deciding about the payment in the form of stock dividends to the stockholders. The expectations of dividends by shareholders help them in determining the share value; therefore, dividend policy is a significant decision taken by the financial management of any company.

Dividend theory

There are various theories which explain the relationship between firm's dividend policy and stock value.

1. Dividend irrelevance theory

This theory states that a firm's dividend policy has no effect on either its value or its cost of capital. Investors do not value dividends with regard to the market price of a share.

a. Modigliani and Miller's hypothesis

According to Modigliani and Miller (MM), dividend policy of a firm is irrelevant as it does not affect the wealth of the shareholders. They argue that the value of the firm depends on the firm's earnings which result from its investment policy.

ASSUMPTION OF MM MODEL

1 The firm operates in perfect capital market.
2 Taxes do not exist.
3 The firm has a fixed investment policy.
4 Risk of uncertainty does not exist, that is, investors are able to forecast future prices and dividends with certainty.

2. Dividend relevance theory

It is opposite of the above theory. It proposes that the value of a firm is affected by its dividend policy. The optimal dividend policy is the one that maximises the firm's value. High-growth firms with larger cash flows tend to pay more dividends and vice versa.

(a) Walter's model

It states that that the choice of dividend policy affects the value of the enterprise. This model shows the importance of the relationship between the firm's IRR (r) and its cost of capital (k) in determining the dividend policy for maximising the wealth of shareholders.

ASSUMPTIONS OF WALTER'S MODEL

1 The firm finances all investments through retained earnings, that is, debt or new equity is not issued.
2 The firm's IRR (r), and its cost of capital (k) are constant.
3 All earnings are either distributed as dividend or reinvested immediately.
4 The firm has a very long or infinite life.

(b) Gordon's model

This is another popular model which relates the market value of the firm to dividend policy.

ASSUMPTIONS OF GORDON'S MODEL

1 The firm is an all-equity firm.
2 No external financing is available.
3 The IRR (r) of the firm is constant.
4 The appropriate discount rate (K) of the firm remains constant.
5 There are no corporate taxes.

Types of dividends

1 *Cash dividends.* They are dividends which are paid in cash in the form of final dividends or interim dividends.
2 *Bonus shares.* These are shares which are issued free of cost to the shareholders of a company, by capitalising a part of the company's reserves. Bonus issue is also called book entry because it increases the number of shares, on the one hand, and decreases profits, on the other hand. So, it does not affect the net worth in total. Post bonus issue, the share price normally falls in proportion to the bonus issue, thereby making no difference to the personal wealth of the shareholder.
3 *Stock splits.* A stock split is a division of the stock which increases the number of shares in a public company. The price is adjusted such that the before and after market capitalisation of the company remains the same and dilution does not occur. For example, a company with 100 shares of stock priced at Rs 10 per share. The market capitalisation is 100 × Rs 10 = Rs 1,000. The company goes for one to two stock split. There are 200 shares now and each shareholder holds twice as many shares. The price of each share is adjusted to Rs 5. The market capitalisation is 200 × Rs 5 = Rs 1,000, which the same as before the split.
4 *Share buybacks.* A buyback is a tool which is used by the promoters or the management of the company to retain/increase control in their hands. Generally companies buyback for probable take-overs or when they find their own shares to be undervalued or when they have surplus idle cash. Stock buybacks also increase the market valuation.

5 *Rights issue*. A rights issue is an issue of new shares to the existing shareholders in order to raise capital. As a matter of right, new shares are first offered to existing shareholders in proportion to their current shareholding.

Procedure for cash dividend payment

A company which intends to declare and pay dividend adopts the following procedures. Further, in case the company's shares are listed on the Stock Exchanges, additional requirements relating to listing agreements are to be followed.

1) Recommendation by the Board of Directors

Dividend can be declared only on the recommendation of the Board of Directors of the company. The shareholders do not have any power to declare any dividend. The Board of Directors, after considering and approval of the financial statements of the company, determines the rate of dividend to be declared and then recommends the same to the shareholders. For this purpose, a Board Meeting shall be convened to pass the resolution for (a) rate of dividend and the amount of dividend to be paid; (b) book closure date for dividend purposes; (c) date of annual general meeting and (d) bank with which the account shall be opened for the purpose of remittance of dividend.

2) Approval by the shareholders

The dividend recommended by the Board of Directors is declared by a resolution passed at the Annual General Meeting by the shareholders. The declaration of dividend should form part of an ordinary business item to be transacted in the notice of the Annual General Meeting. While approving the rate of dividend at the Annual General Meeting, the shareholders have power to declare a lower rate of dividend than what is recommended by the Board but they have no power to increase the amount or the rate of dividend so recommended by the Board of Directors. Dividend when declared becomes debt against the company.

3) Dividend – interim dividend

Pursuant to the Companies (Amendment) Act 2000, interim dividend is now recognised as a part of final dividend (clause 14A of Section 2).

Interim dividend can be declared by the Board of Directors and they have authority to do so. Further, the provisions contained in Sections 205, 205A, 205C, 206, 206A and 207[1] shall apply to interim dividend.

4) Dividend to be deposited in a separate bank account

The company should deposit the dividend amount (including interim dividend) within five days of its declaration in the separate bank account opened for this purpose. It means that the interim dividend will have to be deposited in a bank account within five days of the Board Meeting whereas final dividend will have to be deposited within five days from the date of Annual General Meeting in which it was approved by the shareholders. Also Section 205 (1B)[2] stipulates that the amount so deposited shall be used only for the purpose of payment of dividend (whether interim or final).

Dividend polices

Various companies adopt different kinds of dividend policies. These policies are determined on the growth stage of the company, how the company wants to use its reserves and surplus. A dividend policy on the basis of a sector is pretty rare and each of the dividend policies may exist across industry sectors. Following are the various dividend policies followed by companies.

Constant payout policy

A constant dividend payment ratio policy is a dividend policy whereby a corporation establishes a dividend payout ratio and applies this to earnings (the fraction of earnings paid out as dividends). This policy ensures that retentions as well as dividends fluctuate with earnings, but with given investment plans, outside finance will sometimes be required and reserves will be affected by dividend policy.

Long-run residual dividend policy

A long-run residual dividend policy is a policy designed to give shareholders some confidence in planning the dividends that might be declared. Such a policy is created by a corporation by first forecasting the relevant variables, such as earnings, investment needs, interest charges and taxation, for a given period, usually five years. Then the dividends from a pure residual dividend policy are determined, total dividends over all years are compared with total earnings over the same period and an average dividend payout ratio is determined. This is then applied to each year's earnings to fix the dividends.

Constant dividend per share policy

In this policy, companies payout a constant dividend per share (DPS) irrespective of their EPS, that is, a change in their PAT (whether increased or decreased) would not affect the dividend paid out to shareholders. This kind of policy is generally adopted by companies that do not have shareholders' interest as one of their primary objectives. This is evident from the constant DPS paid even after an increase in EPS. This kind of policy is generally resorted to companies that have a minimum growth potential and have no scope of any large expansion.

Hybrid dividend policy

A hybrid dividend policy encompasses a combination of the above policies as seen appropriate by the company. Using this approach, companies tend to view the debt to equity ratio as a long-term rather than a short-term goal. In today's markets, this approach is commonly used by companies that pay dividends. As these companies will generally experience business cycle fluctuations, they will generally have one set dividend, which is set as a relatively small portion of yearly income and can be easily maintained. On top of this set dividend, these companies will offer another extra dividend paid only when income exceeds general levels.

Determinants of dividend decision

An optimum dividend policy of an enterprise is determined after taking into consideration the following factors:

(i)   external factors; and
(ii) internal factors.

External factors

Following are the external factors which affect the dividend policy of the firm.

1. General state of economy

The general state of economy affects to a great extent the management's decision to retain or distribute earnings of the firm. In case of uncertain economic and business conditions, the management may like to retain the whole or a part of the firm's earnings for future uncertainties.

2. Capital market access

In case a firm has an easy access to the capital market, it can follow a liberal dividend policy. However, if the firm has no easy access to capital market, it is likely to adopt a more conservative dividend policy.

3. Legal restrictions

A firm may also be legally restricted from declaring and paying dividends. For example, in India the Companies Act 1956 has put several restrictions regarding payment and declaration of dividends.

4. Contractual restrictions

Lenders of the firm generally put restrictions on dividend payment to protect their interests. For example, it may be provided in a loan agreement that the firm shall not declare any dividend so long the liquidity ratio is less than 1:1 or else.

5. Tax policy

The tax policy followed by the government also affects the dividend policy. For example, the government may give tax incentives to companies which retain larger share of their earnings. In such a case, the management may be inclined to retain a larger amount of the firm's earnings.

Internal factors

The following are the internal factors which affect the dividend policy of a firm.

1. Desire of the shareholders

The desire of the shareholders cannot be overlooked by the Directors while deciding about the dividend policy. The shareholders expect two forms of return from their capital investment, namely, (i) capital gains and (ii) dividends.

In most cases, the shareholders' desire to get dividends take priority over the desire to earn capital gains because of the less uncertainty and sometimes due to the need for current income.

2. Financial needs of the company

The financial needs of the company may conflict with the desires of the shareholders. Managerial insight tends to give more weightage to the financial needs of the company. However, retained earnings should be used as a source of financing only when the company has profitable investment opportunities.

3. Nature of earnings

A firm having stable income can afford to pay higher amount of dividends as compared to a firm with not such stable earnings.

4. Desire of control

Dividend policy is also influenced by the desire of shareholders or the management to retain control over the company. The issue of additional equity shares for procuring funds dilutes control. So, this factor also needs to be considered before arriving at a dividend decision.

5. Liquidity position

It is also important for the management to take into account the cash position and overall liquidity position of the firm before and after payment of dividends while taking the dividend decision.

Discussion questions

1 Discuss the relevance of dividend policy in a corporate.
2 What are the different theories of dividend policy? Explain in detail.

3   Discuss the various form of dividend payment.
4   Explain the procedure for dividend payment to shareholders.
5   'Every company decides its own dividend policy'. Examine the statement in the light of different dividend policies.
6   What are the various factors which influence the dividend decision of the company?

Notes

1 Available at http://www.mca.gov.in/Ministry/pdf/Companies_Act_1956_13jun2011.pdf (accessed on 21 February 2013).
2 Ibid.

24

DIVIDEND POLICY OF FMCG SECTOR IN INDIA

The overview of Indian FMCG industry and the companies in the sector have been discussed in the earlier parts.

Scope

Following companies are analysed here:

1 HUL
2 Dabur
3 Marico

Analysis and discussion

The dividend policy depends on the profit position of the company. So, first we have studied the *revenue and profit trend* of the units for their dividend policy. Then, an attempt has been made to find out the type of *dividend policy* followed by the units during the period. Further, examination has been done to find out whether companies have gone for *bonus, stock split* or not during the period. Finally, the impact of dividend policy of the units has been tested on their market price.

Box 24.1 Bonus issue and stock split

'Bonus issue' implies issues of 'extra' shares to existing share-holders. A company distribute these additional shares as an alternative of the dividend payout. New shares are issued to shareholders in proportion to their holdings. For example, the bonus issue of 1:2 means company will give one bonus share for every two shares held.

'Stock split' refers to the division of an existing share into multiple shares with lower face value. This is done by the company to make the share more affordable for the investors. For example, a split of 1:2 means that the stockholder will have two shares for every share held earlier.

1. Revenue picture

(a) HUL

HUL revenue dropped in FY 2010 but has risen back again since then.

(b) Dabur

The company has maintained a strong and consistent growth over the past few years with growth accelerating in the past five years to CAGR of 18.5%. Dabur India has reported continued year on year growth in sales and profit for the past thirty-six quarters.

(c) Marico

Marico achieved a turnover of Rs 3,128 crore during FY 2011, a growth of 18% over FY 2010. The volume growth underlying this

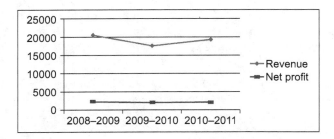

Figure 24.1 Revenue trend of HUL (Rs crore)
Source: HUL Annual Reports.

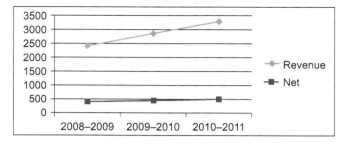

Figure 24.2 Revenue trend of Dabur (Rs crore)
Source: Dabur Annual Reports.

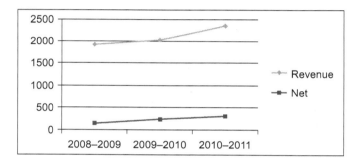

Figure 24.3 Revenue trend of Marico (Rs crore)
Source: Marico Annual Reports.

revenue growth was healthy at 12%. PAT for FY 2011 was Rs 286 crore, a growth of 24% over FY 2010. Marico achieved a turnover of Rs 2,661 crore during FY 2010, a growth of 11% over FY 2009. Over the past five years, the top line and bottom line have grown at a CAGR of 22% and 27%, respectively.

2. Dividend policy

(a) HUL

The company's dividend trends show constant dividend policy. For the year ending March 2011, HUL has declared an equity dividend of 650.00% amounting to Rs 6.5 per share. At the current share price of

Table 24.1 Dividend at a glance of HUL

Announcement date	Effective date	Dividend type	Dividend %	Remarks
17–10–11	04–11–11	Interim	350	–
09–05–11	08–07–11	Final	350	–
14–10–10	01–11–10	Interim	300	–
25–05–10	08–07–10	Final	350	–
15–10–09	06–11–09	Interim	300	–
11–05–09	12–06–09	Final	400	–
15–07–08	04–08–08	Interim	350	–
13–02–08	17–03–08	Final	300	–
23–10–07	07–11–07	Interim	300	Dividend (Platinum Jubilee)
23–07–07	07–08–07	Interim	300	–
20–02–07	20–04–07	Final	300	AGM
10–07–06	08–08–06	Interim	300	–
14–02–06	28–04–06	Final	250	AGM

Source: HUL Annual Reports.

Rs 393.85, this results in a dividend yield of 1.65%. The company has a good dividend track report and has consistently declared dividends for the past five years (Table 24.1).

DIVIDEND PAYOUT RATIO

* FY 2008–9 : 76.47
* FY 2009–10 : 75.20
* FY 2010–11 : 71.20

(b) Dabur

The company has good dividend record and has consistently declared dividends for the past five years (Table 24.2).

The dividend policy at Dabur is that dividend shall be declared or paid only out of

i) current year's profit;
ii) the profits for any previous FY(s);
iii) Out of i) and ii) or both.

245

Table 24.2 Dividend at a glance of Dabur

Announcement date	Effective date	Dividend type	Dividend (%)	Remarks
14–10–11	04–11–11	Interim	55.00	–
27–04–11	29–06–11	Final	65.00	–
13–10–10	02–11–10	Interim	50.00	–
18–06–10	03–08–10	Final	125.00	–
14–10–09	30–10–09	Interim	75.00	–
29–04–09	29–06–09	Final	100.00	–
13–01–09	02–02–09	Interim	75.00	–
30–04–08	19–06–08	Final	75.00	AGM
10–10–07	29–10–07	Interim	75.00	–
05–03–07	16–03–07	Interim	75.00	–
09–10–06	03–11–06	Interim	100.00	–
25–04–06	21–06–06	Final	100.00	AGM

Source: Dabur Annual Reports.

Board shall endeavour to maintain the dividend payout ratio as near as 50% subject to

a company's need for capital for its growth plan; and
b positive cash flow.

DIVIDEND PAYOUT RATIO

- FY 2008–9 : 47.41
- FY 2009–10 : 46.89
- FY 2010–11 : 49.43

(c) Marico

The company has also followed a prudent dividend policy and has been declaring cash dividend on a regular basis thereby providing a regular return on investment to shareholders (cash dividend).

FOR FY 2010–11

First interim dividend paid was of 30% on the equity base of Rs 61.41 crore. Second interim dividend paid was of 36% on the equity base of

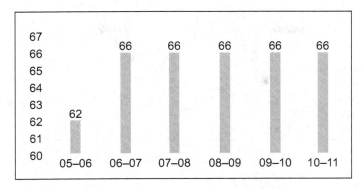

Figure 24.4 Dividend trend of Marico (%)
Source: Marico Annual Reports.

Rs 61.45 crore. The total equity dividend for FY 2011 at 66.0% is thus at par with the dividend paid during FY 2010. The total dividend (including dividend tax) was Rs 47.2 crore (about 16.5 % of the group PAT). This corresponds to a dividend payout ratio of 16.5% (inclusive of dividend distribution tax).

Dividend Payment Date:

16 November 2010 (first interim equity dividend 2010–11)
23 May 2011 (second interim equity dividend 2010–11)

DIVIDEND PAYOUT RATIO

- For FY 2011, the dividend payout ratio was 16.5%.
- For FY 2010, the dividend payout ratio was 20%.
- Although the dividend paid was same at 66%, the payout ratio has decreased due to increasing profit base.

3. Bonus issue

(a) HUL

The last bonus that HUL had announced was in 1991 in the ratio of 1:2. The share has been quoting ex-bonus from 19 July 1991. No bonus shares have been issued in the past three years (Table 24.3).

Table 24.3 Bonus issue of HUL

Announcement date	Bonus ratio	Record date	Ex-bonus date
30–09–91	1:2	21–08–91	19–07–91
22–06–87	1:1	–	–
22–06–83	3:5	–	–
22–06–79	1:3	–	–

Source: HUL Annual Reports.

Table 24.4 Bonus issue of Dabur

Announcement date	Bonus ratio	Record date	Ex-bonus date
26–07–10	1:1	10–09–10	08–09–10
31–10–06	1:2	29–01–07	25–01–07
24–10–05	1:1	20–01–06	19–01–06
30–09–93	4:1	01–12–93	16–11–93

Source: Dabur Annual Reports.

(b) Dabur

EFFECT OF BONUS ON CAPITAL STRUCTURE OF DABUR

1   Capitalisation of a sum of Rs 87,01,29,834 out of general reserves of the company for allotment of bonus shares.
2   Increasing of authorised share capital of the company from Rs 145 crore divided into 145 crore equity shares of Re 1 each to Rs 2 crore divided into 2 crore equity shares of Re 1 each.
3   Alteration in the Article 4 of the Articles of Association of the Company regarding the increase in authorised share capital from Rs 145 crore to Rs 2 crore (Table 24.4).

4 Stock split

(a) HUL

HUL had last split the face value of its shares from Rs 10 to Rs 1 in 2000. The share has been quoting on an ex-split basis from 3 July 2000 (Table 24.5).

Table 24.5 Stock split of HUL

Announcement date	Old face value	New face value	Ex-split date
05–07–00	10	1	03–07–00

Source: HUL Annual Reports.

Table 24.6 Stock split of Dabur

Announcement date	Old face value	New face value	Ex-split date
03–11–00	10	1	27–11–00

Source: Dabur Annual Reports.

Table 24.7 Dividend and market performance of HUL

Date of declaration	Effect on stock price
04–04–08	−0.65 (0.27%)
25–07–08	+12.5 (5.69%)
03–07–09	+7.85 (2.96%)
31–10–09	+2.45 (0.87%)
27–07–10	−4.55 (1.71%)
25–10–10	+3.45 (1.16%)

Source: HUL Annual Reports.

(b) Dabur

Dabur India had last split the face value of its shares from Rs 10 to Rs 1 in 2000. The share has been quoting on an ex-split basis from 27 November 2000 (Table 24.6).

(c) Marico

As already indicated Marico has been following conservative dividend policy. So for the past three years it has not issued any bonus shares nor has it done any stocks splits or reverse stock splits.

5 Dividend and its impact on share price

(a) HUL

Most of the times, stock of the company reacted positively to the dividend announcement (Table 24.7).

(b) Dabur

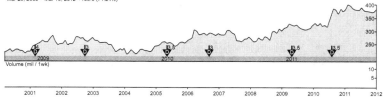

393.25 0.00 (0.00%)

Mar 19 - Close
BOM real-time data - Disclaimer
Currency in INR

Range	388.20 - 399.00	Div/yield	3.50/1.78
52 week	264.50 - 420.00	EPS	7.49
Open	389.00	Shares	2.16B
Vol.	0.00	Beta	-
Mkt cap	849.83B	Inst. own	-
P/E	52.51		

BSE Sensex 17,273.37 0.00%
500696   393.25 0.00%

1day 5day 1month 3month 6month YTD 1year 5year 10year All
Mar 20, 2009 - Mar 19, 2012 +163.6 (71.24%)

Figure 24.5 Market trend of HUL
Source: BSE (www.bseindia.com).

Table 24.8 Dividend and market performance of Dabur

Date of declaration	Effect on stock price
14–10–11	0.15 (0.15%)
27–4–11	0.80 (0.76%)
13–10–10	–2.4 (–2.2%)
03–08–10	–7 (–6.62%)
14–10–09	–3.18(–3.14%)
29–4–09	3.27(5.71%)
13–1–09	1.9(4.49%)
30–04–08	–1.22(–2.23%)

Source: Dabur Annual Reports.

1day 5day 1month 3month 6month YTD 1year 5year 10year All
Apr 04, 2008 - Mar 25, 2011 +41.98 (78%)

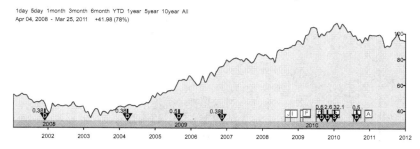

Figure 24.6 Market trend of Dabur
Source: BSE (www.bseindia.com).

(c) Marico

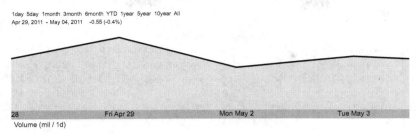

Figure 24.7 Dividend and market performance FY 2011 of Marico
Source: BSE (www.bseindia.com).

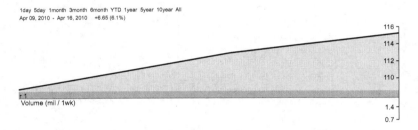

Figure 24.8 Dividend and market performance FY 2010 of Marico
Source: BSE (www.bseindia.com).

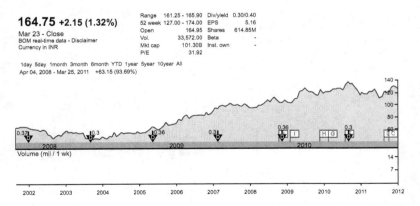

Figure 24.9 Market trend of Marico
Source: BSE (www.bseindia.com).

Conclusion

After doing the analysis, we have come to a conclusion that most of the companies in the FMCG sector in India have paid handsome returns to the shareholders. Companies have chosen the cash dividends and bonus shares as the most common way of rewarding the shareholders. Despite being in this high-growth sector, companies like Marico have followed a very conservative dividend distribution policy. On the other hand, there are companies like Dabur which have consistently declared dividends for the shareholders. Since, the sector is in growth phase, a responsible and generous dividend distribution policies by the FMCG companies can lead to more investment in this sector.

Discussion questions

1 Analyse the revenue trend of HUL, Dabur and Marico.
2 Comment on the dividend policy of the above units. Examine the dividend–payout ratio in this context.
3 What are the types of dividend theories? Which dividend theory can be related to the present case?
4 Discuss the various dividend incentives announced by the above companies for shareholders' interest and their effect on the capital structure:

   (a) bonus issue
   (b) stock split

5 'Bonus issue is book adjustment'. Explain.
6 Discuss the procedure followed by corporate for cash dividend payment.
7 'Dividend policy varies with the sector'. What type of dividend policy is followed by the above business units?
8 Evaluate the impact of dividend policy of these companies on the market performance.

25

DIVIDEND POLICY OF CHEMICAL SECTOR IN INDIA

Indian chemical industry

Chemical industry is one of the oldest industries in India with an estimated size of around US$30 billion. India is the third-largest producer of chemical in Asia and the twelfth-largest producer in the world. The industry, comprising both small scale and large units (including MNCs) produces several thousands of products and by-products, ranging from plastics and petro-chemicals to cosmetics and toiletries. It contributes about 13% share in the manufacturing sector and around 5% in total exports of the country.

Scope

The following companies are analysed here:

1. *Pidilite Industries Ltd*

Pidilite Industries Ltd is the largest adhesive manufacturer in India. Its most famous product is the Fevicol range of adhesives. Its other famous brands are Dr. Fixit, Ranipal, M-seal and Acron.

2. *Tata Chemicals Ltd*

Tata Chemicals Ltd is a global company with presence in segments such as, chemicals, crop nutrition and consumer products. The company is one of the largest chemical companies in India and a part of Tata Group.

3. Gujarat Fluorochemicals Ltd

Gujarat Fluorochemicals Ltd (GFL) is a part of the $2 billion INOX Group of Companies. INOX has diverse businesses including industrial gases, refrigerants, chemicals, carbon credits, cryogenic engineering and renewable energy.

Analysis and discussion

The *dividend trend* of the units has been examined for all the dividend payments by them during the period, interim and/or final. Dividend policy is seen as a market influencer. So, the *impact of dividend policy* of the units has been tested on their market price. An examination has also been done to find out whether companies have gone for *bonus*, *stock split* or not during the period.

1. Dividend policy

(a) Pidilite Industries

The directors recommend a dividend of Rs 1.75 per equity share of one each out of the current year's profit, on 506.1 million equity shares of one each (previous year at Rs 1.50 per equity share including 0.50 per equity share as 'Golden Jubilee Special Dividend'), amounting to Rs 886 million (previous year Rs 759.2 million). The dividend payout amount has grown at a CAGR of 23.68% during the past five years.

The year 2009–10 is the Golden Jubilee year of the company and recognising its significance, the company has issued *bonus equity shares* in the ratio of 1:1 in March 2010. The Board has also recommended a Golden Jubilee *Special Dividend* of Re 0.50 per equity share on the enhanced share capital after bonus Issue. The company has reached its present position with the support of its valued customers and all stakeholders. The company places on record its deep appreciation for their support.

The company has repurchased bonds of face value of US$2.8 million which were cancelled and extinguished. The FCCB holders are entitled to a right to convert their holdings into equity shares of the company on or after 16 January 2008. Those FCCB holders who exercised this right till the record date, that is, 17 March 2010 were eligible to receive the bonus shares on par with the other shareholders. Furthermore, those FCCB holders who opt for conversion after the record date are, under the terms on which the FCCBs were offered, entitled to a proportionately higher number of equity shares as if the conversion had taken place prior to the record date.

The dividend declared by the company during the past seven FYs are as follows.

Figure 25.1a clearly depicts the fact that company has been giving dividends for the past many years. Also we can see from Figure 25.1b

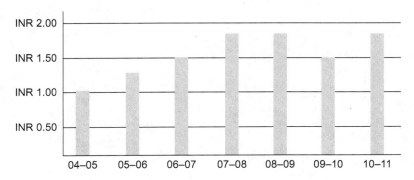

Figure 25.1a Dividend trend of Pidilite
Source: Pidilite Annual Reports.

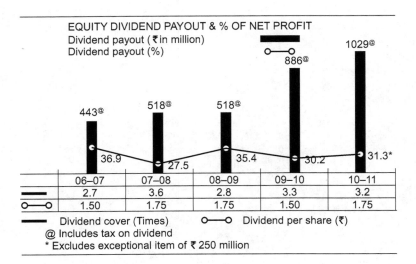

EQUITY DIVIDEND PAYOUT & % OF NET PROFIT
Dividend payout (₹ in million)
Dividend payout (%)

	06–07	07–08	08–09	09–10	10–11
▬	2.7	3.6	2.8	3.3	3.2
⚬—⚬	1.50	1.75	1.75	1.50	1.75

▬ Dividend cover (Times)   ⚬—⚬ Dividend per share (₹)
@ Includes tax on dividend
* Excludes exceptional item of ₹ 250 million

Figure 25.1b Dividend view-up of Pidilite
Source: Pidilite Annual Reports.

that the dividend payout ratio has also been more or less the same in the past five years although the dividend payment has increased. Figure 25.1b shows the dividend payout for the company in the past five years.

The increasing dividend payments and almost constant dividend payout ratio indicates the growth of the company and its increasing profits (Table 25.1).

Table 25.1 Dividend history of Pidilite

Announcement date	Effective date	Dividend type	Dividend (%)	Remarks
19–05–11	08–07–11	Final	175	Rs 1.75 per share (175%) dividend
20–05–10	26–07–10	Final	150	Rs 0.50 per share (50%) special dividend and Rs 1.00 per share (100%) dividend
21–05–09	17–07–09	Final	175	
30–05–08	11–08–08	Final	175	AGM
23–05–07	14–08–07	Final	150	AGM
23–05–06	21–07–06	Final	125	AGM
18–05–05	22–07–05	Final	100	AGM
24–05–04	16–07–04	Final	80	AGM
28–05–03	18–07–03	Final	75	AGM
26–06–02	20–08–02	Final	70	AGM
26–05–01		Final	45	AGM
19–05–00		Final	10	
28–02–00		Interim	70	70% interim dividend (10% first interim and 30% second interim dividend)
20–05–99		Final	70	AGM and dividend
17–07–98		Final	50	
11–07–97		Final	40	

Bonus shares:

Announcement Date	Bonus ratio	Record date	Ex-bonus date
28–01–10	1:1	17–03–10	15–03–10
27–01–00	1:1	N/A	05–06–00
01–10–96	1:1	05–11–96	07–10–96

Stock split:

Announcement date	Old face value	New face value	Record date	Ex-split date
02–07–05	10	1	27–09–05	20–09–05

Source: Pidilite Annual Reports.

(b) TATA Chemicals

The company followed a policy of constant DPS or dividend rate. For the past ten years, the company has consistently given dividend at a rate of not less than 50%. For the year 2010–11, the company paid a rich dividend of 100% to its shareholders. This shows that the company has made profits invariably (Table 25.2).

From Figures 25.2a and 25.2b, we see that the dividend/share given by Tata Chemicals has increased over the years. Also, the 'dividend payout ratio' has shown a significant increase with time.

(c) Gujarat Fluorochemicals Ltd

2010–11

The company had paid an interim dividend of Re 1 per share and the directors now recommend a final dividend of Rs 2.50 per share (250%) subject to approval of the shareholders. The total dividend payout (including dividend distribution tax) for the year will be Rs 4,472.71 lakh (Tables 25.3a, b and 25.4).

Table 25.2 Dividend and effect on market performance of Tata Chemicals

Year	Turnover (Rs crore)	Net operating income (Rs crore)	PAT/ net income (%)	EPS- basic (₹)	DPS (₹)	Gross gearing (%)	Return on capital employed (%)	Return on net worth (%)	Fixed assets cover (no. of times)	Working capital turnover (%)	Market capitalisation as of March 31 (Rs crore)
2000–01	1,470.00	1,405.25	12	9.13	5.00	37	11	9	0.51	52	687.33
2001–02	1,387.10	1,357.68	9	7.02	5.00	34	10	7	0.48	50	839.97
2002–03	1,612.42	1,535.27	13	10.88	5.50	28	12	12	0.54	41	1,190.41
2003–04	2,632.79	2,544.15	9	10.25	5.50	24	12	12	0.84	34	2,293.62
2004–05	3,097.91	3,008.14	11	15.83	6.50	36	14	17	0.98	39	3,260.96
2005–06	3,638.23	3,518.59	10	16.41	7.00	37	14	17	1.12	48	5,675.48
2006–07	4,107.08	3,985.03	11	20.65	8.00	28	17	19	1.24	22	4,451.55
2007–08	4,207.13	4,075.62	23	42.82	9.00	38	24	32	1.24	23	6,570.55
2008–09	8,537.21	8,399.65	5	19.25	9.00	48	12	12	2.33	13	3,328.82
2009–10	5,512.54	5,476.64	8	18.38	9.00	40	11	11	2.48	12	7,982.45
2010–11	6,352.14	6,332.43	6	16.32	10.00	36	10	9	1.60	21	8,715.62

Source: Tata Chemicals Annual Reports.

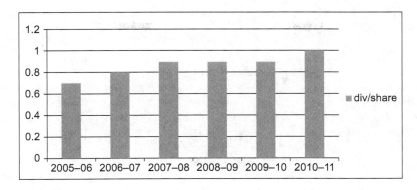

Figure 25.2a Dividend trend of Tata Chemicals
Source: Tata Chemicals Annual Reports.

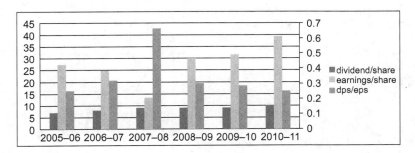

Figure 25.2b Dividend view-up of Tata Chemicals
Source: Tata Chemicals Annual Reports.

Table 25.3a Dividend history of GFL

FY	Interim I (%)	Interim II (%)	Final (%)	Total (%)
2009–10	100	100	150	350
2008–9	0	0	350	350
2007–8	150	100	100	350
2006–7	100	100	50	250
2005–6	0	–	100	100
2004–5	0	–	50	50

Source: GFL Annual Reports.

Table 25.3b Dividend detailed view of GFL

Announcement date	Effective date	Dividend type	Dividend (%)	Remarks
07–12–11	16–12–11	Interim	200.00	First interim dividend
30–05–11	07–07–11	Final	250.00	Rs 2.50 per share (250%) final dividend
31–01–11	10–02–11	Interim	100.00	–
24–05–10	06–07–10	Final	150.00	–
25–01–10	05–02–10	Interim	100.00	–
30–10–09	13–11–09	Interim	100.00	–
22–05–09	18–06–09	Final	350.00	–
12–06–08	11–09–08	Final	100.00	AGM
24–03–08	10–04–08	Interim	100.00	Second Interim Dividend
19–12–07	03–01–08	Interim	150.00	–
19–06–07	20–09–07	Final	50.00	–
07–03–07	22–03–07	Interim	100.00	–
31–10–06	16–11–06	Final	100.00	–
17–06–06	14–09–06	Final	100.00	AGM

Source: GFL Annual Reports.

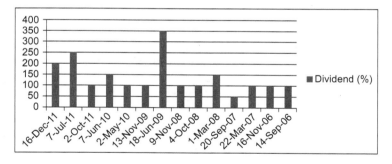

Figure 25.3 Dividend payout of GFL
Source: GFL Annual Reports.

Table 25.4 Splits history of GFL

Announcement date	Old face value	New face value	Record date	Ex-split date
30–07–05	10	2	18–10–05	10–10–05
19–12–07	2	1	08–02–08	01–02–08

Source: GFL Annual Reports.

BONUS HISTORY

The company has not issued bonus shares yet.

Conclusion

The previous discussion clearly indicates that all companies under study have been following more or less a constant dividend payout ratio. This is a good sign for shareholders.

Discussion questions

1 What type of dividend policy is followed by the business units in the chemical sector?
2 Analyse the dividend policy of Pidilite, Tata Chemicals and GFL. Examine the dividend–payout ratio in this context.
3 Discuss the bonus issues announced by the above companies for shareholders' interest and its effect on the capital structure.
4 'Stock split makes shares more affordable'. Discuss in the light of the above case.
5 Evaluate the impact of dividend policy of these companies on the market performance.
6 Which dividend theory can be related to the present case?

26

DIVIDEND POLICY OF POWER SECTOR IN INDIA

The overview of Indian power industry has already been discussed in Part II.

Companies for analysis

Following power companies are selected for the dividend analysis:

1 NTPC
2 NHPC
3 TATA Power
4 Power Grid
5 Torrent Power

Analysis

The *dividend trend* of the units has been analysed with the help of dividend payout ratio and its trend. *Earning potential* has been evaluated by analysing their EPS trend. This helps to find out the interrelationship among these two indicators for shareholders' interest (Table 26.1).

(a) NTPC Ltd

Type	State-owned enterprise Public company
Traded as	BSE: 532555
	NSE: NTPC; BSE SENSEX Constituent
Industry	Electric utility
Founded	1975

Table 26.1 Dividend picture of NTPC

Year	Dividend paid	PAT (Rs crore)	No. of shares	DPS (D/N)	EPS (PAT/N)	Payout ratio
2010	3,133.2	8,728.2	82,454.64	3.8	10.59	35.88
2011	3,133.26	9,102.59	82,454.64	3.8	11.04	34.42
2012	3,298.73	9,223.73	82,454.64	4	11.19	35.74

Source: Company's Annual Reports.

Headquarters	New Delhi, India
Key people	Arup Roy Choudhury
Products	Electrical power, natural gas
Services	Electricity generation and distribution, natural gas exploration, production, transportation and distribution
Revenue	Increase Rs 690.36 billion (US$12 billion) (2011–12)[2]
Net income	Increase Rs 98.14 billion (US$1.7 billion) (2011–12)[2]
Employees	26,000 (2012)

From the data it is evident that the number of shares is fixed, that is, constant. For the two years 2010 and 2011 the dividend paid is constant and thus DPS is same for these two years. For the year 2012, there is increase in dividend paid and thus there is an increase in the DPS. Increase in DPS means that the company is wooing their shareholders by giving more dividends to them in the year 2012. As PAT is increasing continuously from 2010 to 2012, the EPS is also increasing.

This is a very good sign for a company because the numbers of shares are constant and PAT is increasing. This means that the company is doing well in terms of making profit. Next comes the payout ratio, that is, an indication that what the company is doing with their earnings. It implies that how much share of PAT the company is giving as a dividend and how much of it the company has reserved as its surplus, that is, for its expansion mode. From Figure 26.1, it is evident that the payout ratio is almost constant for all the three years. Lower the payout ratio of a company is, more secure the dividend payment is.

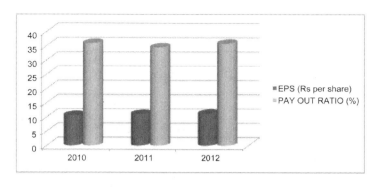

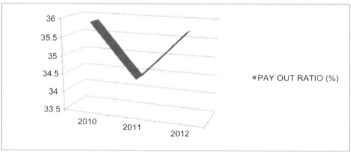

Figure 26.1 Dividend trend of NTPC

(b) NHPC

Type	Sate-owned enterprise public company (BSE: 533098, NSE: NHPC)
Industry	Electric utility
Founded	1975
Headquarters	Faridabad, India
Key people	G. Sai Prasad
Products	Electricity generation, energy trading
Revenue	$1.1 billion (2010)
Net income	$485 million (2010)

From the data it is evident that the number of shares is fixed, that is, constant. For all the three years 2010, 2011 and 2012 the dividend paid has increased continuously and thus DPS increased for these three years. Increase in DPS means that the company is wooing their shareholders by giving more dividends to them in all the three years.

Table 26.2 Dividend picture of NHPC

Year	Dividend paid	PAT (Rs crore)	No. of shares	DPS (D/N)	EPS (PAT/N)	Payout ratio
2010	676.54	2,090.5	123,007.43	0.55	1.7	32.35
2011	738.04	2,166.67	123,007.43	0.6	1.76	34.09
2012	861.06	2,771.77	123,007.43	0.7	2.25	31.11

Source: Company's Annual Reports.

As PAT slightly increases from 2010 to 2011, the EPS is almost constant for these two years (Table 26.2).

In the year 2012 there is much increase in PAT and thus EPS is very high because the number of shares is constant. This is a very good sign for a company because the number of shares is constant and PAT is increasing. This means that the company is doing well in terms of making profit. Next comes the payout ratio, that is, an indication that what the company is doing with their earnings. It implies that how much share of PAT the company is giving as a dividend and how much of it the company has reserved as its surplus, that is, for its expansion mode. From Figure 26.2 it is evident that the payout ratio has increased from year 2010 to 2011 which means that the dividend paying security is decreasing. In 2012, the payout ratio has increased.

(c) TATA Power

Type	Public company
Traded as	BSE: 500400
	BSE SENSEX Constituent
Industry	Electric utility
Founded	1911
Founder(s)	Dorabji Tata
Headquarters	Mumbai, Maharashtra, India
Key people	Cyrus Pallonji Mistry
Products	Electrical power, Natural gas
Services	Electricity generation and distribution Natural gas exploration, production, transportation and distribution
Revenue	Increase Rs 194.5076 billion (US$3.3 billion) (2011)[1]
Net income	Increase Rs 21.4753 billion (US$370 million) (2009–10)[1]
Employees	3,809 (2010)

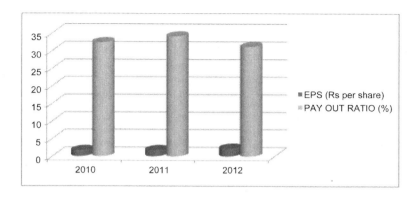

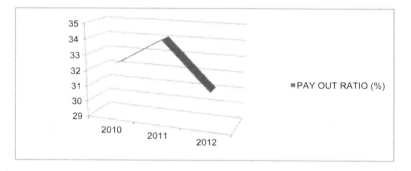

Figure 26.2 Dividend trend of NHPC

From the data it is evident that the number of shares is fixed, that is, constant. From year 2010 to 2011 the dividend paid has increased and thus DPS has increased for these two years. For year 2012 the dividend paid has not increased and thus DPS is same for the two years but here stock split took place thus increasing the number of shares and consequently the DPS. As PAT is slightly decreasing from 2010 to 2011, the EPS has also decreasing. But PAT is increasing from 2011 to 2012. This is a very good sign for a company because the number of shares are constant and PAT is increasing. This means that the company is doing well in terms of making profit. But here also, stock split took place and thus the EPS decreased because the number of shares is increasing (Table 26.3).

Next comes the payout ratio, that is, an indication that what the company is doing with their earnings. It implies that how much share

Table 26.3 Dividend picture of Tata Power

Year	Dividend paid	PAT (Rs crore)	No. of shares	DPS (D/N)	EPS (PAT/N)	Payout ratio
2010	285.05	947.65	2,373.07	12	39.93	30.05
2011	296.92	941.49	2,373.07	12.5	39.67	31.5
2012	296.92	1,169.7	23,730.72	1.25	4.93	25.35

Source: Company's Annual Reports.

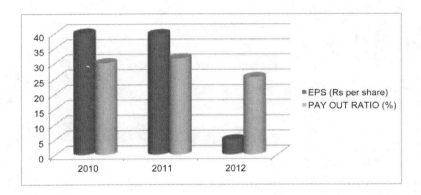

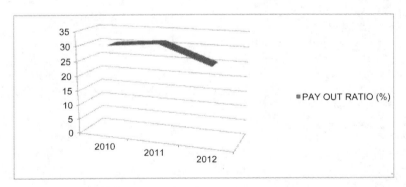

Figure 26.3 Dividend trend of Tata Power

of PAT the company is giving as a dividend and how much of it the company is reserved as its surplus, that is, for its expansion mode. From Figure 26.3 it is evident that the payout ratio is increasing from year 2010 to 2011 but it is increasing from year 2011 to 2012 considerably. There is no effect on payout ratio of stock split. Lower the payout ratio of a company is, more secure the payment of the dividend is.

(d) Power Grid

Type	State-owned enterprise public company
Traded as	NSE: Power Grid
	BSE: 532898
Industry	Electric utility
Founded	23 October 1992
Headquarters	Gurgaon, India
Area served	India
Key people	Shri R. N. Nayak (chairman and managing director)
Products	T&D; energy trading
Revenue	Increase Rs 13,329 crore (US$2.3 billion) (2012–13)[1]
Net income	Increase Rs 4,234 crore (US$730 million) (2012–13)[2]
Employees	10,000 (2012)

From the data it is evident that the number of shares is fixed, that is, constant. From year 2010 to 2011 the dividend paid has increased and thus DPS has increased for these two years. For the year 2012, the dividend paid has not increased and thus DPS has been the same for the two years but here stock split took place thus increasing the number of shares and consequently the DPS. As PAT slightly decreased from 2010 to 2011, the EPS also decreased. But PAT is increasing from 2011 to 2012 (Table 26.4).

Table 26.4 Dividend picture of Power Grid

Year	Dividend paid	PAT (Rs crore)	No. of shares	DPS (D/N)	EPS (PAT/N)	Payout ratio
2010	631.34	2,040.94	46,297.3	1.5	4.85	30.92
2011	810.23	2,696.89	46,297.3	1.75	5.83	30.02
2012	976.89	3,254.95	46,297.3	2.11	7.03	30.02

Source: Company's Annual Reports.

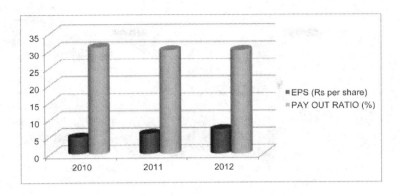

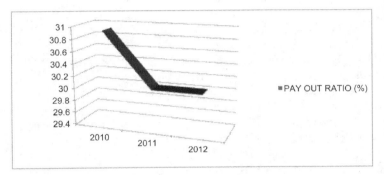

Figure 26.4 Dividend trend of Power Grid

This is a very good sign for a company because the number of shares is constant and PAT is increasing. This means that the company is doing well in terms of making profit. But here also stock split took place and thus the EPS is decreasing because the number of shares is increasing. Next comes the payout ratio, that is, an indication that what the company is doing with their earnings. It implies that how much share of PAT the company is giving as a dividend and how much of it the company has reserved as its surplus, that is, for its expansion mode. From Figure 26.4, it is evident that the payout ratio is increasing from year 2010 to 2011 but it is increasing from year 2011 to 2012 considerably. There is no effect on payout ratio of stock split. Lower the payout ratio of a company is, more secure the payment of the dividend is.

(e) Torrent Power

Type	Public company
Traded as	BSE: 532779
	NSE: TORNTPOWR
Industry	Energy
Founded	1996
Headquarters	Ahmedabad, India
Products	Natural gas production, sale and distribution, electricity generation and distribution, hydro-electricity, wind power, energy trading
Revenue	Increase Rs 23 billion (2006)
Net income	Increase Rs 1.2 billion (2006)
Employees	4,000
Parent	Torrent Group

From the data it is evident that the number of shares is fixed, that is, constant. For all the three years the dividend paid has increasing and thus DPS increased for these three years. Increase in DPS means that the company is wooing their shareholders by giving more dividend to them in all the three years. As PAT increased continuously from 2010 to 2012, the EPS also increased. This is a very good sign for a company because the number of shares is constant and PAT is increasing. This means that the company is doing well in terms of making profit. Next comes the payout ratio, that is, an indication that what the company is doing with their earnings. It implies that how much share of PAT the company is giving as a dividend and how much of it the company has reserved as its surplus, that is, for its expansion mode. From Figure 26.5, it is evident that the payout ratio is considerably increasing from year 2010 to 2011 and slightly increasing from year 2011 to 2012 (Table 26.5).

Table 26.5 Dividend picture of Torrent Power

Year	Dividend paid	PAT (Rs crore)	No. of shares	DPS (D/N)	EPS (PAT/N)	Payout ratio
2010	141.73	836.55	4,724.48	3	17.71	16.93
2011	259.85	1,065.72	4,724.48	5.5	22.56	24.37
2012	307.08	1,237.46	4,724.48	6.5	26.19	24.81

Source: Company's Annual Reports.

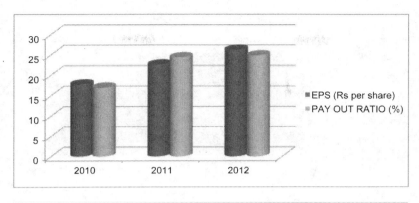

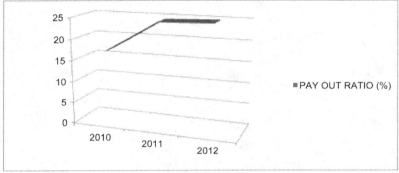

Figure 26.5 Dividend trend of Torrent Power

Conclusion

From the analysis of all the five companies, we found that their payout ratios are in the range of 25–35, which is considered a very good ratio. The companies have distributed their almost one-third of their profit as their dividend and rest are retained as surplus.

But, there is no fixed pattern in the distribution of dividend of the industry, whereas a stable dividend pattern is always positive from the shareholders' point of view. So companies should try to increase their DPS but at a consistent rate to woo the shareholders to invest more and more in them.

Discussion questions

1 Analyse the dividend policy of NTPC, NHPC, Tata Power, Power Grid and Torrent Power. Study the dividend–payout ratio in this context.

2 Comment upon the dividend policy for shareholders' wealth maximisation.

3 Which dividend theory can be related to the present case?

4 What are the various determinants of dividend policy?

5 What type of dividend policy is generally followed in power sector in India?

27

DIVIDEND POLICY AND MARKET RETURN

The type of dividend policy followed by the company has a strong impact on the market price of the share of the company. This is also one of the most important factors in deciding the dividend policy of a company.

This chapter looks at the eight leading Indian companies' dividend policy for the period 2006–10 and its effect on their market price. These companies are taken from diverse sectors to have a better insight into changing dividend policy with the changing sector. Correlation analysis has also been done to determine the relationship between the policy and market price.

The correlation coefficient is self-explanatory to indicate the relationship between dividend and market return.

Analysis

Let us now look at select companies and analyse the effect of DPS on stock price.

1. Tyre

MRF Ltd

Correlation of stock price with respect to dividend: 0.44
Correlation of stock price with respect to Sensex: 0.9748

Table 27.1 Dividend and market return of MRF (Rs)

Year	Stock price	Dividend paid	Sensex
2006	3,160	20	9,323.25
2007	4,331	20	13,846.34
2008	7,045	20	20,296.95
2009	1,981	20	9,533.52
2010	6,159	25	17,464.81

Source: Annual Report of MRF and BSE.

Table 27.2 Dividend and market return of Bharat Bijlee (Rs)

Year	Stock price	Dividend paid	Sensex
2006	681.8	13.50	9,323.25
2007	1,205.4	25	13,846.34
2008	3,562.85	30	20,296.95
2009	510.15	25	9,533.52
2010	924.6	25	17,464.81

Source: Annual Report of Bharat Bijlee and BSE.

2. Engineering

Bharat Bijlee Ltd

Correlation of stock price with respect to dividend: 0.620695208
Correlation of stock price with respect to Sensex: 0.8006

3. Textiles

Victoria Mills Ltd

Correlation of stock price with respect to dividend: None
Correlation of stock price with respect to Sensex: 0.986351

4. Electrical equipment

Nippo Batteries Company Ltd

Correlation of stock price with respect to dividend: 0.341155
Correlation of stock price with respect to Sensex: 0.7895

Table 27.3 Dividend and market return of Victoria Mills (Rs)

Year	Stock price	Dividend paid	Sensex
2006	1416	50	9,323.25
2007	2,467.6	50	13,846.34
2008	5,832.15	50	20,296.95
2009	1,300	50	9,533.52
2010	4,290	50	17,464.81

Source: Annual Report of Victoria Mills and BSE.

Table 27.4 Dividend and market return of Nippo (Rs)

Year	Stock price	Dividend paid	Sensex
2006	405.75	20	9,323.25
2007	343.45	12.5	13,846.34
2008	612.95	20	20,296.95
2009	300.5	20	9,533.52
2010	420.5	20	17,464.81

Source: Annual Report of Nippo and BSE.

Table 27.5 Dividend and market return of Karur Vysya (Rs)

Year	Stock price	Dividend paid	Sensex
2006	111.57	12	9,323.25
2007	151.9	10	13,846.34
2008	238.73	12	20,296.95
2009	121.78	12	9,533.52
2010	224.73	12	17,464.81

Source: Annual Report of Karur Vysya and BSE.

5. Banking

Karur Vysya Bank

Correlation of stock price with respect to dividend: 0.169896
Correlation of stock price with respect to Sensex: 0.981397

6. *Capital goods*

Kaycee Industries Ltd

Correlation of stock price with respect to dividend: 0.089
Correlation of stock price with respect to Sensex: 0.767436

7. *FMCG*

Procter & Gamble Hygiene and Healthcare Ltd

Correlation of stock price with respect to dividend: 0.152569
Correlation of stock price with respect to Sensex: 0.362582

Table 27.6 Dividend and market return of Kaycee (Rs)

Year	Stock price	Dividend paid	Sensex
200	3,517.5	0	9,323.25
2007	1,997.1	10	13,846.34
2008	7,978.4	10	20,296.95
2009	2,070	10	9,533.52
2010	3,965	10	17,464.81

Source: Annual Report of Kaycee and BSE.

Table 27.7 Dividend and market return of P&G (Rs)

Year	Stock price	Dividend paid	Sensex
2006	844.3	25	9,323.25
2007	855	20	13,846.34
2008	765.75	20	20,296.95
2009	751.95	22.5	9,533.52
2010	1740	22.5	17,464.81

Source: Annual Report of P&G and BSE.

Table 27.8 Dividend and market return of Novartis (Rs)

Year	Stock price	Dividend paid	Sensex
2006	589.65	15	9323.25
2007	354.8	10	13846.34
2008	417.95	10	20296.95
2009	274.8	10	9533.52
2010	555.55	10	17464.81

Source: Annual Report of Novartis and BSE.

8. Pharmaceuticals

Novartis India Ltd

Correlation of stock price with respect to dividend: 0.635019
Correlation of stock price with respect to Sensex: 0.121806

Discussion questions

1 'Dividend policy is defined by the sector'. What type of dividend policy is followed by the above business units?

2 Analyse the dividend policy of following companies in different sectors and study the impact of dividend on the market return with the help of correlation analysis:

1 MRF in tyre sector
2 Bharat Bijlee in engineering
3 Victoria Mills in textiles
4 Nippo Batteries in electrical equipment
5 Karur Vysya Bank in banking
6 Kaycee Industries in capital goods
7 P&G in FMCG
8 Novartis in pharmaceuticals.

3 Which dividend theory can be related to the sectors in the present case?

4 'Dividend policy aims at maximising the shareholders' value'. Explain.

REFERENCES

Ahmed, A. S. 1982. 'The Losses in Public Enterprises: Why and How' in Zia U. Ahmed (ed.), *Financial Profitability and Losses in Public Enterprises of Developing Countries*. Ljubljana, Slovenia: ICPE.

Altman, E. 1968. 'Financial Ratios, Discriminant Analysis and the Prediction of Corporate Bankruptcy', *Journal of Finance* 23(4) (September): 589–609.

Annual Reports of the Selected Corporate Enterprises for the period 2006–7 to 2010–11.

Archer, Stephen H., and Charles A. D'Ambrosio. 1972. *Business Finance: Theory and Management*. New York: Macmillan Publishing Co.

Arsdell, Paul M. Van. 1968. *Corporation Finance: Policy, Planning, Administration*. New York: The Ronald Press Co.

Anthony, R. N. *et al.* 1975. *Principles of Management Accounting*. Illinois: Richard Irwin Inc.

Barberis, Nicholas, A. Shleifer and R. Vishny. 1998. 'GA Model of Investor Sentiment', *Journal of Financial Economics* 49: 307–43.

Batty, J. 1966. *Management Accountancy*. London: MacDonald and Evans Ltd.

Bierman Harold Jr. *et al.* 1986. *Financial Management for Decision Making*. New York: Macmillan Publishing Co.

Bogen, Jules I. (ed.). 1964. *Financial Handbook*, Fourth Edition. New York: The Ronald Press Co.

Brigham, Eugene F. *et al.* 1997. *Financial Management: Theory and Practice*, Eighth Edition. Florida: The Dryden Press.

Bryce, M. D. 1960. *Industrial Development*. New York: McGraw-Hill.

Chaturvedi, T. N. 1984. *Public Enterprises*. New Delhi: Indian Institute of Public Administration.

Clarkson, Geoffrey P. E. *et al.* 1983. *Managing Money and Finance*, Third Edition. Aldershot, England: Gower Publishing Co. Ltd.

Clement, M. B. and S. Y. Tse. 2005. 'Financial Analyst Characteristics and Herding Behavior in Forecasting', *The Journal of Finance* 60(1): 307–41.

Committee on Public Undertakings (Fourth Lok Sabha). 1968. *Fifteenth Report on Financial Management in Public Undertakings*. New Delhi: Committee on Public Undertakings.

Curran, W. S. 1970. *Principles of Financial Management*. New York: McGraw-Hill.

Dean, J. 1951. *Capital Budgeting*. New York: Columbia University Press.

Dewing, A. S. 1914. *Corporate Promotions and Re-organisations*. Cambridge, MA: Harvard University Press.

Donaldson, Elvin F. *et al*. 1975. *Corporate Finance*, Fourth Edition. New York: The Ronald Press Co.

Donaldson, Gordon 1960. 'Looking around: Finance for the Non-Financial Managers', *Harvard Business Review* 37 (January–February).

———. 1961. *Corporate Debt Capacity*. Boston: Division of Research, Harvard Business School.

Eiteman, Wilford J. *et al*. 1953. *Essays on Business Finance*. Ann Arbor, MI: Masterco Press Inc.

Emery, Douglas R. *et al*. 1998. *Principles of Financial Management*. Upper Saddle River, NJ: Prentice Hall.

e-university. June 2013. 'e-university'. Retrieved from Wisdom Jobs Gulf.com, available at http://e-university.wisdomjobs.com/financial-management/chapter-1019–289/the-role-and-objective-of-financial-management_maximizing-shareholder-wealth-as-the-priamry-goal_6311.html.

Fama, E. F. 1965. 'The Behavior of Stock Market Prices', *Journal of Business* 38 (January): 34–105.

Finney, H. A. *et al*. 1972. *Principles of Accounting: An Introduction*. Japan: Prentice Hall.

Foulke, R. A. 1979. *Practical Financial Statement Analysis*. New Delhi: Tata McGraw-Hill Publishing Co.

Francis, David Pitt. 1978. *The Foundations of Financial Management*. New York: Pitman Publishing.

Gerstenberg, Charles W. 1959. *Financial Organisation and Management*, Revised Edition. New York: Prentice Hall, Inc.

Gitman, L. J. 1976. *Principles of Managerial Finance*. New York: Harper & Row.

Gorther, Harold F. 1977. *Administration in the Public Sector*. New York: John Wiley & Sons, Inc.

Greene, T. L. 1897. *Corporation Finance*. New York: Pitman.

Gupta, L. C. 1969. *Changing Structure of Industrial Finance in India*. Oxford: Clarendon Press.

Guthmann, Harry G. *et al*. 1962. *Corporate Financial Policy*, Fourth Edition. Upper Saddle River, NJ: Prentice Hall.

———. 1968. *Analysis of Financial Statements*. New Delhi: Prentice Hall of India.

Howard, Bion B. *et al*. 1953. *Introduction to Business Finance*. New York: McGraw-Hill Book C.

Hunt, Pearson *et al.* 1968. *Financial Management Cases and Readings*. Illinois: Richard D. Irwin Inc.

Johnson, R. L. 1973. *Financial Decision Making*. California: Goodyear Publishing Co.

Kennedy, Ralph D. *et al.* 1968. *Financial Statements: Form, Analysis and Interpretation*. Illinois: Richard D. Irwin Inc.

Lev, B. 1974. *Financial Statement Analysis: A New Approach*. Upper Saddle River, NJ: Prentice Hall.

Markowitz, H. 1952. 'Portfolio Selection', *Journal of Finance* 37 (March): 77–91.

Mckevitt, David *et al.* (eds). 1994. *Public Sector Management Theory, Critique & Practice*. London: Sage Publications.

Miller, Merton H. *et al.* 1961. 'Dividend Policy, Growth and the Valuation of Shares', *Journal of Business* 34 (October): 411–33.

Modigliani, F. *et al.* 1958. 'The Cost of Capital, Corporation Finance and the Theory of Investment', *American Economic Review* 48 (June): 261–97.

Moyer, C. R. *et al.* 1981. *Contemporary Financial Management*. New York: West Publishing Co.

Raj, A.B.C. 1978. *Public Enterprises Investment Decisions in India: A Managerial Analysis*. New Delhi: MacMillan Co. of India Pvt Ltd.

Ramnath, S., S. Rock and P. Shane. 2008. 'The Financial Analyst Forecasting Literature: A Taxonomy with Suggestions for Further Research', *International Journal of Forecasting* 24(1): 34–75.

Sharpe, W. F. 1964. 'Capital Asset Prices: A Theory of Market Equilibrium under Conditions of Risk', *Journal of Finance* 19 (September): 425–42.

Smith, K.V. 1974. *Management of Working Capital*. New Delhi: West Publishing Co.

Solomon, Ezra. 1969. *Theory of Financial Management*. New York: Columbia University Press.

Spiller, E. A. 1977. *Financial Accounting*. Homewood, IL: Richard D. Irwin Inc.

Van Horne, James C. *et al.* 1996. *Fundamentals of Financial Management*, Ninth Edition. New Delhi: Prentice Hall of India.

Walter, James E. 1963. 'Dividend Policy: Its Influence on the Value of the Enterprise', *Journal of Finance* 18(2): 280–91.

Wright, M. G. 1973. *Discounted Cash Flow*, Maidenhead, UK: McGraw-Hill.

Weblinks

http://articles.economictimes.indiatimes.com/2011–0103/news/28426991_1_aviation-airline-industry-gdp.

http://www.bseindia.com/indices.

http://businesstoday.intoday.in/story/private-airlines-on-track-to-achive-bigger-profit-capa/1/187484.html.

REFERENCES

http://www.capitaline.com/new/index.asp.

http://www.colgate.co.in/app/Colgate/IN/Corp/InvestorRelations/Annual Reports.cvsp.

http://www.dabur.com/Investors%20Relation-Reports.

http://www.emamiltd.in/investor-info/index.php.

http://www.foolonahill.com/mbaaviation.html#_Toc83227607.

http://www.godrej.com/godrej/Godrej-ConsumerProducts/cpanualreport. aspx?id=381&menuid=2296.

http://www.gsk-india.com/investor-annualreports.html.

http://www.hul.co.in/investorrelations/AnnualReports/.

http://www.ibef.org/industry/india-automobiles.aspx (accessed on 18 June 2013).

http://www.icra.in/Files/ticker/Indian%20Aviation%20Industry%20(NEW). pdf.

http://info.shine.com/Industry-Information/Aviation/140.aspx.

http://Infosys.com.

http://www.itcportal.com/about-itc/shareholder-value/annual-reports/itc-annual-report-2013/ITC-brands-national-assets.aspx.

http://knowindia.net/aviation3.html.

http://www.livemint.com/Industry/LyNBizkuOMdmThw6iaoGbN/Five-trends-that-will-drive-FMCG-growth-in-2013.html (accessed on 25 June 2012).

http://www.marico.com/html/investor/annual-reports.php.

http://www.mca.gov.in/Ministry/pdf/Companies_Act_1956_13jun2011.pdf (accessed on 21 February 2013).

www.mfiles.pl/en.

http://www.moneycontrol.com/.

www.morganstanleycontent.intuition.com.

http://www.nasscom.in/domestic-itbpo.

http://www.nestle.in/investors/stockandfinancials/annualreports.

www.nhpcindia.com.

www.nobel.org.

www.ntpc.co.in.

http://www.pg.com/en_IN/invest/pghh/annualreports/index.shtml.

www.Powergridindia.com.

http://www.projectguru.in/publications/overview-of-indian-aviation-industry/.

www.svtuition.org.

www.tatapower.com.

http://www.tcs.com.

http://www.techmahindra.com.

www.torrentpower.com.

http://www.wipro.com.

INDEX